Introductory Criminal Justice Statistics and Data Analysis

Second Edition

IRINA R. SODERSTROM
Eastern Kentucky University

KRISTIE R. BLEVINS
Eastern Kentucky University

WAVELAND PRESS, INC.
Long Grove, Illinois

For information about this book, contact:
 Waveland Press, Inc.
 4180 IL Route 83, Suite 101
 Long Grove, IL 60047-9580
 (847) 634-0081
 info@waveland.com
 www.waveland.com

Copyright © 2016, 2008 by Waveland Press, Inc.

10-digit ISBN 1-4786-2709-3
13-digit ISBN 978-1-4786-2709-8

All rights reserved. No part of this book may be reproduced, stored in a retrieval system, or transmitted in any form or by any means without permission in writing from the publisher.

Printed in the United States of America

7 6 5 4 3 2 1

To my loving husband, John M. Powell, who provided the patience
and encouragement needed to tackle this project once again.
Also, to my late parents, Harry and Sue Soderstrom,
who always made me believe that anything is possible
if you simply fly the course.
Irina S. Soderstrom

To my husband, John Gassett,
and to my parents, Luther and Sharon Blevins.
Thanks for all your love and support.
Kristie R. Blevins

Contents

Preface   xi

SECTION ONE
DESCRIPTIVE STATISTICS

1 Introduction to Statistics   3
   Why Study Statistics?   4
   Learning to Think Statistically   5
   The Role of Statistics in Scientific Inquiry   5
   Basic Elements of Statistics   6
      Cases, Subjects, and Units of Analysis   6
      Qualitative versus Quantitative Data   7
      Continuous versus Discrete Variables   8
      Independent versus Dependent Variables   8
      Descriptive versus Inferential Statistics   9
      Measurement   9
   Levels of Measurement   10
      The Nominal Level of Measurement   10
      Ordinal Level of Measurement   12
      Interval Level of Measurement   13
      Ratio Level of Measurement   14
   Summary   15
      Notes   15
      ■ KEY TERMS 15   ■ MULTIPLE-CHOICE QUESTIONS 16

2 Displaying and Graphing Distributions — 19

Frequency Distributions 19
   Generating Frequency Distributions 20
   Cumulative Frequency Distributions 20
   Percentage Distributions 21
   Cumulative Percentage Distributions 22
   Working with Grouped Data 23

Graphing and Charting Distributions 25
   Charts for Displaying Discrete Data 25
   Graphs for Displaying Continuous Data 27
   Interpreting Charts and Graphs 28

Summary 30
   ■ Key Terms 30 ■ SPSS Application 30
   ■ Sample Write-Up for SPSS Application 32
   ■ SPSS Assignment 32 ■ Multiple-Choice Questions 33

3 Descriptive Statistics: Measures of Central Tendency and Dispersion — 37

Importance of Quantitative Descriptive Statistics 37

Measures of Central Tendency 38
   The Mode (Mo) 38
   The Median (Md) 40
   The Mean ($\bar{X}$) 40

Measures of Dispersion 45
   The Index of Qualitative Variation (IQV) 45
   The Range (R) and the Interquartile Range (Q) 46
   The Standard Deviation (s, σ) 49

Summary 52
   Notes 53
   ■ Key Terms 53 ■ SPSS Application 53
   ■ Sample Write-Up for SPSS Application 55
   ■ SPSS Assignment 56 ■ Multiple-Choice Questions 56

4 The Normal Curve and Standard Scores — 59

The Normal Curve 59

Standard Scores (z-Scores) 62

The Standard Normal Curve 64

Summary 66
   Note 66
   ■ Key Terms 67 ■ SPSS Application 67
   ■ SPSS Assignment 69 ■ Multiple-Choice Questions 70

SECTION TWO
INFERENTIAL STATISTICS: TESTS OF GROUP DIFFERENCES

5 Introduction to Inferential Statistics — 75

Probability Sampling   75
   Simple Random Sampling   76
   Systematic Random Sampling   77
   Stratified Sampling   77
   Multistage Cluster Sampling   78
Sampling Distributions   79
Confidence Intervals   85
Summary   89
■ KEY TERMS 90   ■ SPSS APPLICATION 90
■ SPSS ASSIGNMENT 92   ■ MULTIPLE-CHOICE QUESTIONS 92

6 Hypothesis Testing — 95

Role of Hypothesis Testing in
  Criminal Justice Research   95
Methods of Hypothesis Testing   97
   The Research Question   97
   The Five-Step Model for Hypothesis Testing   97
Type I and Type II Errors   107
Statistical versus Practical Significance   110
Summary   111
■ KEY TERMS 111   ■ HOMEWORK ASSIGNMENT 111
■ MULTIPLE-CHOICE QUESTIONS 112

7 Nonparametric Tests: Chi-Square Tests — 115

Purpose and Types of Chi-Square Tests   115
Research Examples   117
The Chi-Square ($\chi 2$) Goodness-of-Fit Test   118
   Purpose of the Chi-Square Goodness-of-Fit Test   118
   Five-Step Model For Hypothesis Testing   118

The Chi-Square (χ^2) Test for Independence   125
 Purpose and Elements of the Chi-Square Test
  for Independence   125
 Five-Step Model For Hypothesis Testing   126
Summary   132
- KEY TERMS   133
- SPSS APPLICATION ONE: CHI-SQUARE GOODNESS-OF-FIT TEST   133
- SPSS APPLICATION TWO: CHI-SQUARE TEST FOR INDEPENDENCE   134
- SPSS ASSIGNMENT   135   ■ MULTIPLE CHOICE QUESTIONS   136

8 Mean Difference Tests: *t*-Tests   139

Purpose of *t*-Tests   139
The One-Sample *t*-Test   140
 Purpose of the One-Sample *t*-Test   140
 Five-Step Model For Hypothesis Testing   140
Important Concepts Related to Independent
 and Dependent Samples *t*-Tests   147
 Independent and Dependent Sampling   148
 Homogeneity of Variance   150
The Independent Samples *t*-Test   151
 Purpose of the Independent Samples *t*-Test   151
 Five-Step Model for Hypothesis Testing   151
The Dependent Samples *t*-Test   158
 Purpose of the Dependent Samples *t*-Test   158
 Five-Step Model for Hypothesis Testing   159
Summary   165
- KEY TERMS   165
- SPSS APPLICATION ONE: ONE-SAMPLE *t*-TEST   166
- SPSS APPLICATION TWO: INDEPENDENT SAMPLES *t*-TEST   167
- SPSS APPLICATION THREE: DEPENDENT SAMPLES *t*-TEST   168
- SPSS ASSIGNMENT   168   ■ MULTIPLE CHOICE QUESTIONS   170

9 Significant Differences: 173
One-Way Analysis of Variance (ANOVA)

Purpose of ANOVA Tests   173
Important Concepts Related to Analysis of Variance   174
 The F-Ratio and Logic of ANOVA   174
 Homogeneity of Variance   175
 Efficiency and the Type I Error Rate   176

Research Example 176
    Five-Step Model for Hypothesis Testing 177
Post Hoc Probing 183
Summary 187
 ■ KEY TERMS 187 ■ SPSS APPLICATION: ONE-WAY ANOVA 188
 ■ SPSS ASSIGNMENT 188 ■ MULTIPLE-CHOICE QUESTIONS 189

SECTION THREE
INFERENTIAL STATISTICS: TESTS OF ASSOCIATION

10 Significant Relationships: Bivariate Correlation — 195

Purpose of Tests of Association 196
Important Concepts Related to
  Bivariate Correlation 196
    Measures of Association 196
    Scatterplots 197
    Covariation 197
    Outliers 202
    Nonlinearity 202
    Homoscedasticity 203
    Restricted Range 204
    Research Example 204
    Five-Step Model for Hypothesis Testing 205
Statistical Significance versus
  Practical Significance 211
Summary 212
    Note 212
 ■ KEY TERMS 212
 ■ SPSS APPLICATION: BIVARIATE CORRELATION 213
 ■ SPSS ASSIGNMENT 213 ■ MULTIPLE-CHOICE QUESTIONS 214

11 Significant Relationships: Simple Linear Regression — 217

Purpose of Simple Linear Regression 217
Important Concepts Related to
  Simple Linear Regression 218
    Scatterplots 218
    The Regression of Y on X 219
    Errors of Prediction 223
    Predictive Accuracy 225

Five-Step Model for Hypothesis Testing   230
Summary   231
■ KEY TERMS 231
■ SPSS APPLICATION: SIMPLE LINEAR REGRESSION 232
■ SPSS ASSIGNMENT 233   ■ MULTIPLE-CHOICE QUESTIONS 234

12 Significant Relationships: Multiple Linear Regression   237

Purpose of Multiple Linear Regression   237
Important Concepts Related to
 Multiple Linear Regression   238
  Scatterplots   238
  Multiple Correlation   239
  The Regression of Y on X_1 and X_2 244
  Errors of Prediction   247
  Predictive Accuracy   248
Types of Multiple Linear Regression   252
  Direct Enter Method   252
  Stepwise Regression Methods   252
Handling Nominal Level Variables   253
Summary   255
  Note   256
■ KEY TERMS 256
■ SPSS APPLICATION: MULTIPLE LINEAR REGRESSION 256
■ SPSS ASSIGNMENT 257   ■ MULTIPLE-CHOICE QUESTIONS 258

Appendices: Statistical Tables   261
Index   269

Preface

As was the case with the first edition of this textbook, the words and efforts contained herein represent a labor of love. We have always wanted to write a user-friendly, applied statistics and data analysis textbook for criminal justice. Because we both teach data analysis courses in our criminal justice program at Eastern Kentucky University, we realize how challenging it is for students to grasp analytical concepts and to apply them to real-world research applications in our field. The primary goal of this textbook is to teach this material in a manner that is simply explained and demonstrated through examples to which students can relate. We both have many years of experience successfully teaching research-related courses like research methodology and criminal justice data analysis. We also have many years of experience doing research consulting and working on both large and small research projects of our own. Furthermore, we have solid training in traditional social science techniques. Thus, we believe we are uniquely suited to provide a textbook that can serve undergraduate and graduate students in learning the quantitative skills so important in our discipline.

From the inception of the first edition, it was recognized that we have a great need in criminal justice for an applied statistics and data analysis textbook produced by, and for, a criminal justice professional. Too often, criminal justice professors who teach statistics have been forced to use statistics textbooks written for the social sciences in general, or maybe even some other, non-criminal justice discipline. The reason for this is there has been a paucity of statistics textbooks written specifically for criminal justice. Oftentimes one can find a criminal justice statistics book that has been combined with traditional social science research methodology. In this era of increasing demands for program and policy evaluation in all criminal justice sub-disciplines, a combined statistics/research methods course is no longer sufficient to provide criminal justice students with the statistical and methodological skills required by our profession. A guiding principle in the development of this statistics book has been to provide a thorough presentation of statistical techniques, from basic through advanced levels, that are commonly employed by criminal justice academics and professionals when conducting criminal justice research.

The primary changes to the second edition include: (1) bringing on a second author who is very skilled in data analysis and has considerable experience teaching and conducting quantitative research, thus, allowing this book to reflect some fresh ideas and approaches; and (2) reorganizing/re-writing chapters 7 and 8 so they are more uniform and efficient with content (e.g., similar tests grouped together in a family-wise fashion) and so they reflect the order that SPSS presents various families of statistical tests. Furthermore, all chapters have received homework "face-lifts," and the Instructor's Manual has been redone to reflect those changes in multiple choice and SPSS assignments throughout the book.

The book begins with the basic statistical principles and techniques, and increasingly builds on that foundation all the way through to some of the most advanced statistical procedures employed in our field. Each chapter presents an overview of a particular topic, a clear example of its application in the criminal justice field, step-by-step instructions regarding the use of the statistical technique both with and without the use of a computer, an SPSS example accompanied by an example of how to interpret and write-up the results, and another computer project for students to work on outside of class. While mathematical computations of each statistical test are demonstrated, as well as the SPSS output, it is common for instructors using this book to ignore the mathematical computations entirely and simply focus on the computer output provided by SPSS. The math is included for instructors who want their students to gain more in-depth knowledge of the mathematical operations involved in the data analysis. Therefore, the inclusion of mathematical computations makes the content more complete and allows instructors to decide the manner in which they wish to teach data analysis courses. Moreover, the book is well-designed for teaching statistics/data analysis courses online, and we both use it in that manner, as well as in the traditional classroom.

As mentioned above, the book covers the entire continuum of elementary to advanced statistics to serve both undergraduate and graduate criminal justice students. When used for an undergraduate course, the instructor may opt to ignore mathematical computations and focus on SPSS output. Also, a sixteen-week undergraduate course most likely would not get into the advanced chapters in the latter third of the book. For a master's level data analysis course, the book allows for in-depth examination of mathematical computations so students truly understand what the computer is doing when performing statistical analyses. The graduate course would cover the entire book, as graduate students would still need to review the more elementary chapters at the beginning of the text, but would move through that material quickly. Whether for undergraduate or graduate students, this book is an essential reference for statistics and research conducted after graduation.

Thus, we present to you the second edition of our applied statistics textbook, which meets the following objectives: (1) presents data analysis techniques in a logical fashion; (2) provides a meaningful context for all data analysis techniques regarding their application in the field of criminal justice; (3) builds statistical knowledge and data analysis skills in a manner that lends to an understanding of statistical reasoning; (4) develops an appreciation for the essential role that statistics/data analysis plays in contributing to scientific knowledge; and (5) makes the learning of statistics as painless as possible and hopefully even fun. We believe this textbook can be an essential tool for criminal justice departments and programs desirous of building strong quantitative components in their curricula.

Last, but certainly not least, we would like to thank our publishers at Waveland Press, Inc., Carol and Neil Rowe, who have been so supportive, kind, and patient throughout both editions of this textbook. We wish to extend considerable gratitude to our editor, Jeni Ogilvie, for her hard work, helpful suggestions, and patience throughout the editing process. We also would like to thank Dr. Victor Kappeler for his friendship, leadership at EKU, and unwavering support from the inception of this project. Lastly, we would like to thank our mentors who got us this far in life—they know who they are!

Section One

DESCRIPTIVE STATISTICS

1

Introduction to Statistics

Statistics can be defined broadly as a set of mathematical techniques used to accomplish two primary activities—answering questions and testing ideas. Statistics allow us to perform these activities by providing ways to organize and manipulate information. The information collected in order to test ideas and answer questions are called **data**.

Basically, statistics is a family of mathematical procedures that allow us to reduce a large amount of data to a more efficient and useable form. Statistics also are employed when we want to ask questions of the data and to generalize the answers to some larger population. For example, you could collect information on a randomly selected sample of students from your university. Next, you could perform a descriptive analysis, which would entail reducing the data down to some summary pieces of information that would describe the characteristics of your sample of students (e.g., average age, percent male versus female, most typical major, average grade point average). You could follow this up with a statistical analysis that compared grade point averages for females and males. All of these activities would be done in such a way as to allow you to generalize the findings from your sample to the larger population of all students at your university.

One might wonder about the purpose of going through such an exhaustive process. Yet, the statistical process is one of the most efficient ways of obtaining knowledge. The only other way that you could determine the profile of the average student at your university, or the relationship between gender and grade point average, would be to collect that information on the entire population of university students—a rather formidable task indeed! It is much quicker and less expensive to use the statistical process to find out what we want to know about the university student body.

Why Study Statistics?

Students often question why they are required to take statistics. They believe incorrectly that the career paths they are pursuing will not require a working knowledge of statistics. I cannot emphasize enough how wrong this perception is!

There are four primary reasons to study statistics. The first has to do with the fact that criminal justice professionals are consumers of research. It will be essential that you be able to interpret research findings relevant to your field and that you know how to apply those findings to your work. This is particularly true for supervisory positions. Supervisors often must interpret research in order to make decisions that affect day-to-day operations. You can imagine the importance of having statistical knowledge when the decision being made involves large expenditures or major changes in professional approaches and techniques.

Another reason for studying statistics is that criminal justice professionals are producers of research. For example, probation officers may decide to conduct an experiment to test new approaches to client supervision and/or counseling. Or a researcher for the Federal Bureau of Prisons may be asked to determine the effects of changes in sentencing policies on jail and prison populations. Or perhaps a large police department will conduct a crime analysis to determine the most efficient and effective ways to deploy patrol and special investigative police units in the community. The point of these examples is to impress upon you the notion that there will be times in your professional career when you will be asked to generate some statistics.

Possibly the best reason to study statistics is the fact that your job marketability will increase as your statistical skills increase. No one would argue the fact that the demand for employees with quantitative abilities far exceeds the supply of sufficiently skilled professionals in all disciplines. Criminal justice is no exception to this rule. Whenever funding is sought for new criminal justice programs, or whenever support is sought for new criminal justice policies, evaluation components are required. And the evaluation components require statistical abilities. Serving as a program or policy evaluator is a very lucrative business. As your knowledge of statistics and research increases, you will exponentially increase the number of good-paying job opportunities for which you can compete.

A final, and perhaps more intrinsic, reason for studying statistics is the flexibility and creativity it enables you to apply in designing research projects. The broader your statistical background the more you will be able to explore many interesting ideas about criminal justice. A broad statistical background is the equivalent of a tool bag full of versatile tools that can be utilized to test those ideas. A working knowledge of how all of the tools work will help you decide which tool is best for a particular situation.

LEARNING TO THINK STATISTICALLY

In my experience, most students avoid statistics courses, waiting until the end of their academic programs to take any such required coursework. This avoidance is usually the result of math anxiety. Let me allay those fears right now. This is not a math course. I prefer that students think about statistics as a mathematical language. As long as students acquire a solid foundation in the basic terminology and techniques, they will begin to *think statistically* with a little practice. While the mechanics of statistics involve elements of applied algebra, the logic behind statistics is not nearly as abstract as the logic behind algebra (or any area of mathematics for that matter).

As you begin to understand the logic of statistical reasoning, and as your repertoire of statistical skills increases, you will be well on your way to learning to think statistically. As this process happens, you will begin to realize that statistics is as much of an art as it is a science. Certainly, a good statistician must be proficient in the mechanics of computing statistical information, but a good statistician must also be able to have a sense or a feel for how to match the appropriate statistical approach to a given research situation. This is not something that can be taught in cookbook fashion. Instead, this is the creative or artistic aspect of being an applied researcher. The only way to acquire this kind of ability is to be exposed to a variety of research situations that require the application of different statistical approaches. The numerous applied examples throughout this book were included to help develop this kind of understanding and ability.

THE ROLE OF STATISTICS IN SCIENTIFIC INQUIRY

The Scientific Inquiry Process diagram in figure 1.1 describes the circular process by which we gain scientific knowledge. This process begins with a theoretical idea about why something works the way that it does. The next step is to formulate specific statements (called **hypotheses**) concerning the theory that will be scientifically tested. Observations are then made or data are collected that provide information related to the hypotheses. Statistical analyses are performed on the data to actually test the hypotheses. Based on the results of the statistical tests performed, conclusions are drawn that can be generalized to some larger population. Finally, the original theoretical ideas

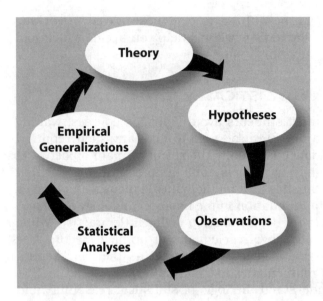

Figure 1.1 Scientific Inquiry Process

are modified to reflect the newly obtained empirical knowledge. The whole process then starts over again.

The newly obtained knowledge resulting from the scientific inquiry process is called **empirical** because it is knowledge that is grounded in actual data. This is in contrast to other ways we have of knowing things such as authoritarian knowledge (knowledge that originates from a source of power or authority), rationalistic knowledge (knowledge that originates from logic, reasoning, and anecdotal evidence), and mystical knowledge (knowledge that originates from faith).[1]

All of the components of the scientific inquiry process, with the exception of the statistical analyses component, are the subject matter for a research methods course. However, it is important that you understand the role that statistics plays in conducting research. Once the research project has completed the stage of collecting empirical data, the research activities switch to the statistical realm.

Basic Elements of Statistics

There are a number of terms that must be defined before we can get into the business of conducting statistical analyses. These definitions are the foundational building blocks of the mathematical language called statistics.

Cases, Subjects, and Units of Analysis

The individual objects of study are often referred to as **cases**. When the object of study is a human being, the cases also may be called **subjects**. For example, if the objects of study were domestic violence arrests that took place within a given year, each arrest would be considered a case.

The **unit of analysis** refers to the types of cases on which the researcher will collect and analyze data. If the researcher decides to have individual offenders serve as the unit of analysis, then each person or subject would serve as a case in the data set that would be generated. For example, if the researcher decides to collect information regarding the incidence of domestic violence arrests, the researcher would collect information about any and all domestic violence arrests associated with each subject. It is likely that this would result in a situation where each case would have more than one domestic violence arrest.

However, if the researcher decides to have domestic violence arrests serve as the unit of analysis, then each domestic violence arrest would serve as one case in the data set that would be generated. It is likely that this would result in a situation where many of the cases in the data set would be the result of the criminal activities of only a few offenders.

While the researcher often has control over the unit of analysis to be utilized in the research project, it is important that once the unit of analysis has been established, all analyses and conclusions refer back to that unit of analysis only. For example, if the unit of analysis is the individual offender, the researcher must be careful not to make generalizations about all domestic violence incidents. Instead the generalizations should characterize the subjects themselves with regard to their domestic violence arrests. Conversely, if the unit of analysis is the domestic violence arrest, the researcher must be careful not to make generalizations about domestic violence offenders. Instead generalizations should characterize only domestic violence arrests.

Qualitative versus Quantitative Data

Qualitative data refers to nonnumerical information obtained on cases or subjects under study. This qualitative data can be in the form of written information such as interview notes or narrative reports. Qualitative data can also refer to things like a person's gender, race, religion, marital status, etc. Basically, qualitative data refers to any information about a case that is not normally quantified.

Quantitative data refers to numerical information obtained on cases or subjects under study. There is an abundance of quantifiable information, including age, number of children, IQ, number of arrests, length of incarceration, etc. Because statistics are more amenable to quantitative data, we often try to code qualitative data in quantitative ways. Later on we will see examples of this, and we will discuss the limitations of working with this kind of data.

Continuous versus Discrete Variables

I often ask my statistics students to define the term variable. The answer is very simple. A **variable** is anything that varies. Basically, any characteristic or attribute of our subjects about which we would like to collect information is a variable, so long as it varies across subjects. For example, if we were doing a study on male sex offenders, it would be illogical to include a variable in the study that identifies the gender of our subjects since all of our subjects would be male. There would be no purpose in including a variable that did not vary across subjects. Without variability, a variable cannot be statistically related to any other variable in the study. If we examined the relationship between gender and number of sex offense arrests, we would obtain statistical results indicating that the two variables are not related. This lack of a relationship would be due to the fact that there was no variability on the gender variable, and not due to a factual lack of relationship between the two variables.

Variables in which the metric of measurement can be subdivided infinitely, at least theoretically, are referred to as **continuous variables**. For example, length of incarceration could be measured in years, or in months, days, hours, minutes, etc. Each metric is a natural division of the metric listed before it. The researcher makes an arbitrary decision about which metric to use, although the choice should be based on a metric that best meets the needs of the specific research project at hand.

Variables in which the metric of measurement cannot be subdivided infinitely are referred to as **discrete variables**. For example, number of children can be measured only in terms of whole units. A person has either zero children, one child, two children, three children, etc. A person cannot have 1.2 children. Frequently, it has been pointed out that we often hear statistics like (hypothetical data) "the typical American couple has on average 2.2 children." This does not represent a violation of the definition of a discrete variable since the value 2.2 represents a statistic, an average, and not the metric in which the variable was originally measured. The average was generated from a variable that was coded as a discrete variable. Other examples of discrete variables include qualitative data such as gender, race, religious affiliation, and type of offense.

Independent versus Dependent Variables

Many times when we formulate our research hypotheses to be tested using statistics, we will make a statement that reflects our theoretical belief that some variable (X) causes an effect on some other variable (Y). The variable that we believe to be the cause of the effect is called an **independent variable** (symbolized by X). The variable that we believe to be influenced by the causal variable is called a **dependent variable** (symbolized by Y). In other words, we are saying that variation in the effect variable depends on the variation observed in the causal or independent variable. This relationship is diagramed in figure 1.2.

X ⟶ Y
(cause) (effect)

Figure 1.2 Relationship between Independent and Dependent Variables

Examples of this cause-and-effect relationship include the observation that poverty (X) causes crime (Y), that having a job (X) increases the likelihood of success on parole (Y), and that receiving therapy while in prison (X) reduces recidivism (Y).

Descriptive versus Inferential Statistics

The field of statistics is often divided into descriptive and inferential techniques. **Descriptive statistics** refer to the analyses performed to reduce a large amount of data down to a few summary pieces of information that describe various features of the data set. There is a very good reason for doing this. If we were to collect information on five different variables for a sample of 100 inmates, we would have 500 separate pieces of information. When we write up a report describing the information collected on our inmate sample, we could present all 500 pieces of information—a very inefficient way of presenting our data. However, if we computed a descriptive statistic for each of the five variables, we could more efficiently and effectively describe our sample using only these five pieces of information. The first part of this book is devoted to instruction in descriptive statistics.

Inferential statistics refer to the analyses performed to test our research hypotheses and to make inferences back to the larger population being represented by the sample. Thus, hypothesis testing is a major feature of the family of inferential statistics. For example, if we wanted to test whether participation in a sex offender treatment program while in prison resulted in lower recidivism than among those who did not participate in the program, we would employ inferential statistics. The last two parts of this book are devoted to instruction in inferential statistics.

Measurement

Measurement refers to the process of assigning numbers to cases in order to represent the presence or absence, or the actual amount, of some attribute that a case has. Thus, the measurement process is a fundamental part of defining a variable before it can be included in a data set. The measurement strategy may be as simple as counting the number of arrests that an offender has had. On the other hand, it may be as complicated as applying a formula to determine the seriousness of an offender's criminal history; the formula would differentially weigh each count of arrest by the seriousness of the offense in order to assign a composite seriousness score.

Measurement gets particularly complicated when we attempt to measure things that cannot be observed or calculated directly. It is easy to measure a person's age when we know that person's birthday—it can be calculated directly. In a similar fashion, it is easy to measure the number of arrests that an offender has had as long as a rap sheet is available—it can be counted directly. But when we want to measure an offender's levels of anxiety, self-esteem, or depression, for example, the measurement strategy becomes much more complicated. That is not to say that we cannot measure these characteristics, but the fact that they have to be measured indirectly presents some unique statistical implications for the measurement strategy selected.

While a thorough discussion of the techniques used to develop these types of personality inventories are beyond the scope of this textbook, it is important to note that there is an exhaustive statistical process required to develop these kinds of inventories; thus, you are encouraged to assess the statistical properties (sometimes referred to as psychometric properties) of any personality inventories prior to utilizing them in a research project.

▰ LEVELS OF MEASUREMENT

When we decide how we want to measure a given variable for a research project, we measure that variable at one of four possible levels of measurement. With each successive level of measurement, the mathematical properties of the variable increase. Accordingly, the statistical procedures allowable for a given variable increase as the level of measurement increases. An important implication of this is that given the choice, the researcher should always measure variables at the highest level possible.

The Nominal Level of Measurement

The lowest and most basic level of measurement is the **nominal level**. This measurement strategy simply categorizes cases into the discrete categories of the variable being measured. Thus, variables measured at the nominal level of measurement are often referred to as categorical data, reflecting the qualitative nature of the underlying information being collected. There are many examples of nominal level data: gender, race, religious affiliation, and marital status, to name a few.

Because the nominal level of measurement does not provide any quantitative or numerical information about the cases, mathematical computations of the data are not permitted. Instead, most statistical analyses of nominal level data involve simply counting the number of cases that fall into each category of the nominal level variable. It should be noted, however, that we typically assign numerical labels to the categories of a nominal level variable. The primary reason for this is to simplify computer data entry.

Another reason is that there are times when numerically coded qualitative data can be treated as quantitative data, if coded in a particular manner (called dummy coding) that we will discuss later in this book. Let me provide a brief illustration of this point. Pretend that we took a sample of 50 police officers, 15 of whom were female and 35 of whom were male, and we assigned a zero to all females and a one to all males for the variable called gender. The zeros and ones in the data set would simply represent the categorical labels of the gender variable (i.e., 0 = female; 1 = male). If we were to compute a mathematical average of the gender variable, we would get an average of .70, a value which does not make sense for a qualitative variable like gender. How can we have an average gender of .70? But because this dichotomous variable was coded with zeros and ones, it turns out that the average of the values for the variable simply indicate the proportion of the sample that were assigned a one on the gender variable. Thus, our average of .70 indicates that 70% of the sample was male. We will revisit this issue of specially coding nominal data for statistical purposes as it becomes relevant to other procedures covered in this textbook.

There are three criteria that must be met in order for a nominal level variable to be measured adequately:

1. The categories must be mutually exclusive. This means that there can be no overlap between the categories of the variable. Each case must fit into one and only one category of the variable. See table 1.1 for an example of a nominal level variable that does not meet this criterion.

    As can be seen in table 1.1, the first variable for religious affiliation does not meet the "mutually exclusive" criterion since a subject who is Baptist would be unsure as to whether to identify himself/herself with the first category labeled "Protestant" or the second category labeled "Baptist." The problem is solved by eliminating the category "Baptist," which overlaps with the category "Protestant."

2. The categories must be exhaustive. This means that every case must fall into some category, even if it is a category labeled "Other." As can be seen in table 1.1, the categories "None" and "Other" were

Table 1.1 Nominal Level Variable and Violation of the Mutually Exclusive Criterion

Religious Affiliation

Protestant
Baptist
Catholic
Jewish
None
Other

included in the definition of the variable called religious affiliation so that any person responding to the variable could be assigned a category. If either of these categories had been excluded from the definition of the variable, it would be concluded that this variable had not been adequately defined since the "exhaustive" criterion had been violated.

3. The categories must be homogeneous. This means that all cases within a category are similar with respect to the attribute being represented by the category. Thus, in the example of the religious affiliation variable, all subjects labeled "Protestant" really need to be Protestants, and all subjects labeled "Catholic" really need to be Catholics. The cases do not need to be similar in any other respects except those indicated by the category label of the variable.

A final point should be made regarding nominal data. Because of the categorical nature of response options for nominal level variables (i.e., an underlying metric of measurement that cannot be subdivided infinitely), nominal data are always discrete data.

Ordinal Level of Measurement

The next highest level of measurement is the **ordinal level**. Ordinal data have all of the same properties of nominal data—mutually exclusive, exhaustive, and homogeneous categories—in addition to the characteristic of ranking the categories in order to indicate increasing amounts of the attribute being measured by the variable. Thus, ordinal variables not only classify cases into categories, they allow cases to be ranked with respect to how much of the trait being measured they possess. Because of this ranking feature, ordinal data are sometimes referred to as ranked data.

An example of an ordinal variable can be found in the following severity of crime scale:

1. Vice (or Victimless) Crimes
2. Petty Property Crimes
3. Serious Property Crimes
4. Violent Crimes

Clearly, this variable classifies cases into four mutually exclusive, exhaustive, and homogeneous categories. Additionally, as one moves across the categories of the scale, the attribute of severity of crime increases.

It should be noted, however, that while each successive category reflects a more severe criminal act, we do not know the exact amount of increase in severity as we move from category to category. This inability to determine the exact distances between the categories of the variable severely limit their submission to statistical analyses. This is due to the fact that the operations of addition, subtraction, multiplication, and division all assume equal intervals between scores (something that we cannot determine with ordinal data). Thus, ordinal data are limited to statistical analyses based on the rankings of cases.

Some additional examples of ordinal scales include: (a) a simple ranking of a list of items with regard to some attribute; (b) semantic differential scales (e.g., happy/sad; satisfied/dissatisfied); and (c) Likert-type scales (e.g., strongly disagree, disagree, neutral, agree, strongly agree).[2] It should be noted that there are times when researchers treat Likert-type scales as though they actually have equal distances or intervals between scale scores, thus allowing for the application of more sophisticated statistical techniques when analyzing the data. It is often assumed that the use of these types of scales have become so common that the distances have taken on a standardized meaning. While "purists" in the measurement field would object to such an assumption, we find that applied researchers make this assumption all the time.

A final point to be made regarding ordinal level variables is similar to a point made previously with regards to nominal data. Because of the categorical nature of response options for ordinal level variables (i.e., an underlying metric of measurement that cannot be subdivided), ordinal data are always discrete data. The only exception is in the case where Likert-type scales are being treated as interval level data (i.e., data that have equal distances between scale scores).

Interval Level of Measurement

The next highest level of measurement is the **interval level**. Interval level data have all of the properties of the two levels below it (mutually exclusive, exhaustive, homogeneous, and ranking categories or scores), in addition to the property of equal distances between the categories or scores. This means that equal score differences on the interval level variable actually reflect equal differences in the amount of the attribute being measured. For example, if a subject has six prior arrests, that is two more than the subject who has four prior arrests. And that difference of two prior arrests is the same amount of difference that would be observed between a subject who had ten prior arrests and a subject who had eight prior arrests.

However, a variable measured at the interval level of measurement does not have a true zero point. Having a true zero point means that it is possible for a case to have none of the trait being measured. The most commonly thought of interval level variable is temperature—there are equal distances between values on the Fahrenheit scale, but there is no true zero point (i.e., there is no such thing as having no temperature at all). Another example of an interval level scale is an IQ inventory—there is no such thing as having zero IQ. A final example of an interval level variable is age. Clearly, there are equal distances between the values of a variable recording a person's age, but it is not possible for a person not to have any age at all.

Because there are equal distances between the values on an interval level scale, it is acceptable to employ all mathematical operations when analyzing the data. Thus, the most sophisticated statistics can be applied to data measured at the interval level of measurement.

Ratio Level of Measurement

The highest level of measurement is the **ratio level**. Ratio data have all of the characteristics of the other three levels of measurement (mutually exclusive, exhaustive, and homogeneous categories; ranked categories or scale values; and equal distances between scale values), as well as the property of an absolute zero point. Because ratio data are measured at the highest level of measurement, the most sophisticated statistics are applicable to these data as well.

There are many examples of ratio data. A person's income in dollars, number of prior arrests, length of incarceration in months, and number of years of education, are just a few. In all of these examples, it is possible for a subject to receive a zero value for the variable, since it is possible for a subject not to have had any prior arrests, to have never been incarcerated, and to have never received any education.

Data that are measured at these two highest levels of measurement may be measured either continuously or discretely. If the metric of measurement can be subdivided infinitely (at least theoretically), then the variable is being measured continuously (e.g., time and money). But if the metric of measurement cannot be subdivided infinitely, as is the case when the variable requires the counting of human beings, the variable is being measured discretely. Note that you cannot count human beings in smaller units than integers (whole numbers).

A final point to be made concerns the implications of levels of measurement and the appropriate use of statistics. Because nominal and ordinal data do not meet the mathematical requisite of equal distances between values, they are limited to rather unsophisticated statistical analyses. Since interval and ratio variables do meet the equal distance requirement, they are equally suitable for submission to the most sophisticated statistical procedures. Henceforth, no distinction will be made between these two highest levels of measurement, and they will now be referred to as interval-ratio level variables.

Summary

This chapter broadly defined statistics as being a set of mathematical tools used to answer questions and to test ideas. We also discussed four primary reasons for learning statistics: to be informed consumers of research; to produce meaningful research; to increase job marketability; and to become a more creative and capable researcher.

Students learn to think statistically once they realize that statistics is as much an art as it is a science. Becoming statistically proficient requires exposure to a number of applied experiences. In this textbook, we will simulate a variety of experiences from across the criminal justice discipline.

To begin the process of building a strong foundation of statistical knowledge, we defined a number of key terms. Further, the four levels of measurement were defined and illustrated through the use of hypothetical examples. Now you should be ready to begin learning both the logic and mechanics of statistics.

Notes

[1] For a more complete discussion of these approaches to knowledge see Chava Frankfort-Nachmias and David Nachmias (1996). *Research Methods in the Social Sciences*. New York: St. Martin's Press.

[2] For a more detailed illustration of these types of ordinal scales see Chava Frankfort-Nachmias and David Nachmias (1996). *Research Methods in the Social Sciences*. New York: St. Martin's Press.

Key Terms

Statistics	Qualitative Data	Descriptive Statistics
Data	Quantitative Data	Inferential Statistics
Hypothesis	Variable	Measurement
Empirical	Continuous Variable	Nominal Level
Cases	Discrete Variable	Ordinal Level
Subjects	Independent Variable	Interval Level
Unit of Analysis	Dependent Variable	Ratio Level

Section One: Descriptive Statistics

MULTIPLE-CHOICE QUESTIONS

1. Information that is easily reduced to numbers is known as _____ data.
   A. Qualitative
   B. Independent
   C. Quantitative
   D. Dependent

2. Race is an example of a _____ variable.
   A. Discrete
   B. Quantitative
   C. Continuous
   D. Dependent

3. Exact number of prior arrests is a variable measured at the _____ level of measurement.
   A. Nominal
   B. Ordinal
   C. Interval
   D. Ratio

4. A variable that has been measured in such a way that it can be subdivided infinitely is called a continuous variable.
   A. True
   B. False

5. Type of religion is a variable measured at the _____ level of measurement.
   A. Nominal
   B. Ordinal
   C. Interval
   D. Ratio

6. Variability in a variable is not required for that variable to be statistically related to another variable.
   A. True
   B. False

7. Opinion about mandatory sentencing laws measured as "strongly agree," "agree," "neutral," "disagree," and "strongly disagree," is measured at the _____ level of measurement.
   A. Nominal
   B. Ordinal ✓
   C. Interval
   D. Ratio

8. A variable that is assumed to cause another variable is called the _____ variable.
   A. Qualitative
   B. Independent ✓
   C. Quantitative
   D. Dependent

9. Knowledge that is grounded in actual data is called _____.
   A. Theoretical
   B. Qualitative
   C. Quantitative
   D. Empirical ✓

10. Nonnumerical information obtained on subjects is called _____.
    A. Qualitative ✓
    B. Independent
    C. Quantitative
    D. Dependent

2

Displaying and Graphing Distributions

The first step in any data analysis component of a research project is to examine the distributions of the data collected. The researcher must have a feel for how observations are distributed across the score or value ranges of each variable. This initial data screening process often results in the researcher identifying variables that have extreme scores, too little variability in responses, or other problematic characteristics of distributions. The best way to obtain a quick overview of any data set is to generate frequency distributions, cumulative frequency distributions, percentage distributions, and cumulative percentage distributions for all of the variables. The first half of this chapter will provide instruction in the generation of these frequency and percentage distributions, both for ungrouped as well as grouped data.

Additionally, it is very useful to generate graphs of distributions of data since many of the problems that can arise with a variable's distribution can often be spotted immediately when the data are presented in a visual format. The generation of graphs and charts of distributions will be the focus of the second half of this chapter. A general discussion of the kinds of things to look for when observing graphed or charted data will be provided as well.

▬ FREQUENCY DISTRIBUTIONS

Frequency distributions are tables that summarize the number of cases contained in each category or score level of a variable. In fact, the construction of frequency distributions is the most common initial step in conducting any statistical analysis of a data set. Frequency distributions provide an overview of the distributions of the variables contained in a data set, and they allow the researcher to make sure the data have been coded properly. They do this by reducing a large amount of data to the point where it is easy to discern general patterns in responses. This allows the researcher to get to know the data set a little better before conducting any further analyses. For example, an examination of a frequency distribution for a variable would allow for the immediate detection of any extremely high or extremely low scores (called **outliers**) on that variable.

Frequency distributions also allow the researcher to identify variables on which subjects' data were coded outside the range specified by the definition of the variable. For example, if the variable called gender was coded with zeros representing females and ones representing males, a quick glance at this variable's frequency distribution would make it possible to detect if a subject had been given a code of two accidentally. We often refer to this activity of examining frequency distributions for miscoded data as **data cleaning**.

Generating Frequency Distributions

The following steps should be followed when generating frequency distributions for nominal, ordinal, and interval-ratio data:

Step 1: List values of the variable in ascending order.
Step 2: List the counts of cases that correspond to each value.
Step 3: Total the frequency column.

Using the data set reported for the ten law enforcement officers in table 2.1, frequency distributions were generated for the variables "type of agency" and "years of service." The resulting frequency distributions are located in column (a) of table 2.2. A quick examination of the frequency distributions provides us with a couple of noteworthy observations about the data set. First, a large majority of the cases in the sample were local law enforcement officers. Second, most officers had between 11 and 18 years of service, except for one outlier, an officer who had 28 years of service. Finally, we can see that the data appear to be "clean" in terms of coding, since no unreasonable values were recorded for any of the cases.

Table 2.1 Data Set for 10 Law Enforcement Officers

Officer's Last Name	Type of Agency	Years of Service
Whiteson	Local	17
James	Local	11
Shepherd	State	14
Cramer	Local	15
Martin	Local	18
Sanchez	Local	13
Black	Local	18
Baird	State	13
Snowden	Local	28
Thomas	State	13

Cumulative Frequency Distributions

When generating frequency distributions, we often add a column for the **cumulative frequency distribution** of the data. Cumulative fre-

Table 2.2 Frequency Distributions for the Law Enforcement Data Set Presented in Table 2.1

Variable Name	Values	(a) f	(b) f_c	(c) %	(d) $\%_c$
Type of Agency	Local	7	7	70.0	70.0
	State	3	10	30.0	100.0
		10		100.0	
Years of Service	11	1	1	10.0	10.0
	12	0	1	00.0	10.0
	13	3	4	30.0	40.0
	14	1	5	10.0	50.0
	15	1	6	10.0	60.0
	16	0	6	00.0	60.0
	17	1	7	10.0	70.0
	18	2	9	20.0	90.0
	19	0	9	00.0	90.0
	20	0	9	00.0	90.0
	21	0	9	00.0	90.0
	22	0	9	00.0	90.0
	23	0	9	00.0	90.0
	24	0	9	00.0	90.0
	25	0	9	00.0	90.0
	26	0	9	00.0	90.0
	27	0	9	00.0	90.0
	28	1	10	10.0	100.0
		10		100.0	

quency distributions can be defined as the frequency count of cases scoring at and below each listed category or score of a variable. Thus, you would compute them by taking the frequency count for a given value of the variable, and then add all previous frequency counts to the current category's frequency count. Column (b) of table 2.2 presents the cumulative frequency distributions for the two variables in the law enforcement officer data set. While not particularly informative, cumulative frequency distributions simply illustrate another way of summarizing the data. In fact, the most useful piece of information that can be derived from the cumulative frequency distribution of the variable named years of service is the fact that a cumulative frequency of nine was observed for many of the variable's score levels. This pattern would alert the researcher to the fact that the value 28 years of service represents an outlier.

Percentage Distributions

In addition to reporting the frequency distributions for the data, additional columns can be added to more completely describe the characteristics of the variables. The **percentage distribution** is reported in column (c) of table 2.2 and can be defined as the percentage of cases that correspond to each category or score level on a given variable. This column is computed by simply converting the frequencies listed in column (a) to percentages using the following formula:

FORMULA 2.1:

$$\% = \frac{f}{N} \times 100$$

Where: f = frequency count for category
N = sample size

The application of this formula requires the following two steps:
Step 1: for each value of the scale, divide the frequency count by the total sample size.
Step 2: multiply that value by 100.

A primary purpose for including a percentage column when generating frequency distributions is that it allows for comparisons across samples of different sizes. For example, the data listed in table 2.3 would suggest that Town B has a more serious drug problem than Town A, since there were three times as many arrests for drugs in Town B. However, when the percentage column is added to the frequency distribution (see table 2.4), we see that Town A really has the more serious drug problem since 50.6% of its arrests are drug-related, while only 27.1% of the arrests in Town B are drug-related.

Table 2.3 Frequency Distributions for Total Number of Arrests

Type of Crime	Town A f	Town B f
Drugs	42	127
Property	27	285
Violent	14	57
	83	469

Table 2.4 Percentage Distributions for Total Number of Arrests

Type of Crime	Town A %	Town B %
Drugs	50.6	27.1
Property	32.5	60.8
Violent	16.9	12.1
	100.0	100.0

Cumulative Percentage Distributions

Cumulative percentage distributions are percentiles; that is, they indicate the percentage of cases that fall at or below a given category or score level of the variable. They are computed simply by converting each cumulative frequency to a percentage using the following formula.

FORMULA 2.2:

$$\%_c = \frac{f_c}{N} \times 100$$

Where: f_c = cumulative frequency for a category or score
N = sample size

The application of this formula requires the following two steps:

Step 1: for each value of the scale, divide the cumulative frequency count by the total sample size.
Step 2: multiply that value by 100.

Because cumulative percentages are percentiles, they inform us rather quickly as to how a subject's score sits in relation to other scores in the distribution. Column (d) in table 2.2 presents the cumulative percentage distributions of the two variables contained in the data set for law enforcement officers. In that table, we can see that once the value of 18 years of service had been taken into consideration, we had accounted for 90% of the sample; thus, only 10% of the sample could fall in the score range above 18 years of service.

Working with Grouped Data

Sometimes when working with interval-ratio data, it becomes desirable to collapse score ranges of a variable in order to report more concisely what was observed. For instance, in the data set presented in table 2.1, the frequency and percentage distributions for the years of service variable could be reported in a more efficient manner if we collapsed the data into score intervals.

The advantage of score intervals is that they describe the data in a more parsimonious fashion, which means that the reader has less information to process when looking at the tabled distributions. The wider the score intervals, the more the data have been condensed, and the easier the results are to interpret.

Of course, there is a trade-off involved when we collapse data. The trade-off is the fact that grouped data preclude the reader from determining exactly how many cases were observed for each specific score on the variable. It is the responsibility of the researcher to determine how wide the score intervals will be and to select a score interval width that will be wide enough to summarize the responses in a concise manner and that will be narrow enough to prevent the loss of too much detailed information.

The following three rules must be followed when determining the width of the score interval: (1) all score intervals must be of equal width; (2) score intervals must be exhaustive—all cases must belong to some score interval; and (3) score intervals must be mutually exclusive—a case must belong to only one score interval. You should note the similarity of rules (2) and (3) to the characteristics of nominal level data. This is logical since we are collapsing interval-ratio data into score categories. Since the score intervals will maintain a ranking of observations with respect to the attribute being measured by the variable, the grouped data meet the ranking requirement of ordinal level data. As long as interval-ratio data are collapsed into equal-width score intervals, the collapsed data can be used as interval-ratio level data as well.

All of the frequency and percentage distributions that we covered in the first half of this chapter can be computed for grouped data as well. Table 2.5 presents the four distributions for the years of service variable after it was collapsed into score intervals with a width of two. Table 2.6 presents the four distributions for this same variable using score intervals with a width of five. Given the choice between the two score interval widths, a researcher probably would choose the interval width of two since the resulting distributions were easier to interpret than was the case for the ungrouped data (see table 2.2 for ungrouped distributions). Further, the distributions based on score intervals of five resulted in data that were condensed too much, which had the effect of making it difficult to discern in what ways observations differed across cases.

A helpful guide for determining the width of the score intervals is to subtract the lowest score from the highest score in the distribution; then divide that number by the desired number of score intervals. The resulting number will indicate the required width of the score intervals.

Table 2.5 Frequency and Percentage Distributions for Years of Service (Score Interval Width = 2)

Variable Name	Values	(a) f	(b) f_c	(c) %	(d) %$_c$
Years of Service	11–12	1	1	10.0	10.0
	13–14	4	5	40.0	50.0
	15–16	1	6	10.0	60.0
	17–18	3	9	30.0	90.0
	19–20	0	9	00.0	90.0
	21–22	0	9	00.0	90.0
	23–24	0	9	00.0	90.0
	25–26	0	9	00.0	90.0
	27–28	1	10	10.0	100.0
		10		100.0	

Table 2.6 Frequency and Percentage Distributions for Years of Service (Score Interval Width = 5)

Variable Name	Values	(a) f	(b) f_c	(c) %	(d) %$_c$
Years of Service	11–15	6	6	60.0	60.0
	16–20	3	9	30.0	90.0
	21–25	0	9	00.0	90.0
	26–30	1	10	10.0	100.0
		10		100.0	

Chapter Two ■ Displaying and Graphing Distributions   **25**

▬ GRAPHING AND CHARTING DISTRIBUTIONS

As stated at the beginning of this chapter, it is often helpful to graph or chart distributions of variables in order to visually detect a number of characteristics of the data. There are certain kinds of charts that are appropriate for discrete data typically observed for nominal and ordinal variables. Other kinds of graphs are more suitable for continuous data typically observed for interval-ratio variables. Once these various charts and graphs have been described, a brief discussion regarding the visual inspection and interpretation of graphs will be presented.

Charts for Displaying Discrete Data

The two most commonly used charts for visually displaying nominal, ordinal, or any discrete data are pie charts and bar charts. Both types of charts are easy to construct, either by hand or with the assistance of a computer program like SPSS or Excel. The SPSS Application at the end of this chapter demonstrates both.

The following steps should be followed to generate a pie chart by hand:

Step 1: Compute the percentage distribution for the variable.
Step 2: Draw a circle (i.e., pie) and divide into segments (i.e., slices) proportional to the percentages calculated for each category of the variable.
Step 3: Label the slices of the pie with the corresponding category labels and the percentages.

The nominal variable, type of agency, in the law enforcement officers' data set presented in table 2.1 is well-suited for the application of the pie chart. See figure 2.1 for a pie chart of this discrete variable. As can be seen in the pie chart for this variable, the vast majority of officers included in the data set worked for local law enforcement agencies. Basically, this chart provides a visual description of the information contained in the frequency and percentage distributions for the years of service variable.

A bar chart would be appropriate for visually dis-

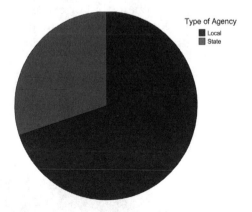

Figure 2.1   Pie Chart for Type of Agency (N = 10)

playing this nominal data as well. The following steps should be followed when generating a bar chart:

Step 1: Array category labels at equal distances across the horizontal axis.
Step 2: Array frequencies (or percentages) along the vertical axis.
Step 3: For each category of the variable, draw a rectangular bar such that the height of the bar corresponds to the frequency (or percentage) count for that category.
Step 4: Keep the bars the same width and leave a distinct space between each bar.
Step 5: Label each axis of the chart.

The bar chart of the nominal variable, type of agency, is displayed in figure 2.2. Similar to the interpretation of the pie chart, the bar chart also indicates that the vast majority of the sample of officers worked for local law enforcement agencies. An additional feature of the bar chart is the distinct space between each of the bars, accentuating the discrete nature of the data.

The choice of whether to use a pie chart or a bar chart to visually display the distribution of a discretely measured variable is at the discretion of the researcher. However, if the variable has several categories, the bar chart may be a better choice since pie charts become difficult to interpret when there are more than five slices in the pie.

Similarly, the choice of whether to report the frequency counts or the percentages for each category is another matter left to the discretion of the researcher. It is recommended that when the sample size is very small (20 or fewer cases), the researcher should report the actual frequencies rather than the percentages. The reason for this is that percentages change very dramatically when the observation for only one case is changed. For example, if we changed the type of agency for one of the local law enforcement officers, our percentage distribution would

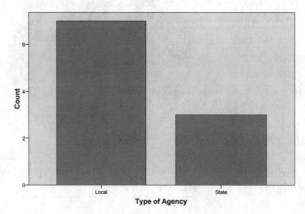

Figure 2.2 Bar Chart for Type of Agency (N = 10)

change from a report of 70% local law enforcement to a report of 60% local law enforcement. By changing the type of agency for only one case in the data set, we saw a 10% change in the percentage distribution. This is why it might be misleading to report percentages when the data were generated from small samples. On the other hand, percentages are very useful for comparing distributions of data across samples of different sizes, since the percentages standardize sample sizes to a base of 100.

Graphs for Displaying Continuous Data

Different types of graphs are required for continuous data since the visual display of the distribution needs to reflect the nondiscrete nature of the data. Since only interval-ratio level variables can be measured continuously, the two types of graphs discussed in this section, the histogram and the frequency polygon (often called a line graph), are not appropriate for use with nominal or ordinal data. Since the histogram and frequency polygon are more difficult to generate by hand than the pie and bar charts, a computer program (like SPSS) typically is used instead. Instructions for generating histograms and frequency polygons can be found at the end of the chapter in the SPSS Application.

The only visual difference between a bar chart and a histogram is the fact that the bars touch each other in the histogram, whereas they do not touch each other in the bar chart. This is because the bars in the bar chart reflect the discrete categories of the nominal or ordinal variable being charted. In the histogram, the bars reflect the previously collapsed score intervals of the variable, wherein each bar (and score interval) picks up where the last bar (and score interval) left off. A histogram for the years of service variable is displayed in figure 2.3.

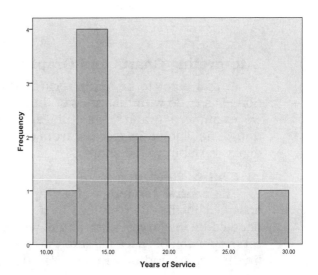

Figure 2.3 Histogram for Years of Service (N = 10)

Notice how the first four bars touch each other, reflecting the continuous underlying nature of the variable.

The final graph to be discussed in this chapter is the frequency polygon. This graph is sometimes simply referred to as a line graph, since the graph consists of a line connecting dots that represent either the actual continuous data points or the midpoints of the score intervals. A frequency polygon for the years of service variable is presented in figure 2.4.

While it is simply a matter of preference in regard to which graph to use, it seems that the histogram does a better job of representing the distribution of the variable than does the line graph, particularly since the histogram allows values of the variable that contain no cases to be identified at a glance.

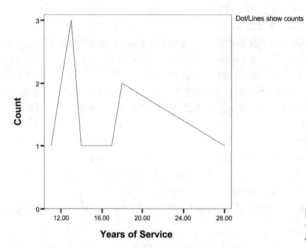

Figure 2.4   Line Graph for Years of Service (N = 10)

Interpreting Charts and Graphs

A final point to be made regarding the visual display of distributions has to do with the kinds of things we should be looking for when we examine a graph. Generally speaking, there are three primary things that should be gleaned from a graph interpretation: central tendency, variability, and shape.

Central Tendency

The **central tendency** of a graph refers to the most typical value observed in the distribution. In a pie chart, the central tendency is denoted by the largest slice of pie, which reflects the fact that the largest proportion of cases fell into that particular category of the variable. In a bar chart and in a histogram, the central tendency is denoted by the tallest bar, reflecting the fact that the category (or score interval) represented by the tallest bar contained the largest proportion of cases. Finally, the central tendency in a frequency polygon is denoted by the highest point in the line graph.

Observations of the pie and bar charts indicate that local law enforcement agency is the central tendency point for this nominal variable. Observations of the histogram indicate that the score range of 12.5–17.5 years (midpoint = 15) represents the central tendency of this ratio level variable. The central tendency is much less clear in the frequency polygon due to the outlier of 28.

Variability

Variability has to do with the amount of spread or dispersion of cases around the point of central tendency. If cases are dispersed widely on either or both sides of the central tendency point, this would be an indication of data with high variability. Conversely, if cases are all quite close in value to the central tendency point, this would be an indication of data with low variability.

In a pie chart, high variability is indicated by lots of pie slices that are all about the same size; low variability is indicated by one very large slice of pie accompanied by a few tiny slices. In a bar chart and a histogram, high variability is indicated by all bars being about the same height; low variability is indicated when there is a single bar that is considerably taller than all of the other bars. Finally, in a frequency polygon, high variability is denoted by a fairly smooth line graph; low variability is denoted by a rather jagged line graph.

Observations of the pie and bar charts suggest that the type of agency variable suffers from low variability, given the fact that one slice/bar was much bigger/taller than the other slice/bar. Observations of the histogram and frequency polygon indicate that little variability was observed in the years of service data, given the fact that the bars in the histogram were of various heights and the line graph was rather jagged.

Shape

The final interpretation feature of graphs has to do with the overall **shape** of the distribution. This particular feature only applies to graphs of interval-ratio data (i.e., histograms and frequency polygons). While in the next chapter we will learn the specific terminology for describing the shape of a distribution, some general points can be made here. First, we often look for a bell-shaped appearance in the outline of the graph. In particular, we make note of whether the distribution has only one peak, multiple peaks, or no peak. Second, we make observations regarding the symmetry of the distribution; the right side of the distribution should be a near mirror-image of the left side of the distribution for it to be symmetrical. Finally, we make note of the degree of flatness or peakedness of the distribution.

▬ Summary

This chapter described four distributions (frequency, cumulative frequency, percentage, and cumulative percentage) that can be used to summarize the way that cases are distributed across each category or score level of a variable. In addition, instruction was given on the generation of these same four distributions for use with data that have been collapsed or grouped into score intervals.

Four types of graphs and charts were introduced, along with the rationales and instructions for generating them. Pie charts and bar charts were offered as appropriate graphs for discrete level data (i.e., nominal, ordinal, and some interval-ratio variables), while histograms and frequency polygons were suggested as being the most appropriate graphs for continuously measured interval-ratio level data.

Finally, a brief discussion of the interpretation of these charts and graphs was provided. The focus of the discussion was on the three primary features (central tendency, variability, and shape) of a distribution of data, which can be gleaned immediately from a quick perusal of the graphs.

Key Terms

Frequency Distribution
Outliers
Data Cleaning
Cumulative Frequency Distribution
Percentage Distribution
Cumulative Percentage Distribution
Central Tendency
Variability
Shape

SPSS Application

1. Create the officer data set displayed in table 2.1.
2. Label the variables:

Variable Name	Variable Label	Value Labels and Other Codings
officer	Officer's Name	(Type = string; width = 25)
type	Type of Agency	(0 = State Police; 1 = Municipal Police)
yrsserv	Years of Service	

Chapter Two ■ Displaying and Graphing Distributions   31

Analysis Steps (indented steps indicate submenus in SPSS):
1. Run frequencies for "type" and "yrsserv"
   i. Analyze
      ii. Click on "Descriptive Statistics"
      iii. Click on "Frequencies"
         iv. Click each of the two variables (type and yrsserv) over to the "variables" list
         v. Click "OK"
         v. Click "OK"
2. Generate pie chart for "type"
   i. Click on "Graphs"
      ii. Click on "Legacy Dialogs"
      iii. Click on "Pie"
         iv. Click on "Define"
            v. Move "type" variable into the "Define Slice By" box
            vi. Click "OK"
3. Generate bar chart for "type"
   i. Click on "Graphs"
      ii. Click on "Legacy Dialogs"
      iii. Click on "Bar"
         iv. Click on "Simple"
         v. Click on "Define"
            vi. Move "type" variable into the "Category Axis" box
            vii. Click "OK"
4. Generate histogram for "yrsserv"
   i. Click on "Graphs"
      ii. Click on "Legacy Dialogs"
      iii. Click on "Histogram"
         iv. Move "yrsserv" into the variable box
         v. Click "OK"

5. Generate frequency polygon (line graph) for "yrsserv"
   i. Click on "Graphs'
   ii. Click on "Legacy Dialogs"
      iii. Click on "Line"
      iv. Click on "define"
         v. Move "yrsserv" into the category axis box
         vi. Click "OK"

Sample Write-Up for SPSS Application

Data were collected for 10 officers regarding the type of agency that employed them, as well as the number of years they had served as law enforcement officers. A pie chart and a bar chart were generated for the variable "type of agency" since it is a discrete variable. A histogram and a line graph were generated for the variable "years of service" since it is a continuous variable.

A visual inspection of the pie and bar charts indicated that most officers worked for local law enforcement agencies. There was low variability in the variable "type of agency" as indicated by unequal slices and bars.

A visual inspection of the histogram and line graph indicated that most officers had between 12.5 and 17.5 years of service. There was low variability in the "years of service" variable as indicated by the few tall bars in the histogram and the jagged line in the line graph. Finally, the graphs for the "years of service" variable indicated that the distribution was not very symmetrical and displayed at least two peak points of service time (13 and 18).

SPSS Assignment

1. Create the offender data set below:

Data Set for 10 Offenders

Offender's Last Name	Gender	Race	Age	# of Prior Arrests
Brown	0	3	21	5
Marietta	1	2	24	14
Sampson	0	2	26	15
Williams	0	3	28	18
Cooper	0	2	23	13
Watson	1	3	23	13
Ferguson	0	2	28	18
Lopez	1	1	23	13
Carson	0	2	38	16
Booker	0	2	27	17

Chapter Two ■ Displaying and Graphing Distributions

2. Label the variables:

Variable Name	Variable Label	Value Labels and Other Codings
name	Offender's name	(Type = string; width = 25)
gender	Offender's Gender	(Value labels: 0 = male; 1 = female)
race	Offender's Race	(Value Labels: 1 = Hispanic; 2 = White; 3 = Black)
age	Offender's Age	
Priorarr	# of Prior Arrests	

3. Generate the following analyses:
   i. Run frequency, percentage, and cumulative percentage distributions for the following variables: gender, race, age, and prior arrests
   ii. Generate pie and bar charts for the following variables: gender and race
   iii. Generate histograms and line graphs for the following variables: age and prior arrests

4. Based on the charts and graphs, write a paragraph describing what the four variable distributions look like in terms of central tendency, variability, shape, and any potential outliers in the two continuous variables.

MULTIPLE-CHOICE QUESTIONS

1. Graph interpretations involve examining a variable's shape, variability, and _____.
   A. Central Tendency
   B. Direction
   C. Score Intervals
   D. Unit of Analysis

2. The appropriate types of graphs for the variable age (measured as exact number of years) are _____.
   A. Histograms and Pie Charts
   B. Bar Charts and Line Graphs
   C. Histograms and Line Graphs
   D. Bar Charts and Pie Charts

3. Extremely low or high scores on a variable are called _____.
   A. Histograms
   B. Outliers *(circled)*
   C. Frequencies
   D. Exhaustive

4. A statistics exam had scores that ranged from 0 to 100. The researcher wants to generate a frequency distribution that has five score intervals. How wide should the score intervals be?
   A. 10
   B. 20 *(circled)*
   C. 30
   D. 40

5. _____ are tables that summarize the number of cases contained in each category of a variable.
   A. Variabilities
   B. Outliers
   C. Histograms
   D. Frequency Distributions *(circled)*

6. A researcher collapsed the variable age into five categories: 1 = Younger than 25, 2 = 25–35, 3 = 35–45, 4 = 46–55, 5 = Older than 55. What mistake did the researcher make?
   A. The categories are not exhaustive
   B. The variable should not have been collapsed
   C. The categories are not mutually exclusive *(circled)*
   D. The score intervals are not realistic

7. The shape of a distribution is something that needs to be examined for variables measured at the _____ and _____ levels.
   A. Nominal, Ordinal
   B. Ordinal, Interval
   C. Nominal, Ratio
   D. Interval, Ratio *(circled)*

Chapter Two ■ Displaying and Graphing Distributions   35

8. An appropriate type of graph to use for the variable race, measured as 1 = white, 2 = black, 3 = Hispanic, 4 = other is a _____.

   A. Bar Chart ⟵
   B. Line Graph
   C. Histogram
   D. None of the Above

9. A _____ allows the reader to determine at a glance the 75th percentile of a score distribution.

   A. Cumulative Percentage Distribution
   B. Frequency Distribution ⟵
   C. Cumulative Frequency Distribution
   D. Percentage Distribution

10. When researchers are working with a small number of cases they report raw numbers rather than percentages because _____.

    A. It is too difficult to compute percentages for small sample sizes
    B. It allows the researcher to perform the statistical analysis without the use of a computer
    C. It is misleading to report percentages when a change of a few cases can appear large when reported as percentages ⟵
    D. It is easier to interpret the statistical findings

3

Descriptive Statistics
Measures of Central Tendency and Dispersion

A primary purpose of descriptive statistics is to reduce a large amount of data down to a few concise summary pieces of information. This activity is referred to as **data reduction**. Any time one uses a few numbers, a table, or a graph to summarize a larger set of data, data reduction is taking place. This chapter will focus on quantitative statistics used to describe distributions of data. You will be instructed in the computation and interpretation of measures of central tendency, measures of dispersion, and other measures commonly used to describe the shape of a score distribution.

▄ IMPORTANCE OF QUANTITATIVE DESCRIPTIVE STATISTICS

Before getting into the mechanics of computing descriptive statistics, it is important that you acquire an appreciation of the rationale for using them. For example, if you had to generate a report describing the number of felony arrests that are handled through plea negotiations in state courts, would it be easier to convey that information by reporting each felony arrest and its corresponding disposition, or simply reporting the summary statistic that 91% of all felony arrests are handled through plea negotiations?[1] Obviously, it is much more efficient and meaningful to simply report a descriptive statistic that summarizes the larger data set.

Of course we use descriptive statistics all of the time in criminal justice research. When we read that in 2011, 53% of state prisoners were sentenced for a violent crime, as compared to 16.8% for a drug crime, and 18.3% for a property crime, we are benefitting from descriptive statistics.[2] Or when we read that in 2011, society spent an average of $28,323 per inmate for state prison operating costs, we also are benefitting from descriptive statistics.[3]

However, it should be noted that there is a trade-off involved when we reduce a large amount of data down to a few summary statistics. That trade-off is the loss of specific or detailed information contained in the complete data set. For example, how typical or representative is an average of $28,323 for all states? Do most states have average operating costs per inmate that are close to the overall average of $28,323? Or do some states have averages considerably lower than that amount, while other states have averages considerably higher than that amount (meaning that the overall average is simply a result of some low state averages canceling out some high state averages)? Because only a descriptive statistic, the average, was reported, we have no way of answering these questions. Fortunately, there are other descriptive statistics that can be provided, in addition to the average, that can assist in describing the kinds of information that tend to get lost when we use descriptive statistics to perform data reduction and summarization activities.

The key point here is that the researcher has the responsibility to be knowledgeable about the kinds of descriptive statistics that are appropriate to use so that the data will not be interpreted incorrectly. Thus, the researcher must make decisions about how to present the data and about what kinds of detailed information can be obscured or hidden safely. These kinds of decisions, like many decisions that must be made when conducting research, illustrate the creative or artistic aspect of statistics that must develop simultaneously with the more scientific techniques presented in this textbook.

■ MEASURES OF CENTRAL TENDENCY

As discussed in the interpretation of graphs section of chapter 2, it is desirable to be able to describe the point of central tendency in a score distribution. Basically, we are asking "where is the center of the score distribution?" This **central tendency** point is intended to tell us what score in the distribution is the most typical, or representative, value for all of the cases in the data set. As will be the case with most statistics, the appropriate measure of central tendency to report depends on the level of measurement of the variable.

The Mode (Mo)

The **mode** is the least sophisticated measure of central tendency, and hence the easiest to determine. It is the only central tendency statistic appropriate for variables measured at the nominal level, but also may be calculated for variables at higher levels of measurement. The mode is determined by identifying the most frequently occurring category or score in the distribution.

Table 3.1 presents hypothetical data for the three types of variables (nominal, ordinal, and interval-ratio). The mode for the nominal variable "race" is white, meaning that white is the most frequently occurring race in the distribution of the "race" variable. The mode for the ordinal variable "security level" is medium, meaning that the most typical security level for the sample is medium security. Note that there are two modes (1 and 2) for the variable "# of disciplinary infractions" since there are two most frequently occurring scores in the distribution (each score appears twice).

Because the mode is a rather unsophisticated measure of central tendency, there are some limitations with its use:

1. The distribution may not have a mode. For example, a data set with 20 cases may have 10 males and 10 females, thus, there will not be a mode since all values of the variable occurred the same number of times.

2. The distribution may have two or more modes. This occurs when there is variability in the number of cases for each category or score of the distribution, yet there are two or more values that are equally the most frequently occurring. An example of this is presented in table 3.1 where the variable "# of disciplinary infractions" has two modes (1 and 2).

3. The mode may be very misleading as a measure of central tendency since multiple occurrences of a value at either the low end or the high end of the distribution may cause a value to be identified as the mode when most of the cases really fall in the mid-

Table 3.1 Hypothetical Data Set for Nine Prison Inmates

Inmate's Last Name	Race	Security Level	# of Disciplinary Infractions
Thompson	Black	Minimum	0
Jones	White	Medium	2
Rothfuss	White	Medium	1
Gonzalez	Hispanic	Minimum	5
Bunch	White	Maximum	1
Lewis	Black	Medium	7
Minor	White	Maximum	4
Garcia	Hispanic	Medium	2
Tevis	Black	Medium	3
Measures of Central Tendency:	Mo = White	Mo = Medium Md = Medium	Mo = 1, 2 Md = 2 $\bar{X}$ = 2.78

dle of the score distribution. An example of this would be if one of the inmates identified as having 2 disciplinary infractions in table 3.1 was changed to having 7 disciplinary infractions. This would cause the mode to be 7, yet we can see that most of the inmates have a considerably lower number of infractions.

The Median (Md)

The **median** is very easy to determine; it is the middle score in the score distribution. It is the category or score that splits the score distribution exactly in half so that 50% of the cases lie below, and 50% lie above, that score. To calculate it all scores must be placed in chronological order, and then the middle score is selected. Because calculation of the median requires that scores be placed in chronological order, it is not possible to compute the median for nominal level data since there is no possible ordering of the categories of a nominal level variable. The median can be determined for both ordinal and interval-ratio level variables. Table 3.1 displays the median for "security level" (medium) and "# of disciplinary infractions" (2).

A point needs to be made about what to do if one is trying to determine the median of an interval-ratio variable (like "# of disciplinary infractions") when there are an even number of cases. Note that in the table there are nine cases. The chronologically ordered values of this variable are: 0, 1, 1, 2, 2, 3, 4, 5, 7. The 5th ordered case (2) is the median. But what if there had been 10 cases? In such a situation the median is computed by taking the average of the two middle scores. For example, if a 10th inmate were added to the table and he had eight disciplinary infractions, the ordered values of this variable would be: 0, 1, 1, 2, 2, 3, 4, 5, 7, 8. Then the median would be the average of the 5th and 6th ordered cases. The median would now be 2.5, resulting from adding the 5th ordered case (2) and the 6th ordered case (3), and then dividing by 2. Typically, these calculations are done on a computer but it is important that you understand how the resultant statistics are derived.

The Mean ($\bar{X}$)

The **mean** is the most sophisticated measure of central tendency; therefore, it can only be computed for variables measured at the interval-ratio level of measurement. It is symbolized in formulas as , and it is the arithmetic average of all of the scores in the distribution. Throughout the rest of the book formulas, like the one below for the mean, will be presented for two reasons: (1) to allow for hand calculations of the statistic and (2) to allow for the conceptual understanding of how the formula works even when processed through a statistical software package such as SPSS.

There are many Greek letters and mathematical symbols in statistics. They will always mean the same thing across formulas. Learning to read them is an important part of learning how to read and use all statistics textbooks. The uppercase Greek letter sigma (Σ) always means to sum up whatever comes after it. The letter X is a generic symbol to indicate a variable. The subscript "i" indicates an individual score in the distribution of the X variable. The letter N always refers to the total number of cases.

The formula for the mean is displayed below.

FORMULA 3.1:

$$\bar{X} = \frac{\Sigma X_i}{N}$$

Where: ΣX_i = the sum of all the individual scores on variable X
N = the total number of cases

Simply interpreted, this formula instructs us to add up all of the scores for the variable and then to divide by the total number of cases. While this type of notation seems to be a complicated way to instruct the computation of a mean (since we commonly know how to compute an average), it is important that you start learning how to read and work with formulas early on. This will assist in your ability to interpret formulas and to gain a conceptual understanding of what they are doing with the data.

Table 3.1 presents the mean for the only interval-ratio variable, "# of disciplinary infractions," which is 2.78. The calculation of the mean for this variable is as follows:

$$\bar{X} = \frac{\Sigma X_i}{N} = \frac{(0+2+1+5+1+7+4+2+3)}{9} = \frac{25}{9} = 2.78$$

It should be noted that all three of the measures of central tendency for the "# of disciplinary infractions" variable differ in value. This fact in and of itself is providing important information about not only the point of central tendency in the score distribution, but also about the shape of the distribution. This will become clearer as you think about the following three important characteristics of the mean:

1. The mean is always the exact point of central tendency in a score distribution. We know this because the scores above the mean always cancel out the scores below the mean. We prove this by creating deviation-from-the-mean scores (called **deviation scores**). A deviation score is created by subtracting the mean from a raw score. Once all of the deviation scores have been computed they are summed up; they will always total to

zero (or within plus/minus 2 one-hundredths of a point, with the slight difference from zero resulting from rounding error). Table 3.2 demonstrates this with the "# of disciplinary infractions" data from table 3.1.

It may be helpful to think of the mean as the center of a teeter-totter that is balanced because there is an equal weight of scores on each side, even if there are more scores on one side than the other. Five of the cases in table 3.2 were below the mean, while only four were above it. Yet they are balanced by the mean; the positive deviation scores cancel out the negative deviation scores.

Table 3.2 Illustration of Deviation Scores

# of Disciplinary Infractions (X)	Deviation Scores $(X - \bar{X})$	Squared Deviation Scores $(X - \bar{X})^2$
0	−2.78	7.73
2	−0.78	0.61
1	−1.78	3.17
5	2.22	4.93
1	−1.78	3.17
7	4.22	17.81
4	1.22	1.49
2	−0.78	0.61
3	0.22	0.05
	−0.02	39.57

2. If we square all of the deviation scores and then sum them up (called **squared deviation scores**) we will have what is referred to as a minimum value. That means that the variability of the scores around the mean is smaller than around any other point in the distribution. In the example in table 3.2 we see that the sum of the squared deviation scores is 39.57. If deviation scores, and subsequently squared deviation scores, were generated by subtracting a value besides the mean from each X score, the sum of the squared deviation scores would be a value greater than 39.57. Algebraically, this means that the mean simultaneously lies closer to all other scores in the distribution than does any other score. And that means that the mean is the most accurate in describing the score distribution than any other value we could think of. The importance of this feature becomes clearer later in the text, but suffice it to say that it is the reason that the mean is found so frequently in other statistical formulas; it is the best measure of central tendency when there

is a need for a summary measure that is the most typical or representative of all other scores in the distribution.

3. The mean is affected by every score in the distribution. Note that the mode and the median only make use of the most frequently occurring score, or the middle score, respectively. Only the mean uses every score in the distribution in its calculation. This has its advantages and disadvantages. The advantage is that it obviously utilizes all of the information contained in a variable since that is required in its calculation. And that is a desirable feature of a descriptive statistic since it means that the loss of information from data reduction has been minimized.

The disadvantage of this utilization of every score in the computation of the mean becomes apparent when the score distribution contains one or more extremely high or extremely low scores (called **outliers**). These outliers can cause the mean to be extremely misleading with respect to the central point of the score distribution. In fact, the outlier pulls the mean in its direction, which we call a skew in the data. If the outlier is at the low end of the score distribution, the mean will get pulled below (to the left of) the median; we call this a **negative skew**. If the outlier is at the high end of the score distribution, the mean will get pulled above (to the right of) the median; we call this a **positive skew**. The more that the median and the mean differ from each other, the more that skewness is a problem for that particular variable. A perfectly symmetrical, nonskewed distribution is identified by having a median and a mean that are equal.

The relationship between the three measures of central tendency and the shape of the score distribution is illustrated in figure 3.1. Panel A depicts a symmetrical, bell-shaped score distribution (called a normal distribution) where there is no skewness, so the three measures of central tendency are all the same. Panel B depicts a symmetrical, bimodal distribution where there is no skewness so the median and the mean are the same. Panel C depicts a uniform distribution (meaning all scores in the distribution occurred with the same frequency) where there is no mode and no skewness, thus the median and the mean are the same. Panel D depicts a positively skewed distribution where the mean is pulled in the direction of the outlier, to the right of the median. Panel E depicts a negatively skewed distribution where the mean is pulled in the direction of the outlier, to the left of the median. As illustrated, the only time the median and the mean are the same value is when the distribution is perfectly symmetrical and without outliers.

There is a statistic that measures how skewed a score distribution is. A nonskewed distribution will have a skewness statistic of zero. If the

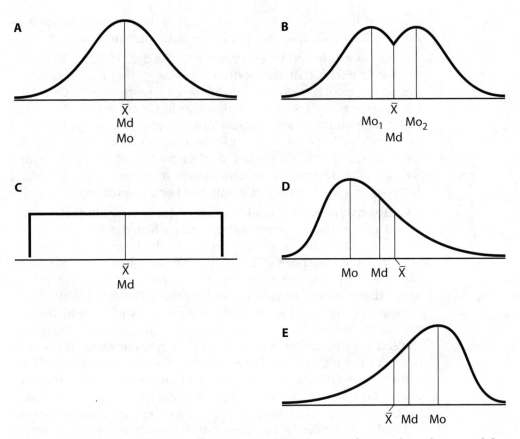

Figure 3.1 The Relationship between the Three Measures of Central Tendency and the Shape of the Distribution

skewness statistic is positive in value, the data are positively skewed (indicating one or more positive outliers). If the skewness statistic is negative in value, the data are negatively skewed (indicating one or more negative outliers). Skewness statistics greater than +/− 1.0 indicate that the score distribution should be examined for outliers. Skewness statistics greater than +/− 2.0 indicate a serious skewness problem. There are a number of complex formulas that are used to measure the skewness of a score distribution. They all vary slightly in their estimates of skewness but should be in agreement regarding the determination of a skewness problem using the guidelines provided here. Because the formulas are complex and not very intuitive in terms of how they manipulate the data, they will not be provided here. We will rely on SPSS to perform the calculation of the skewness statistic and base our interpretations of that statistic on the guidelines just presented.

In the inmate data set presented in table 3.1 the median was 2 and the mean was 2.78. Because the median and the mean do not differ much in value, we have our first indication that skewness is not a problem in the variable "# of disciplinary infractions," even though the case with seven disciplinary infractions appears to be much greater in value than most of the other data points in that variable. In the SPSS exercise at the end of this chapter you will use SPSS to generate the skewness statistic for the "# of disciplinary infractions" variable. The resultant value will be .796. Because this value is less than the 1.0 guideline, we can feel confident that skewness is not a problem with this variable. However, if the data had been highly skewed, it would be necessary to make a decision about whether to throw out the outlier case(s) causing the problem. Other, more statistical, remedies exist for handling outliers but are outside the realm of this introductory textbook.

Measures of Dispersion

As discussed in the interpretation of graphs section of chapter two, it is desirable to be able to describe the way that scores are dispersed around the point of central tendency in a score distribution. Basically, we are asking "how much variability is there in the score distribution?" The measure of dispersion is intended to tell us the degree to which the point of central tendency is the most typical, or representative, value for all of the cases in the data set. The lesser the variability in the distribution, the more representative the central tendency point is for all of the scores in the distribution, and conversely, the more variability observed in the distribution, the less representative the central tendency point is for all of the scores in the distribution. As was the case with the measures of central tendency, the appropriate measure of dispersion to report depends on the level of measurement of the variable. Table 3.3 on p. 47 presents the hypothetical data set found in table 3.1, but now includes the measures of dispersion that go with each of the measures of central tendency.

The Index of Qualitative Variation (IQV)

The **Index of Qualitative Variation** (IQV) is the only measure of dispersion that can be used to describe the variation in a nominal level variable. It can be used with ordinal variables that are treated as nominal data, as well as with interval-ratio data that have been collapsed into discrete categories. While found infrequently in the criminal justice research literature, the IQV should be reported with the mode. Most statistical packages (including SPSS) do not include the IQV as a statistical analysis option, so it generally must be computed by hand using the following formula.

Formula 3.2:

$$IQV = \frac{k(N^2 - \Sigma f^2)}{N^2(k-1)}$$

Where: k = the number of categories in the variable
N = the total number of cases
Σf^2 = the sum of the squared frequencies of each category

The IQV ranges from 0.0 to 1.0. An IQV of 0.0 means that there is absolutely no variation in the variable. This would occur if all of the cases fell in only one category of the variable. An IQV of 1.0 means that there is maximal variation across the categories of the variable. This would occur if all of the cases were evenly distributed across all of the categories of the variable. Typically, the IQV statistic falls somewhere in between these two extremes and values close to 0.0 cause the researcher to conclude that the variable has very little variation, while values close to 1.0 cause the researcher to conclude that the variable has considerable variation. Using the nominal variable "race" from the inmate data set displayed in table 3.3, the frequency distribution and IQV computations are provided below:

Variable	Categories	f	f^2
Race	Black	3	9
	White	4	16
	Hispanic	2	4
		9	29

$$IQV = \frac{k(N^2 - \Sigma f^2)}{N^2(k-1)} = \frac{3(9^2 - 29)}{9^2(3-1)}$$

$$= \frac{3(81-29)}{81(2)} = \frac{3(52)}{162} = \frac{156}{162} = .96$$

Given the high value of .96 for the IQV, it is clear that this variable has a considerable amount of variation since the sample cases are distributed almost evenly across its categories. And this makes intuitive sense since a glance at the frequency distribution shows that the nine cases are fairly evenly distributed across the three categories of the variable.

The Range (R) and the Interquartile Range (Q)

The **range** (R) and the **interquartile range** (Q) are the most appropriate measures of dispersion for variables measured at the ordinal level of measurement; thus, they should be reported with the median. As was the case with measures of central tendency, statistics that are

Table 3.3 Hypothetical Data Set for Nine Inmates and the Appropriate Descriptive Statistics

Inmate's Last Name	Race	Security Level (codes in parentheses)	# of Disciplinary Infractions
Thompson	Black (1)	Minimum (1)	0
Jones	White (2)	Medium (2)	2
Rothfuss	White (2)	Medium (2)	1
Gonzalez	Hispanic (3)	Minimum (1)	5
Bunch	White (2)	Maximum (3)	1
Lewis	Black (1)	Medium (2)	7
Minor	White (2)	Maximum (3)	4
Garcia	Hispanic (3)	Medium (2)	2
Tevis	Black (1)	Medium (2)	3
Measures of Central Tendency:	Mo = White (2)	Mo = Medium (2) Md = Medium (2)	Mo = 1, 2 Md = 2 $\bar{X}$ = 2.78
Measures of Dispersion:	IQV = 0.96	R = 2.0 Q = 1.0	R = 7.0 Q = 3.5 s = 2.22

appropriate for lower levels of measurement are also applicable with variables measured at higher levels. However, the opposite is not true; statistics appropriate for higher levels of measurement generally are not appropriate for the lower levels. When working with an ordinal variable that is a string (computer lingo for a nonnumeric or alphanumeric) variable, the ordinal categories need to be numbered before computing R and Q. This is demonstrated for the ordinal variable "security level" in table 3.3.

The range is very simple to calculate. It simply is the highest value minus the lowest value in the score distribution. The range can easily be computed for both the ordinal variable of "security level" and the interval-ratio variable of "# of disciplinary infractions":

Security Level:
    R = Highest Value − Lowest Value = 3 − 1 = 2

# of Disciplinary Infractions:
    R = Highest Value − Lowest Value = 7 − 0 = 7

The interpretation of the ranges for these data is that there is considerable variability in both variables. "Security level" varied from the central tendency point by two categories, and of course there were only three categories comprising the variable; the variable "# of disciplinary infractions" varied considerably as well with a dispersion of seven around its central tendency point.

But there are problems with the range. Because R is based on extreme values in the score distribution, it can be very misleading as a measure of dispersion when outliers are present. For example, in the distribution for "# of disciplinary infractions" the case with seven infractions appears to be somewhat of an outlier, thus inflating the variability of the score distribution. We can see that most of the scores fall well below seven. One answer to this problem is to use a truncated range called the Interquartile Range (Q). Essentially, the interquartile range is the range of the middle 50% of cases, cropping off the lower 25% and the upper 25% of cases where outliers could occur.

If we take a score distribution and divide it in half, the middle point is the median and the 50th percentile, as well as the second quartile (Q_2). If we take the lower half of the full score distribution and divide it in half, the middle of that lower half is the 25th percentile, as well as the 1st quartile (Q_1). Similarly, if we take the upper half of the full score distribution and divide it in half, the middle of that upper half is the 75th percentile and the third quartile (Q_3). This is demonstrated in figure 3.2.

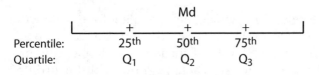

Figure 3.2   Percentiles and Quartiles

The interquartile range is computed by subtracting the 1st quartile (Q_1) from the 3rd quartile (Q_3), thereby giving us the range of the middle 50% of cases. If computing Q by hand, simply find the median of the full score distribution to split the distribution in half. Then find the median of the lower half to get Q_1, and find the median of the upper half to get Q_3, and then subtract the two. Most statistical packages will compute the quartile values for you but not do the subtraction for the value of the interquartile range; however, once the computer has identified the quartiles for you, generating Q is a simple matter of subtraction. The calculations of Q for the ordinal and interval-ratio variables in table 3.3 are:

Security Level:
$Q = Q_3 - Q_1 = 2.5 - 1.5 = 1.0$

# of Disciplinary Infractions:
$Q = Q_3 - Q_1 = 4.5 - 1.0 = 3.5$

Given the low number of categories in the ordinal variable "security level" a Q of 1.0 is not really that meaningful; however, the truncated range Q may be very useful in an ordinal variable with many categories. The value of Q is very helpful for the interval-ratio variable "# of disciplinary infractions" because it lets us know that the middle 50% of cases are dispersed around the median by only 3.5 infractions. And this information would be even more beneficial if it were describing the distribution for hundreds or thousands of inmates instead of only nine.

The Standard Deviation (s, σ)

The **standard deviation** is only appropriate for use with data measured at the highest level of measurement, interval-ratio variables. It should always be reported with the mean, because its calculation (like the mean) requires mathematical operations that require equal distances between the values of the variable. Also like the mean, it is more difficult to compute and interpret than its measures-of-dispersion counterparts. Another similarity to the mean is the fact that it uses all of the scores in the distribution in its calculation, thus resulting in a statistic that summarizes the dispersion in a score distribution with a minimal amount of lost information. However, the same disadvantage that applied to the mean regarding possible outliers also applies to the standard deviation; if outliers exist they will distort the picture of how much variability exists in the variable.

Note that there are two symbols that are used to denote the standard deviation. When the standard deviation is computed using data from the entire population, the lower-case Greek letter sigma (σ) is employed. (Remember that you have already been exposed to the upper-case Greek letter sigma [Σ], which means "the summation of.") When the standard deviation is computed using data from a sample of cases from a population, the letter s is employed. Rarely do we have population data to work with (typically because they are difficult to access, expensive, and time-consuming; usually we only have access to population data when the population is very small or when population statistics are provided, as is the case in our knowledge that the national average ACT score is 20 with a standard deviation of 5). In fact, most computer statistical packages (including SPSS) assume that the data being entered are from a sample and only calculate s rather than σ. As you soon will see, the formulas differ only slightly.

The standard deviation describes the average or typical deviation of a score from the point of central tendency, the mean. And the standard deviation increases in value as the scores in the distribution become more variable and dispersed from the mean. The greater the standard deviation, the more **heterogeneous** the score distribution, meaning the more dispersed the scores are around the mean. The smaller the standard deviation, the more **homogeneous** the score distribution, meaning the more concentrated scores are around the mean. Thus, the standard deviation is a very useful statistic because when coupled with the mean, the researcher is able to picture what the score distribution looks like.

For example, if I teach two statistics classes and both classes have an average midterm exam grade of 77, I am tempted to conclude that both classes performed similarly on the exam. But if I observe that the first class had a standard deviation of 5 points, while the second class had a standard deviation of 10 points, then I can conclude that the midterm average of 77 is much more typical and representative of the students in the first class than for those in the second class. Why? Because there is twice as much variability around the mean in the second class ($s = 10$) as in the first class ($s = 5$). That means that the mean of 77 for the second class is more a result of high test scores canceling out low test scores, whereas the mean of 77 for the first class is more a result of most test scores being close to the mean.

The formulas for the standard deviation (see formula 3.3) reveal that the standard deviation is the square root of the average squared deviation of scores around the mean. The average comes from summing up all the squared deviation scores ($\Sigma(X - \bar{X})^2$) and dividing by N (N – 1 when working with sample data). The reason that the deviation scores must be squared before summing them up is because summing the deviation scores themselves will always total to zero. And if we divided the summed deviation scores by N (as we intuitively would want to do to generate an average deviation of scores from the mean) we also would always get zero. Thus, the squared deviation scores are used instead. Since we don't typically describe variability in a score distribution in squared units, we take the square root of the squared-unit average to return the statistic to raw score units. It should be noted that before we take the square root of that average, we call it the **variance** of the score distribution (see formula 3.3).

FORMULA 3.3:

	Population	Sample
Variance:	$\sigma^2 = \dfrac{\Sigma(X - \bar{X})^2}{N}$	$s^2 = \dfrac{\Sigma(X - \bar{X})^2}{N-1}$
Standard Deviation:	$\sigma = \sqrt{\dfrac{\Sigma(X - \bar{X})^2}{N}}$	$s = \sqrt{\dfrac{\Sigma(X - \bar{X})^2}{N-1}}$

Note that the only difference between the population and sample formulas is the N – 1 in the denominator. Why do we use N – 1 instead of N when working with sample data? The reason is that s is considered to be a **biased estimator** of σ when working with sample data.

What that means is that when the sample standard deviation (s) is used to estimate the population standard deviation (σ) over many repeated trials using different samples drawn from the same population, the estimator (s) either under- or overestimates σ. Statisticians learned long ago that by using N − 1 in the denominator instead of N, the bias was corrected. Again, computer programs like SPSS err on the side of caution by always making that correction (using N − 1 instead of N) when calculating the standard deviation. As can be seen in table 3.3, the standard deviation for the interval-ratio variable "# of disciplinary infractions" is 2.22. As stated earlier, the interpretation of the standard deviation is not as straightforward as other measures of dispersion. Chapter 4 will discuss the intricacies of the standard deviation in more depth. The hand calculation of the standard deviation for the "# of disciplinary infractions" variable is demonstrated below, with the sum of squared deviations computations having already been performed in table 3.2.

$$s = \sqrt{\frac{\Sigma(X - \bar{X})^2}{N - 1}} = \sqrt{\frac{39.57}{9 - 1}} = \sqrt{\frac{39.57}{8}} = \sqrt{4.946} = 2.22$$

There are algebraic reworkings of this formula that are easier to compute by hand but yield the same result. However, these will not be demonstrated here since, as in real-life research situations, we typically will be using the computer to do most computations throughout the rest of the textbook. As stated earlier, the benefit of including formulas (particularly those that are intuitive in terms of their manipulations of the data) in this text is that you gain a conceptual understanding of what the formula is doing with the data. Additionally, the formulas provide a reference for you to work the formulas by hand if necessary.

There is one final measure of dispersion that is underutilized in the research literature. It is the kurtosis statistic. Think about the normal curve displayed in A of figure 3.1. This curve is mesokurtic because the scores are distributed around the mean in an expected, probabilistic way (we'll learn more about probability expectations later on). SPSS standardizes the kurtosis formula so that mesokurtic distributions yield kurtosis statistics of 0. However, if the raw scores are too concentrated around the mean and not distributed throughout the distribution in an expected probabilistic way, the curve will be narrower and much more peaked than the normal curve; this is called a leptokurtic distribution and will yield a kurtosis statistic greater than 0. If the raw scores are spread throughout the distribution and not concentrated around the mean as probabilistically expected, the curve will be wider and flatter than the normal curve; this is called a

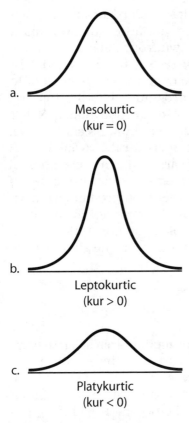

Figure 3.3 Examples of Mesokurtic, Leptokurtic, and Platykurtic Distributions

platykurtic distribution and will yield a kurtosis statistic less than 0. If the kurtosis statistic falls between −1 and 1, it is close enough to normal to assume normality. In the social sciences, we often treat distributions with kurtosis values of −2 to 2 as normal. Anything below −2 or above +2, however, indicates that we cannot assume normality for the distribution. Figure 3.3 illustrates an example of the effects of kurtosis on a score distribution.

As was the case with the skewness statistic, there are a number of formulas used to determine the kurtosis of a score distribution. These formulas vary in terms of the value of the statistic, so it is important to verify the interpretation of results (for example, the formula may not be standardized to 0 and may be interpreted around a value of 3, which was the old way of interpreting kurtosis when computations of the statistic were routinely done by hand). Because the kurtosis formula is complex and not at all intuitive in terms of how it manipulates the data, we will use SPSS to generate the kurtosis statistic for the "# of disciplinary infractions" variable. After working through the SPSS Application at the end of this chapter, you will find that the kurtosis statistic for this variable is .081, which indicates that the distribution is technically leptokurtic. However, since the kurtosis value falls between 0 and 1, we can treat it as a normal distribution.

▄ SUMMARY

This chapter taught you the importance of using descriptive statistics to describe variables in terms of their central tendency and dispersion. You learned that the level of measurement of the variable is important in determining which descriptive statistics to use. You also observed the advantages and disadvantages of each of the statistics. Finally, you learned how to calculate and interpret several statistics used to describe score distributions.

Chapter Three ■ Descriptive Statistics

The information found in chapters 1 and 3 regarding levels of measurement and the appropriate use of descriptive statistics can be summarized in the following table:

Level of Measurement	Discrete or Continuous?	Most Appropriate Measure of Central Tendency	Most Appropriate Measure of Dispersion
Nominal	Discrete	Mo	IQV
Ordinal	Discrete	Md	R or Q
Interval-Ratio	Discrete or Continuous	$\bar{X}$	s or σ

Notes

[1] Victim Input into Plea Agreements, Legal Series, Bulletin #7, November 2002. Retrieved online 2/23/06 at http://www.ojp.usdoj.gov/ovc/publications/bulletins/legalseries/bulletin7/1.html

[2] Bureau of Justice Statistics Criminal Offender Statistics. Retrieved online 9/9/14 at http://www.ojp.usdoj.gov/bjs/crimoff.htm

[3] U.S. Department of Justice. Office of Justice Programs. Bureau of Justice Statistics. Special Report. State Prison Expenditures, 2001. Retrieved online 9/9/14 at www.ojp.usdoj.gov/bjs/pub/ascii/spe01.txt.

KEY TERMS

Data Reduction
Central Tendency
Mode
Median
Mean
Deviation Scores
Squared Deviation Scores
Outliers
Negative Skew

Positive Skew
Index of Qualitative Variation
Range
Interquartile Range
Standard Deviation
Heterogeneous
Homogeneous
Variance
Biased Estimator

SPSS APPLICATION

1. Create the inmate data set displayed in table 3.1.

2. Label the variables:

Variable Name	Variable Label	Value Labels and Other Codings
Inmate	Inmate's Name	(Type = string; width = 25)
race	Inmate's Race	(1 = Black; 2 = White; 3 = Hispanic)
security	Security Level	(1 = Minimum; 2 = Medium; 3 = Maximum)
infractions	# of Disciplinary Infractions	

Analysis steps:
1. Run frequencies for "race," "security," and "infractions"
    i. Analyze
    ii. Descriptive Statistics
    iii. Frequencies
        iv. Click each of the three variables (race, security, and infractions) over to the "variables" list
        v. Click on the "Statistics" button
        vi. Check the boxes of the following:
            Quartiles
            Mean
            Median
            Mode
            Standard Deviation
            Range
            Skewness
            Kurtosis
        vii. Click on the "Continue" button
    viii. Click on the "OK" button

2. This will generate the following output:

Statistics

		Race	Security Level	# of Disciplinary Infractions
N	Valid	9	9	9
	Missing	0	0	0
Mean		1.89	2.00	2.78
Median		2.00	2.00	2.00
Mode		2	2	1[a]
Std. Deviation		.782	.707	2.224
Skewness		.216	.000	.796
Std. Error of Skewness		.717	.717	.717
Kurtosis		-1.041	-.286	.081
Std. Error of Kurtosis		1.400	1.400	1.400
Range		2	2	7
Percentiles	25	1.00	1.50	1.00
	50	2.00	2.00	2.00
	75	2.50	2.50	4.50

a. Multiple modes exist. The smallest value is shown

Be sure to interpret only the appropriate statistics for each variable. It is easier to generate all of the statistics for each variable at the same time, but only the appropriate statistics are reported in a research report; inappropriate statistics should be ignored. Specifically, for "race" the mode is the only appropriate statistic. For "security level" the mode, the median, the range, and the 25th and 75th percentiles, which can be subtracted to get the interquartile range, are appropriate. For "# of disciplinary infractions," all of the statistics are appropriate. The interquartile range must be computed by hand. Be sure to match the printout with table 3.3 to see what statistics go with which variables.

SAMPLE WRITE-UP FOR SPSS APPLICATION

Data were collected for nine prison inmates on three variables: race, security level, and number of disciplinary infractions. Descriptive statistics revealed that the most typical inmate in the sample was white (Mo = white) and was serving time in a medium security facility (Md = medium). The number of disciplinary infractions ranged from 0–7 with an average of 2.78 (s = 2.22) infractions. There was considerable variation across all three variables. Hand calculation of the IQV for race yielded a .96, indicating that inmates were almost equally distributed across the three racial categories. The range of 2 for the security level variable also indicated high variability across the three security level categories. Considerable variation occurred with respect to how many disciplinary infractions an inmate had received, as noted by a relatively high standard deviation, a rather large range (R = 7) and interquartile range (Q = 3.5). Finally, the "number of disciplinary infractions" variable was found to be fairly symmetrical and non-skewed (sk = .796, kur = .081) with cases distributed throughout the score distribution rather than being concentrated around the mean.

SPSS Assignment

1. Open the offenders data set created for the chapter 2 SPSS Assignment.
2. Run the descriptive statistics (through the frequencies option) for all four variables.
3. Calculate the IQV and Q by hand for the appropriate variables.
4. Write a paragraph describing the offenders sample with respect to the four variables.

Multiple-Choice Questions

1. The average, or the mathematical center point of a score distribution is called the _____.
   A. Mode
   B. Median
   C. Mean
   D. Range

2. A variable can have more than one mode.
   A. True
   B. False

3. The standard deviation should not be reported for data measured at the _____ level.
   A. Nominal
   B. Continuous
   C. Interval
   D. Ratio

4. The _____ is the midpoint of a distribution.
   A. Mode
   (B) Median
   C. Mean
   D. Range

5. The most appropriate measure of central tendency for the variable race is the _____.
   (A) Mode
   B. Median
   C. Mean
   D. Range

6. If the mean is higher in value than the median, the data are _____.
   A. Symmetrical
   B. Negatively Skewed
   C. Normally Distributed
   (D) Positively Skewed

7. Deviation scores will always total to _____.
   A. +1.0
   B. −1.0
   (C) 0
   D. A minimum of 2.0

8. The most frequently occurring score in a distribution is called the _____.
   (A) Mode
   B. Median
   C. Mean
   D. Range

9. The only appropriate measure of dispersion to be reported with the mode is the _____.
   A. Standard Deviation
   (B) Index of Qualitative Variation
   C. Interquartile Range
   D. Range

10. If education is defined as "less than high school," "high school diploma or GED," "more than high school diploma," the only measure of central tendency that cannot be computed is the _____.

A. Mean ✓
B. Median
C. Mode
D. Standard Deviation

4

The Normal Curve and Standard Scores

This final chapter on descriptive statistics is intended to accomplish two things: (1) to teach you how the normal curve allows us to describe data with respect to the probability associated with certain events and (2) to teach you how to describe and transform data using standard scores.

▬ THE NORMAL CURVE

The **normal curve** is a theoretical (non-empirical) frequency distribution that is a bell-shaped curve when graphed. You have already been exposed to the normal curve when you learned about skewness in chapter 3 (see figure 3.1, panel A). The normal curve has a number of defining features: it's symmetrical, unimodal, and has tails that extend to negative ($-\infty$) and positive infinity ($+\infty$). The normal distribution is so important in statistics that much of the logic of statistics stems from our knowledge of the normal curve. You should think of the normal curve as a measuring device analogous to a ruler. Because we have a standard metric called the 12-inch ruler, we can use it to measure and describe things in ways that are universally and uniformly understood. The normal curve is the ruler in statistics, and we use it to measure and describe score distributions as well as to determine probabilities associated with the events graphed under the curve.

You might wonder why statistics emphasizes the normal curve. Why would that curve be chosen as the ruler rather than the many other curves that are possible? I like to tease my statistics students by telling them that mother nature was a statistician. Most things that occur in nature seem to fit the normal curve. For example, height, weight, IQ, blood pressure, and heart rate are all variables that have a central tendency point where most people in the population tend to fall, but equal and known proportions will have values higher and lower than the mean. When we have a variable that follows the normal curve, we say that our variable is **normally distributed**. In fact, in statistics we typically assume that variables are normally distributed (called the **assumption of normality**) because we know how well the normal curve fits most data distributions.

Having said that, let me express some caution. In criminal justice research we often work with variables that we know are not normally distributed. Instead they may be skewed, or they may be symmetrical but nonnormal (like the uniform and bimodal distributions displayed in chapter 3 in figure 3.1) in shape. For example, variables such as "number of disciplinary infractions," or "time to failure on parole" typically are positively skewed. Most inmates have a low number of disciplinary infractions, but there are some inmates with a very high number of disciplinary infractions, causing the distribution of "number of disciplinary infractions" to be positively skewed. Similarly, most parolees who fail on parole do so early in their time served in the community, but there are some parolees who make it in the community for many months before failing, causing the distribution of "time to failure on parole" to be positively skewed. This means that in our discipline it is important that we examine the distributions of our variables before we submit them to analyses that are based on the assumption of normality. The reason for this is that the extent to which our variables violate the assumption of normality, our assumption of normality-based statistics will be inaccurate.

The most useful thing that the normal curve tells us is the percent of cases that will fall into various areas under the curve. The total area under the curve is 100% and represents 100% of all cases in the population. If the curve were split in half at the central tendency point, 50% of all cases would fall below the mean and 50% above the mean. We also know the specific areas between all points under the curve and those areas correspond to proportions of cases that would fall between those points. The following areas (or percent of cases) that lie between standard deviations around the mean of the normal curve serve as markers that allow for a quick assessment of where a raw score lies in the score distribution:

- 68.26% of the area (cases) under the curve lies between ± 1 standard deviation
- 95.44% of the area (cases) under the curve lies between ± 2 standard deviations
- 99.72% of the area (cases) under the curve lies between ± 3 standard deviations

See figure 4.1 for a visual depiction of these areas. As you can see, 99.72% of all cases will always fall within 3 standard deviations of the mean, regardless of what the variable is measuring as long as it is normally distributed. For example, American women have an average height of 65.5″ with a standard deviation of 2.5″.[1] The normal curve tells us that 68.26% of all American women will have heights between 63″ and 68″ (± 1 standard deviation from the mean). It also tells us that 95.44% of all American women will have heights between 60.5″ and 70.5″ (± 2 standard deviations from the mean). And it tells us almost all (99.72%) American women will have heights between 58″ and 73″ (± 3 standard deviations from the mean). Only 0.28% (100% minus 99.72%) of American women will have heights either shorter than 58″ or taller than 73″ (beyond ± 3 standard deviations from the mean).

An important concept that you should begin to think about has to do with probabilities of events. The area under the normal curve tells us the probability of randomly selecting someone who has some specified value of the normally distributed variable. If 68.26% of American women have heights between 63″ and 68″, then it should make sense that the probability of randomly selecting a woman from all American women who is between the heights of 63″ and 68″ is 68.26%. The probability of randomly selecting a woman who is between the heights of 60.5″ and 70.5″ is 95.44%. And the probability of randomly selecting a woman who is between the heights of 58″ and 73″ is 99.72%. There is only a 0.28% chance that a randomly selected woman will be shorter than 58″ or taller than 73″. You can see how areas (percent of

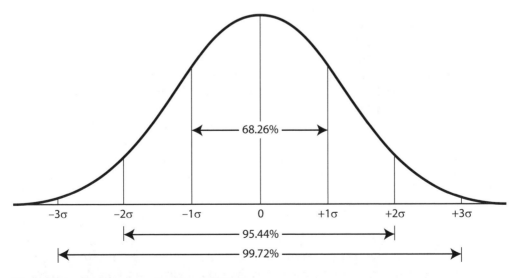

Figure 4.1 Areas under the Normal Curve

cases) under the normal curve are the same as the probability of randomly selecting someone from a population with the specified characteristics being mapped by the curve.

Key to this process of determining the probability of events is the concept of randomization. **Randomization** is a deliberate sampling process that makes the laws of probability work and you will see throughout the rest of the book how central the concept of randomization is to the appropriate use and interpretation of statistics.

▬ STANDARD SCORES (Z-SCORES)

Standard scores (called **z-scores**) involve converting raw scores to units of the raw score distribution's standard deviation. They are useful for two reasons. First, they let us describe an individual raw score in terms of where it lies in the score distribution relative to the point of central tendency and relative to other raw scores in the distribution. For example, a standard score (z-score) will allow us to determine if a person's raw score is close to the mean of the score distribution ($z = 0.00$), or whether that score is far from the mean, as would be the case with a score falling at the 90th percentile of the score distribution ($z = 1.28$). The SPSS exercise at the end of the chapter demonstrates how raw scores can be converted to z-scores and then converted to percentiles.

Second, they allow us to compare and equate scores from two distributions even when the distributions have different score ranges as long as both distributions follow the normal curve. For example, if a college admissions board allowed students to enter the university with an ACT score of 15 or higher, standard scoring would indicate that the equivalent requirement on the SAT would be 400 or higher. The calculations for this example will be demonstrated in a moment.

There are times in criminal justice research when we need to be able to combine data from two different measurement systems so that they can be treated as a single variable. One example from my own research experience involved the measurement of self-esteem of samples from juvenile and adult boot camp inmates using two different self-esteem scales: (1) a 25-item juvenile scale that was age- and reading-level appropriate and (2) a 50-item adult version with a higher reading level. I wanted to be able to determine if self-esteem changed for the adults and juveniles between the point of entry into the boot camp and the point of exit. I needed to be able to treat self-esteem as a single variable, which required combining data from two different scales that had two different score ranges. Standard scoring made it possible to convert juvenile and adult self-esteem scores to values (z-scores) that indicated how many standard deviations each score was from its own mean. Since all scores were now based on a single z-score distribution, the data could be combined into a single variable and then submitted to further statistical analyses to examine the combined adult and juvenile sample.

Specifically, z-scores transform raw scores into standard deviation units. And of course the standard deviation is a measure of how dispersed scores are from the mean. The z-score tells us how many standard deviations a raw score is from the mean. Formula 4.1 instructs us in the transformation of a raw score to a z-score.

FORMULA 4.1:

$$Z = \frac{X - \bar{X}}{s}$$

Where: Z = the standard score that corresponds to the raw score X
X = raw score
$\bar{X}$ = mean of the raw score distribution
s = standard deviation of the raw score distribution

A z-score measures the deviation of the raw score from the mean ($X - \bar{X}$) and then standardizes that difference by dividing by the standard deviation (s). Thus, any score from any score distribution can be transformed into a standard score that reflects its distance from its own distribution's mean in standard deviation units.

There are two things that z-scores tell us. The first is the magnitude of the difference between the raw score and the mean. This difference is measured in standard deviation units. The larger the absolute value of the z-score, the further the raw score is from the mean. The second is the direction of the difference between the raw score and the mean. A negative z-score indicates that the raw score is below the mean. A positive z-score indicates that the raw score is above the mean.

The ACT exam has a mean of 20 and a standard deviation of 5. The SAT exam has a mean of 500 and a standard deviation of 100. A student who receives a score of 15 on the ACT has a z-score of −1.0. Similarly, a student who receives a score of 400 on the SAT has a z-score of −1.0. Both of these students scored 1 standard deviation below the raw score mean, which is why their raw scores are equivalent and why a college admissions board would be able to determine the SAT cut score that would be equivalent to the ACT cut score. Here are the computations:

Student 1: $Z = \dfrac{X - \bar{X}}{s} = \dfrac{15 - 20}{5} = \dfrac{-5}{5} = -1.0$
(ACT)

Student 2: $Z = \dfrac{X - \bar{X}}{s} = \dfrac{400 - 500}{100} = \dfrac{-100}{100} = -1.0$
(SAT)

If we were to conduct a national study of college students and we wanted to use their admissions test scores as a single variable in our study, we could convert ACT and SAT test scores to standard scores and then combine them because we know that a student with a z-score of –1.0 scored 1 standard deviation below the mean on the test taken, regardless of which exam it was.

A final point concerning the transformation of raw scores to z-scores is that the z-score distribution is identical in shape to the raw score distribution. The z-score distribution always retains the shape of the raw score distribution in the process of the standard score transformation. The SPSS Application at the end of the chapter demonstrates this by graphing both a raw score variable and its z-score equivalent. The output presented with the application demonstrates that the only difference in the histograms is the result of the horizontal labeling of the graphs and the fact that so few cases appear in the data set. However, the skewness, kurtosis, and areas of missing data are equally evident in both graphs.

■ THE STANDARD NORMAL CURVE

When we combine our knowledge of z-scores with the normal curve, we get the **standard normal curve**. The standard normal curve is the theoretical normal curve with z-scores serving as the metric along its horizontal axis. The standard normal distribution represents the entire population of scores so the mean, which is always zero, is denoted by the Greek letter µ (pronounced "mu"). In statistics, population values are typically denoted by Greek letters, while sample values are not. The standard normal curve has a population standard deviation (σ) that is always equal to one. Since z-scores are the metric of the standard normal curve, they too have a mean of zero and a standard deviation of 1. As you can see in figure 4.2, z-scores correspond to the standard deviations of the normal curve.

The implications of this are that the things we know about the normal distribution in terms of probabilities associated with events under the curve can be determined for raw scores that come from normally distributed variables. This is accomplished by converting raw scores to the metric of the standard normal curve (z-scores), and then determining the probabilities associated with any given z-score. In a more visual sense the z-score is standardizing the raw score so that it can be mapped onto the standard normal curve and the corresponding probability can be determined. It is determined by translating areas under the curve to proportions, which are the same as the probabilities. Remember the average height example where 68.26% of American women are between 63" and 68"? The mean was 65.5" with a standard deviation of 2.5". Let's convert these two raw scores to z-scores:

Raw Score 1: $Z = \dfrac{X - \bar{X}}{s} = \dfrac{63'' - 65.5''}{2.5''} = \dfrac{-2.5''}{2.5''} = -1.0$
(63″)

Raw Score 2: $Z = \dfrac{X - \bar{X}}{s} = \dfrac{68'' - 65.5''}{2.5''} = \dfrac{2.5''}{2.5''} = 1.0$
(68″)

Remember that z-scores are the metric of the standard normal curve, so a z-score of −1.0 is the same as a standard deviation of −1.0. Similarly, a z-score of 1.0 is the same as a standard deviation of 1.0.

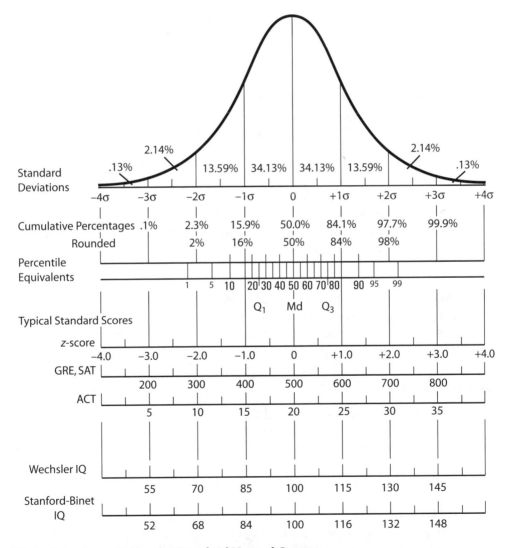

Figure 4.2 Areas Under the Standard Normal Curve

The raw score of 63" is 1 standard deviation below the mean and the raw score of 68" is 1 standard deviation above the mean. And we know from our knowledge of the normal curve that there are 68.26% of cases that fall between ± 1 standard deviation of the mean (see figure 4.1). Since we know that the normal curve maps out probabilities, we know that we have a 68.26% chance of randomly selecting a woman from the American population who will be between 63" and 68" in height. SPSS uses a density function procedure to identify the areas under the standard normal curve corresponding to any given z-score.

When z-scores do not compute to whole numbers, and when a statistical software package like SPSS is unavailable, a statistical table of areas under the normal curve can be used to determine the percentage of cases in the population that would fall between a given z-score and the mean ($z = 0$). Appendix A displays such a table. Using the table for our woman who is 68" ($z = 1.0$) we find that 34.13% of cases fall between that score and the mean. Subtracting that percentage from 50% (half of the curve) we find that 15.87% of American women are taller than 68". Adding 50% to the obtained percentage of 34.13% results in the finding that 84.13% of American women are 68" or shorter.

Other commonly used measurements are mapped on the standard normal curve in figure 4.2. From the figure it is clear that the ACT has a mean of 20 and a standard deviation of 5. This means that 68.26% of the university population scores between 15 and 25 on the ACT. We also can see that the SAT has a mean of 500 and a standard deviation of 100. This allows us to determine that an SAT score of 600 is equivalent to an ACT score of 25 since both scores are 1 standard deviation from their respective means. The same types of equivalencies can be determined for the Wechsler IQ test and the Stanford-Binet IQ test. College admissions boards and school counselors use the standard normal curve in this manner so that correct interpretations of test scores and subsequent decisions can be made.

■ SUMMARY

In this chapter you learned the features of the normal curve, how to convert raw scores to z-scores, and how to use the standard normal curve to determine the probabilities associated with events represented by the areas under the curve. You also were introduced to the concept of randomization that is so crucial to much of the field of statistics.

Note

[1] Mean and Standard Deviation for Height of American Women. Retrieved online 3/13/06 at http://www-stat.stanford.edu/~naras/jsm/NormalDensity/NormalDensity.html.

Key Terms

Normal Curve
Normally Distributed
Assumption of Normality
Randomization
z-Scores
Standard Normal Curve

SPSS Application

In this exercise you will use the "officers" data set created in chapter 2. You will convert the variable "years of service" to z-scores and then you will use the normal curve (normal cumulative density function) to generate percentiles that correspond with the raw scores and z-scores. Then you will graph (using the histogram) both the raw score variable and the z-score variable to see how they conform to the normal distribution and how they conform to each other.

Data Set for 10 Law Enforcement Officers

Officer's Last Name	Type of Agency	Years of Service
Whiteson	Local	17
James	Local	11
Shepherd	State	14
Cramer	Local	15
Martin	Local	18
Sanchez	Local	13
Black	Local	18
Baird	State	13
Snowden	Local	28
Thomas	State	13

Analysis Steps:
1. Create z-scores for the variable "yrsserv"
    i. Click on "Analyze"
        ii. Click on "Descriptive Statistics"
        iii. Click on "Descriptives"
            iv. Click "yrsserv" into variable list
            v. Check the box "Save Standardized Values as Variable"
                vi. Click "OK"

Now look at your data set and you will see that SPSS created a variable called "zyrsserv" that contains the z-scores corresponding to each raw score.

2. Transform z-scores into cumulative percentages of the standard normal curve.
   i. Click on "Transform"
      ii. Click on "Compute Variable"
      iii. Name the new variable as "percyrs" in the target variable box
      iv. Use the "Type and Label" button to label the new variable
      v. Under "Function Group" select "CDF & Noncentral CDF"
         vi. Under "Functions & Special Variables" select "cdf.Normal"
         vii. Click on arrow that puts this function into the "Numeric Expression" Box
      viii. Click on "zyrsserv" and arrow it into the "Numeric Expression" Box to replace the first "?"
      ix. Use number buttons to replace the second "?" with a "0" (mean of the normal distribution)
      x. Use number buttons to replace the third "?" with a "1" (standard deviation of the normal distribution)
         xi. Click "OK"

Now look at your data set and you will see that SPSS created a variable called "percyrs" that contains the percentiles corresponding to each raw score and z-score.

3. Graph the raw score and the z-score variables
   i. Click on "Graphs"
      ii. Legacy Dialogs
      iii. Click on "Histogram"
         iv. Move "yrsserv" into the variable box
         v. Check "Display Normal Curve" box
         vi. Click "OK"

4. Now repeat these graphing steps for the variable "zyrsserv"
   Your data set should contain the following:

Name	Agency	yrsserv	zyrsserv	percyrs
Whiteson	Local	17	.20702	.58
James	Local	11	−1.03510	.15
Shepherd	State	14	−.41404	.34
Cramer	Local	15	−.20702	.42
Martin	Local	18	.41404	.66
Sanchez	Local	13	−.62106	.27
Black	Local	18	.41404	.66
Baird	State	13	−.62106	.27
Snowden	Local	28	2.48424	.99
Thomas	State	13	−.62106	.27

Your output should look as follows:

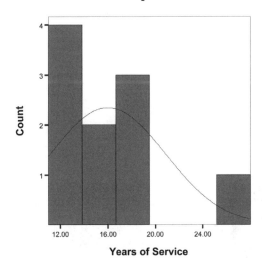
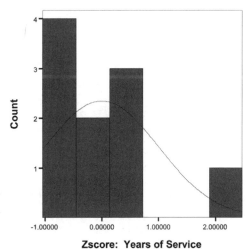

SPSS ASSIGNMENT

1. Open the offenders data set created for both the chapter 2 and chapter 3 assignments.

2. Create z-score variables for the age and prior arrest variables.

3. Transform the two z-score variables (one at a time) into cumulative percent variables.

4. Create histogram graphs for the age and prior arrest variables. Be sure to check the "Display Normal Curve" Box.

5. Answer the following questions:
   a. Using the cumulative percentage variable for age, what percent of cases would one expect to find having an age greater than 28?
   b. Using the cumulative percentage variable for prior arrests, what percentage of cases would one expect to find having 14 or fewer prior arrests?
   c. After examining the histograms, in what ways do the age and prior arrest variables differ from normality?
6. Print out the data set to display transformed variables.

MULTIPLE-CHOICE QUESTIONS

1. What percentage of cases fall between ± 3 standard deviations from the mean?
   A. 49.86%
   B. 68.26%
   C. 95.44%
   D. 99.72%

2. Standard scores convert raw scores to units of the raw score distribution's _____.
   A. Frequencies
   B. Standard Deviation
   C. Range
   D. Mean

3. Why do we often make the assumption of normality about our data?
   A. Because statistical analyses can only analyze normally distributed variables
   B. Because normal data graph neatly
   C. Because all variables are normally distributed
   D. Because the normal curve fits most data distributions

4. The raw score mean will always have a will always have a z-score of _____.
   A. 0
   B. -1
   C. +1
   D. The same value as the raw score mean

Chapter Four ■ The Normal Curve and Standard Scores   71

5. What z-score approximates the 95th percentile of the normal curve?
   A. 3.65
   B. 2.65
   C. 1.65
   D. 0.65

6. What percentage of cases fall between the mean and z = 3.2?
   A. 34.13%
   B. 48.61%
   C. 49.93%
   D. 68.26%

7. Which of the following is not a feature of the normal curve?
   A. Its tails extend to positive and negative infinity
   B. It is bimodal
   C. It is theoretical
   D. It is symmetrical

8. Converting raw data to standard scores normalizes a skewed distribution.
   A. True
   B. False

9. What percentage of cases fall above z = 3.2?
   A. 0.07%
   B. 1.39%
   C. 24.78%
   D. 48.61%

10. The laws of probability work through the process of _____.
    A. Averaging raw scores
    B. Transforming raw data to z-scores
    C. Randomization
    D. Normalization

Section Two

INFERENTIAL STATISTICS
TESTS OF GROUP DIFFERENCES

5

Introduction to Inferential Statistics

This chapter teaches the key concepts and foundations of statistics that are used both to test hypotheses and to make statistical conclusion inferences back to the population from which the study sample was drawn. In order to understand this process you must learn about probability sampling, sampling distributions, and confidence intervals. The remaining chapters in this section will then put this foundational knowledge of inferential statistics to work as you learn the process of hypothesis testing.

PROBABILITY SAMPLING

As mentioned earlier, it is often too time-consuming and expensive to study entire populations. Samples of cases from the population are typically studied instead. And as mentioned in the last chapter, randomization is key to making the laws of probability kick in so that our knowledge about areas under the normal curve and probabilities of events are accurate. **Probability sampling techniques** use random selection methods so that statistical analyses will be accurate. There are also nonprobability sampling techniques. However, only probability sampling techniques are appropriate for the use of inferential statistics, so they will be the only sampling methods discussed in this textbook.

This is how randomization invokes the laws of probability: If we know that 60% of a population is male and 40% female, and if we randomly select a person out of that population, we know that there is a 60% chance that we will select a male and a 40% chance that we will select a female. If we continue randomly selecting subjects from that same population until we have 100 subjects for the study sample, we can feel fairly confident that we will end up with approximately 60 males and 40 females in the final sample. These are the laws of probability at work. But if we move away from random sampling, we interfere with these laws, and the resultant characteristics of the selected sample become uncertain.

Because the field of statistics is driven by laws of probability, it is crucial that probability sampling techniques be used. Think about a situation where a researcher does not use a random sample for his study. He cannot be sure that his sample has the same characteristics of the population from which the sample was drawn. If he continues to collect data from the sample and analyze them, he will not be able to infer the results back to some population. There is no way to know their generalizability because there is no way to know whether his sample accurately represents the population. This is why the primary goal of all probability sampling techniques is **sample representativeness**—obtaining a sample that represents all of the key traits of the population. Sample representativeness can be assured only through the use of probability sampling techniques based on randomization. There are four types of probability sampling techniques: simple random sampling; systematic random sampling; stratified sampling; and multistage cluster sampling.

Simple Random Sampling

Simple random sampling is the purest form of sampling based on randomization. It is the most desirable form of sampling to employ. It is similar to putting the names of every person in the population into a hat and then randomly drawing names out of that hat. This process results in every person in the population having an equal chance of being selected. The two primary ways of selecting a simple random sample are (1) a random digits table (see appendix F) or (2) a random sample generator (as will be demonstrated in the SPSS Application at the end of the chapter).

When using the random digits table to select a sample, perform the following steps:

1. Assign each case in the population an identification number (if there are 50 people in the population, number cases 01–50 so that all identification numbers are the same number of digits).
2. Randomly pick a starting point in the random digits table (close your eyes and point to a starting point).
3. Read as a single number the number of digits that are in the identification numbers (if two-digit identification numbers are used then read two digits as a number).

4. If that first random number matches the identification number of someone in the population, then that subject is selected to be in the sample; if that number is not a match, read the next number to see if it is a match.
5. Keep moving across the random digits table matching identification numbers until the desired number of cases have been selected for sample inclusion. Ignore spacing between columns of random digits since they exist simply for ease of eye purposes.

Systematic Random Sampling

While simple random sampling is the purest and most desirable form of probability sampling, it can be a very tedious method to use. **Systematic random sampling** addresses this problem by making the random sampling process somewhat more efficient. It interferes a little bit with the laws of probability, but often is considered worth the trade-off in sample representativeness due to its efficiency. It frequently is employed with very large samples.

Since systematic random sampling typically is employed when working with very large populations, it is likely that a list of population names (called a **sampling frame**) will be acquired by the researcher. The following steps should be followed to obtain a systematic random sample from the sampling frame:

1. Determine the sampling interval (k) by dividing the number of cases in the population by the desired sample size:

    k = population size/desired sample size

2. Randomly select a case in the sampling frame as the starting point and as the first case for sample inclusion.
3. Pick every kth case thereafter for sample inclusion, wrapping around the list until you come back to your starting point. You should have the desired number of cases for sample inclusion when you get back to the starting point.

It should be noted that when most sampling frames are acquired, they tend to be in alphabetical order. Whenever possible the researcher should try to de-alphabetize the list before drawing the sample. The reason for this is that a quantity of the same surname can inhibit randomization. It is important that every person in the population have an equal chance of being selected to be in the sample.

Stratified Sampling

Stratified sampling is a useful technique that allows the researcher to guarantee that the sample will be representative of the population on a few selected traits. While this sampling method moves us even further away from pure random sampling (compromising sample representativeness), it is used when it is more important that the selected sample have some particular characteristics that could not be guaranteed if left to simple random sampling. For instance, if a researcher wanted to draw a sample of 100 inmates from a prison that housed mainly nonviolent offenders, it is possible that a simple or systematic random sample of that prison would result in few, if any, violent offenders. The researcher could control what proportions of the sample were violent and nonviolent offenders by stratifying the sample on offense type. The researcher would use the following steps to generate a stratified sample:

1. Stratify (divide) the population list into subpopulations based on the selected traits.
2. Employ either simple random sampling or systematic random sampling to each subpopulation list until the desired number of cases have been selected for sample inclusion from each sublist.

In the inmate sample example just given, the researcher would divide the prison sampling frame into a list of violent offenders and a list of nonviolent offenders. If he wanted a sample of 50 violent offenders and a sample of 50 nonviolent offenders, he could use systematic random sampling to determine the sampling interval (k) for each subpopulation list, and then he would use the sampling intervals to obtain 50 names from each respective list. This technique is often used when researchers want to obtain a sample that is demographically similar to another researcher's sample so that their study results can be compared meaningfully.

Multistage Cluster Sampling

Multistage cluster sampling is a probability sampling technique that moves the furthest away from pure random sampling and yields samples that are the most problematic in terms of sample representativeness. In fact, typically it is only used when there is no identifiable population or sampling frame available, thus eliminating the possibility of using the other three probability sampling techniques. Even though this technique is fraught with problems, it is still the best sampling technique available when a population list does not exist. It is used frequently in national survey efforts like the Gallup Poll. The media constantly reports on the public's views on things like approval of the president, support for gun control, and confidence in the economy. Obviously, these polling sources do not contact every American for their opinion, and they never have a complete and accurate list of the population from which to draw a random sample. Instead they use a form of multistage cluster sampling.

Multistage cluster sampling usually involves selecting a random number of geographical units (called a cluster), then smaller units from within that cluster, and then smaller units from within that cluster, until actual cases are selected for sample inclusion. Common stages in the procedure are:

1. Randomly select a certain number of larger geographical units for sample inclusion.
2. From the cluster of selected geographical units in step one, randomly select another cluster of smaller geographical units.
3. From the cluster of selected geographical units in step two, randomly select another cluster of smaller geographical units.
4. Keep doing this cluster sampling until you are selecting sample cases at the same unit of analysis to be studied.

For example, if a polling company wanted to conduct a national survey on public attitudes regarding mandatory minimum sentences and persistent felon (three strikes) laws, and if they wanted to obtain a random sample of 300 Americans to participate in a telephone poll, they could do the following: (1) randomly select six states from a list of all 50 states; (2) randomly select five counties from each of those six selected states; and (3) randomly select 10 households from each of those 30 selected counties (6 states × 5 counties × 10 households = 300). How many units are selected at the various stages is an arbitrary decision that is made by the researcher, as well as the desired overall sample size. While this process is far removed from the notion of all population members having an equal chance of being selected for sample inclusion, it yields surprisingly accurate results and it allows for inferential research that otherwise may not be possible under other sampling techniques.

SAMPLING DISTRIBUTIONS

The concept of the **sampling distribution** is arguably the most abstract and difficult aspect of inferential statistics to master. Once mastered, however, it is the key to gaining a conceptual understanding of how most statistics work. Once you understand how the laws of probability work through sampling distributions, you will understand the logic of all inferential statistics, and the rest of the statistical learning process is simply a matter of application.

When we perform inferential statistical research there are three data distributions in use. The first is the population distribution—it is empirical (based in real data), but its values on any given variable are unknown. We conduct research with the purpose of finding out what those values are in the population. The second distribution is the sample distribution. It also is empirical (again, based in real data), but its values on any given variable are known. We collect data on the sample so that it can inform us on the things we wish to know about the population. The third distribution is the sampling distribution, which is theoretical (not based in real data but rather on laws of probability), and its values are known. We weave the information obtained from the sample distribution (empirical and known) through the sampling distribution (theoretical and known) to obtain knowledge about the population distribution (empirical but unknown). All inferential statistics work in this manner. Figure 5.1 illustrates this process.

The definition of a sampling distribution is that it is a theoretical, probabilistic distribution of all possible sample outcomes for a given sample size (N). Because it contains all possible sample outcomes, it allows us to determine the probability associated with any particular sample outcome. Every statistic has its own sampling distribution that specifies the probability of that statistic taking on any given value.

An example of a sampling distribution of means would be if we drew a random sample of 100 students from a university population, calculated their average GPA, and then replaced the sample of students into the population. Then we randomly draw another sample of 100 students, calculate their average GPA, and again replace the sample of students into the population. We would keep drawing samples of 100 students, calculating their average GPAs, and then replacing them into the population. Once we had exhausted all possible samples (all possible subsets of 100 students) and calculated their average GPA, we would find that the distribution of the many average GPA values (sample means) would follow a normal curve. Most sample mean GPAs would pile up at the center of the distribution of all possible means, while fewer sample means would occur much higher or much lower than the central tendency point.

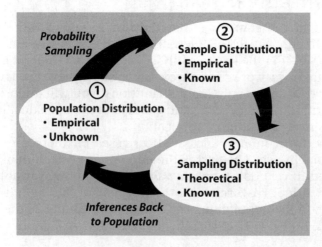

Figure 5.1 The Logic of Inferential Statistics

Why do we expect sample estimates to be accurate at times and inaccurate other times? Each time we draw a sample of individuals, there will be two sources of variation: (1) individual differences that each person uniquely brings to the sample and (2) real differences that reflect reliable relationships between variables in the population. When we draw a sample, the real differences component of the equation is constant since it is reliable (repeatable across samples of the same size from the same population), but the individual differences component of the equation varies from sample to sample. We call this individual variation **random sampling variability**, a concept that we will revisit many times throughout this text. When we calculate a sample mean on a variable for one sample, replace those individuals back into the population, and then draw another sample of the same size and calculate its mean on the same variable, we will get different results. If we keep doing this repeatedly for all of the samples of the same size out of the same population, the result will be a sampling distribution of sample means. Most of the sample means will be piled up around the true population mean, but a small percentage will fall into the negative and positive tails of the distribution, reflecting inaccurate (too low and too high) estimates of the true population mean.

Because we know so much about the theoretical normal curve, we can apply that knowledge to this sampling distribution of means in order to determine the probability of getting a sample mean of any specified value. By using the theoretical tool called the sampling distribution, we can determine these probabilities without having to actually draw all possible samples.

There are two important theorems in statistics that further define the sampling distribution. The first, the **normality theorem**, states that repeated random samples of size N drawn from a *normally* distributed population will have a sampling distribution of means that will be normally distributed with a mean of μ and a standard deviation of $\sigma / \sqrt{N}$ (called the **standard error of the mean**). This first theorem tells us that if we repeatedly draw all possible random samples of some specified size (N) and calculate the mean for each of those samples, the distribution of those sample means will follow the normal distribution. The mean of all possible sample means will be the true population mean (μ). And the standard deviation of this distribution of all possible sample means will be the population standard deviation divided by the square root of N ($\sigma / \sqrt{N}$). The standard deviation of the sampling distribution is called the standard error of the mean so as to distinguish it from a regular standard deviation. Figure 5.2 illustrates the differences between a normally distributed population distribution and the sampling distribution.

Normally Distributed Population Distribution
(contains raw score data)

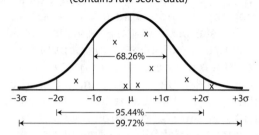

Sampling Distribution
(contains all possible sample means
of a specified N-size from the population)

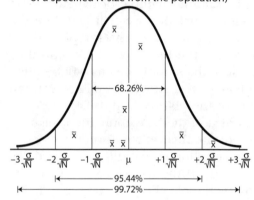

Figure 5.2

The normality theorem is important since it tells us the shape, central tendency, and dispersion of the sampling distribution. It tells us that the sampling distribution of the mean looks like the normal curve, therefore all of the things you learned about the normal curve in chapter 4 in terms of areas and probabilities under the curve also apply to the sampling distribution of the mean. Note, however, that the normality theorem indicates that these characteristics are accurate if we randomly draw samples from a normally distributed population. But what if we do not know whether the population is normally distributed? In fact, it is unlikely that we would know the shape of the population distribution since population distributions tend to be empirical but unknown. If we knew so much about the population distribution we would not need to draw a sample to obtain specific information. So what happens when we are unsure whether the population distribution is normally distributed?

Fortunately, there is a second theorem that addresses this issue. The **central limit theorem** is the most important theorem in the field of statistics. It states that when repeated random samples of size N are drawn from *any* shaped population distribution, the sampling distribution of sample means will approach normality *as N increases*. This theorem gives us assurance that as long as we use a large sample size (N), the sampling distribution of means will be normally distributed regardless of the shape of the population distribution.

Figure 5.3 demonstrates the central limit theorem. In the first row are the three parent population distributions, one being normal, one rectangular, and the other skewed. The second row displays the sampling distributions for N = 2 taken from their respective parent populations. Notice how the sampling distributions at this low sample size maintain much of the nonnormal characteristics of the rectangular

Parent Population (μ = 100, σ = 15)

Normal

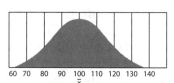

Rectangular

Skewed

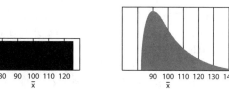

Sampling Distribution with N = 2

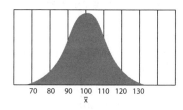
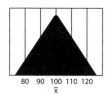
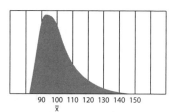

Sampling Distribution with N = 10

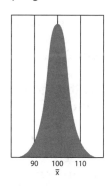

Sampling Distribution with N = 25

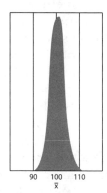

Figure 5.3   Central Limit Theorem Demonstration

and skewed parent population distributions. But once N = 10 (third row of figure) all three sampling distributions become normally distributed; it is difficult to tell which came from nonnormal population distributions. Once N = 25 (fourth row of figure) all three sampling distributions are normal, despite the fact that two of the sampling distributions drew their samples from nonnormal parent populations. It should also be noted that most of the sample means are very close to the true population mean of 100. You can only imagine how much more accurate these sample means become once sample size increases to a more typical number like 100 or greater. This is the central limit theorem at work; it assures us that as long as a sample size is large, the sampling distribution of means will be normally distributed, regardless of the shape of the parent population distribution.

This leads to the obvious question of what sample size is large enough in order to be confident that the sampling distribution of means is normally distributed. Surprisingly, once sample sizes are of at least 15 cases it is difficult to distinguish between the sampling distributions of means obtained from normal, skewed, and uniform population distributions. Most research guidelines suggest using a much more conservative rule of having at least 100 cases in the sample. However, when doing any subsample analysis there needs to be at least 15 cases in each subgroup in order for the central limit theorem assurance to apply.

Returning to our example of the sampling distribution of mean GPAs for all possible samples of 100 university students, we know from these two theorems that the sampling distribution will be normal in shape. We also know that the mean of all the sample means will be equal to the true population mean (μ), and the average dispersion of sample means around μ will be equal to the standard error of the mean ($\sigma / \sqrt{N}$). Remember that our knowledge of the normal curve applies to the sampling distribution of means. Also remember that on the normal curve, 68.26% of cases fall between ±1 standard deviation of the mean, meaning that the probability of randomly selecting a person with a value between ±1 standard deviation of the mean is 68.26%. The same laws of probability apply to the sampling distribution, where the standard deviation is the standard error of the mean. This means that 68.26% of all possible sample means will fall between ±1 standard error of the mean (see figure 5.2). Furthermore, this means that the probability of randomly selecting a sample from the population with a value that falls between ±1 standard error of the mean is 68.26%. The same principles apply when we are determining probabilities of sample outcomes for two, three, or more standard errors from the mean.

CONFIDENCE INTERVALS

When a sample is drawn and the mean for some variable is computed, that sample mean is a **point estimate** for the true population mean (remember, population data typically are unknown and must be estimated from the sample). We often want to know the range of sample mean values that would be likely to contain the true population mean that we are trying to estimate. This range of sample means, called an **interval estimate** or a **confidence interval**, tells us the range of sample mean values that would have a high probability of containing the true population mean, indicating that it is an accurate estimate. These probabilities, of course, come from the sampling distribution of the mean.

The reason we expect sample means to vary around the true population mean is due to random sampling variability—the uniqueness of the individuals in the sample that varies from sample to sample. Typically we want the probability of obtaining a sample estimate that is accurate to be 95%, and sometimes as high as 99% or even 99.9%. The more critical the use of the statistical results (e.g., medical research), the higher the desired confidence level. In the social sciences we tend to use the 95% confidence level.

The confidence interval formula tells us how big of a value to add and subtract to the mean in order to get the appropriate range of mean values. The sampling distribution tells us that 68.26% of all possible sample mean values will fall between ±1 standard error of the mean, and that 95.44% fall between ±2 standard errors of the mean, and that 99.72% fall between ±3 standard errors of the mean. Typically, we want to be much more certain than only 68.26% confident that the population value is within our interval estimate, so we tend to use very high confidence levels of 95% and 99%. If we generate a 95% confidence interval (the level that is the default in SPSS) then we are saying that we are 95% confident that the true population value falls within our interval estimate. If we generate a 99% confidence interval then we are saying that we are 99% confident that the true population value falls within our interval estimate.

A good example of this process comes from the national polls that we see reported in the media everyday. If a poll indicates that the president's approval rating is 49%, ±3% points (using the 95% confidence interval), then we know that the true average population approval rating likely falls between 46% and 52% (49% − 3%, and 49% + 3%). In other words, we can be 95% confident that the true presidential approval rating in the American population falls somewhere between 46% and 52%.

Formula 5.1 instructs the construction of a confidence interval around a mean when the population value of the standard deviation is known:

FORMULA 5.1:

$$\% \text{ C.I.} = \bar{X} \pm Z\left(\frac{\sigma}{\sqrt{N}}\right)$$

Where: % C.I. = desired confidence level
$\bar{X}$ = sample mean
Z = z-score that corresponds with the desired confidence level
$\frac{\sigma}{\sqrt{N}}$ = population standard error of the mean

But we typically do not know the population value of the standard deviation and must use "s" to estimate it. When we use the sample standard deviation (s) as an estimate of the population standard deviation (σ), we must replace the N in the denominator with N – 1 to correct for the fact that "s" is a biased estimator of σ. Thus, the formula for the confidence interval becomes:

FORMULA 5.2:

$$\% \text{ C.I.} = \bar{X} \pm Z\left(\frac{s}{\sqrt{N-1}}\right)$$

Where: % C.I. = desired confidence level
$\bar{X}$ = sample mean
Z = z-score that corresponds with the desired confidence level
$\frac{s}{\sqrt{N-1}}$ = sample standard error of the mean

You may wonder how the z-score corresponds with the desired level of confidence (% C.I.). Let's go back to our knowledge of areas under the normal curve. If we wanted to be 68.26% confident that our interval estimate covers the true population value, we would want to report the z-scores that correspond with the mean minus 1 standard error of the mean and the mean plus 1 standard error of the mean. Remember that ±1 standard error of the mean contains 68.26% of all possible sample values in a sampling distribution. Thus, the z-scores of ±1 would reflect a confidence level of 68.26%.

Any changes in desired levels of confidence require a corresponding change in z-scores. Here are the formulas for the most commonly used confidence intervals of 90%, 95%, and 99%:

FORMULA 5.3:

Population Standard Deviation Known

$$90\% \text{ C.I.} = \bar{X} \pm 1.65\left(\frac{\sigma}{\sqrt{N}}\right)$$

$$95\% \text{ C.I.} = \bar{X} \pm 1.96\left(\frac{\sigma}{\sqrt{N}}\right)$$

$$99\% \text{ C.I.} = \bar{X} \pm 2.58\left(\frac{\sigma}{\sqrt{N}}\right)$$

Population Standard Deviation Unknown

$$90\% \text{ C.I.} = \bar{X} \pm 1.65\left(\frac{s}{\sqrt{N-1}}\right)$$

$$95\% \text{ C.I.} = \bar{X} \pm 1.96\left(\frac{s}{\sqrt{N-1}}\right)$$

$$99\% \text{ C.I.} = \bar{X} \pm 2.58\left(\frac{s}{\sqrt{N-1}}\right)$$

What these z-scores tell us is that 90% of all possible sample means will fall between ± 1.65 standard errors of the population mean; 95% of all possible sample means will fall between ± 1.96 standard errors of the population mean; and 99% of all possible sample means will fall between ± 2.58 standard errors of the population mean.

Note that since we desired a higher confidence interval, our z-scores became larger reflecting the fact that more area under the curve was being accounted for by the interval estimate. There are two things that affect the width of the confidence interval. The first is the desired level of confidence. The more confident we want to be with our estimates, the wider the confidence interval. The second factor affecting the width of the confidence interval is sample size. The larger the sample size, the more narrow the sampling distribution (we know this from the central limit theorem) and the smaller the confidence interval.

Before we get into an application demonstrating the use of confidence intervals, it is important to learn how to interpret a confidence interval. A 95% confidence interval tells us that we can be 95% confident that the true population mean lies within our interval estimate. Another way of saying this is that 95% of all sample means will lie between the low end and high end of the interval estimate. Unfortunately, many people interpret confidence intervals incorrectly by saying that their point estimate ($\bar{X}$) of the population mean (μ) is 95%

accurate. Because statistics are probabilistic we can never say with certainty that our statistics are accurate. We can, however, provide a range of values that have a high probability of containing the true population value that we are trying to estimate. The interpretation of the confidence interval involves observing how wide the range of values is and then making a decision as to whether that range is narrow enough to suggest that the point estimate is likely to be representative of the true population value. This is what confidence intervals allow researchers to do.

For an example of confidence intervals, let us return to our example of a sample of 100 university students. After collecting their GPAs we calculate an average GPA of 3.1 ($\bar{X} = 3.1$), a standard deviation of 0.87 ($s = 0.87$), and of course N = 100. We want to know what the range of sample average GPAs should be in order for us to be 95% confident that our sample mean is inside that range of values. The calculations are as follows:

$$95\% \text{ C.I.} = \bar{X} \pm 1.96 \left(\frac{s}{\sqrt{N-1}} \right)$$

$$95\% \text{ C.I.} = 3.1 \pm 1.96 \left(\frac{0.87}{\sqrt{100-1}} \right)$$

$$95\% \text{ C.I.} = 3.1 \pm 1.96 \left(\frac{0.87}{\sqrt{99}} \right)$$

$$95\% \text{ C.I.} = 3.1 \pm 1.96 \left(\frac{0.87}{9.95} \right)$$

$$95\% \text{ C.I.} = 3.1 \pm 1.96 (0.0874)$$

$$95\% \text{ C.I.} = 3.1 \pm 0.1713$$

$$95\% \text{ C.I.} = 2.93, 3.27$$

Our interpretation of the results is that we can be 95% certain that the true mean GPA for the population of university students lies somewhere in the range of 2.93 to 3.27. If we wanted to know how much wider that interval would have to be so that we could be 99% confident that our interval estimate contained the population mean, we would recalculate using the formula for the 99% confidence interval:

$$99\% \text{ C.I.} = \bar{X} \pm 2.58\left(\frac{s}{\sqrt{N-1}}\right)$$

$$99\% \text{ C.I.} = 3.1 \pm 2.58\left(\frac{0.87}{\sqrt{100-1}}\right)$$

$$99\% \text{ C.I.} = 3.1 \pm 2.58\left(\frac{0.87}{\sqrt{99}}\right)$$

$$99\% \text{ C.I.} = 3.1 \pm 2.58\left(\frac{0.87}{9.95}\right)$$

$$99\% \text{ C.I.} = 3.1 \pm 2.58(0.0874)$$

$$99\% \text{ C.I.} = 3.1 \pm 0.2255$$

$$99\% \text{ C.I.} = 2.87, 3.33$$

Our interpretation of this finding would be that 99% of all samples of size 100 would give us an estimate of the true population average GPA between 2.87 and 3.33. In other words, we can be 99% confident that the true population average GPA lies between 2.87 and 3.33. Note that our confidence interval had to get wider when we changed from 95% to 99% confident in order to cover more area under the sampling distribution curve. Also note that the only thing that changed in the two calculations was the z-score. The sample mean and the standard error did not change. Only the z-score changes to reflect the change of area under the curve, or desired confidence level, of the interval estimate.

SUMMARY

This chapter taught the importance of using probability sampling when performing inferential statistical analyses, as well as the four most common methods of probability sampling. The rather abstract concept of the sampling distribution was presented along with two important theorems, the normality theorem and the central limit theorem, which allow us to conduct inferential analyses even when we are uncertain of the characteristics of the population from which the sample was drawn. The concept and application of confidence intervals was presented. The role of random sampling variability in inferential statistics was explained. Finally, the importance of using a large sample size when conducting inferential statistics was discussed.

KEY TERMS

Probability Sampling Techniques
Sample Representativeness
Simple Random Sampling
Systematic Random Sampling
Sampling Frame
Stratified Sampling
Multistage Cluster Sampling
Sampling Distribution
Random Sampling Variability
Normality Theorem
Standard Error of the Mean
Central Limit Theorem
Point Estimate
Interval Estimate
Confidence Interval

SPSS APPLICATION

1. Open the "inmates" data set created in chapter 3. Use SPSS to select a random sample of three inmates from the population of nine inmates. You will be using the random sample generator, which requires you to specify if you want an approximate user-specified percentage of the population to be selected for sample inclusion, or if you want an exact number. We will use the exact number option. (The purpose of this task is to teach you how to select samples using the random sample generator.)

    The steps are:
    i. Click on "Data"
    ii. Click on "Select Cases"
    iii. Click on "Random Sample of Cases"
    iv. Click "Sample" Button
    v. Click on "Exactly"
    vi. Type "3" in first box (desired sample size)
    vii. Type "9" in second box (population size)
    viii. Click on "Continue"
    ix. Click on "OK"

    The result of this process will be slashes through case numbers in the data set that were not selected for sample inclusion. You can now run descriptive or any other kind of statistics on the data file, and it will only use the remaining cases in the file. You can save the data file under a new name if you want a file with only the sample cases active for data analysis.

2. Generate a confidence interval for the average on the "# of disciplinary infractions" variable using all nine cases in the "inmates" data set.

First, you need to select all cases to be active in the data file:
i. Click on "Data"
   ii. Click on "Select Cases"
   iii. Click on "All Cases"
   iv. Click on "OK"

Now, generate the 95% and 99% confidence intervals for the "average number of disciplinary infractions" variable:
i. Click on "Analyze"
   ii. Click on "Descriptive Statistics"
      iii. Click on "Explore"
         iv. Move the "number of disciplinary infractions" variable to the "Dependent List"
         v. Click on "Statistic" under "Display"
         vi. Click on the "Statistics" Button
         vii. Type in the desired percentage for the confidence interval (default is 95%)
      viii. Click on "Continue"
   ix. Click on "OK"

The results of following this procedure was that the nine inmates had an average of 2.78 disciplinary infractions. The 95% confidence interval was 1.07 – 4.49, and should be interpreted to mean that 95% of all inmate samples of size nine from the population from which they were drawn will yield average estimates ranging from 1.07 to 4.49 disciplinary infractions. Another way to say this is that we can be 95% confident that the true population mean lies in the range of 1.07 to 4.49 disciplinary infractions.

When the procedure was repeated for the 99% confidence interval the results indicated that 99% of all inmate samples of size nine from the population from which they were drawn will yield average estimates ranging from 0.29 to 5.26 disciplinary infractions. Another way to say this is that we can be 99% confident that the true population mean lies in the range of 0.29 to 5.26 disciplinary infractions. Clearly, these confidence intervals are rather large, indicating that we cannot feel very confident that the average for our sample (2.78) is a good estimate of the true population mean. The best way to reduce the widths of the confidence intervals is to increase sample size.

SPSS Assignment

1. Open the "officers" data set created in chapter 2.
2. Use the random sample generator to create a random sample of four law enforcement officers. Print out the data file showing selected and unselected cases.
3. Select all of the cases in the data set.
4. Generate 95% and 99% confidence intervals around the sample mean for the "years of service" variable.
5. Write a couple of paragraphs interpreting the confidence intervals and discussing the issue of sample size and confidence interval width.

Multiple-Choice Questions

1. A listing of all known cases in a population is called a _____.
   A. Sample
   B. Sampling Distribution
   C. Sampling Frame
   D. Representative Sample

2. If a population is comprised of 40% nonwhites and 60% whites, there is a _____ chance that a randomly selected person will be nonwhite.
   A. 20%
   B. 40%
   C. 60%
   D. 80%

3. If a researcher wants to conduct a study on a population for which no population list is available the most appropriate probability sampling technique is _____.
   A. Multistage Cluster Sampling
   B. Systematic Sampling
   C. Stratified Sampling
   D. Simple Random Sampling

4. Provided they use large sample sizes, the _____ allows researchers to use statistics based on the assumption of normality even when they do not know what the shape of the population distribution looks like.
   A. Sampling Frame
   B. Confidence Interval
   C. Normality Theorem
   (D). Central Limit Theorem

5. If a researcher has a very large sampling frame and must select the sample by hand, the most efficient sampling technique is _____.
   A. Multistage Cluster Sampling
   (B). Systematic Sampling
   C. Stratified Sampling
   D. Simple Random Sampling

6. Researchers use the largest samples possible because it ensures that the _____.
   (A.) Sampling distribution of means will be normally distributed
   B. Sampling interval will be large
   C. Sample will be representative of the population
   D. Population mean will fall outside the confidence interval

7. Decreasing the level of confidence in the estimate of the population mean has the effect of _____.
   A. Decreasing the sample size
   (B). Decreasing the width of the confidence interval
   C. Increasing the sample size
   D. Increasing the width of the confidence interval

8. If a researcher is doing a study and wants to select a specific percentage of males and females in the sample, then the researcher should use the _____ technique.
   A. Multistage Cluster Sampling
   B. Systematic Sampling
   (C.) Stratified Sampling
   D. Simple Random Sampling

9. Probability sampling techniques are often preferred by researchers because _____.
   A. They help ensure that the sample is representative of the population
   B. They guarantee that the statistical analyses will be accurate
   C. They keep the laws of probability from being invoked
   D. They are easier to use than nonprobability sampling techniques

10. If a researcher wants to conduct a study where every case in the population has an equal chance of being selected into the sample the researcher should use _____.
    A. Multistage Cluster Sampling
    B. Systematic Sampling
    C. Stratified Sampling
    D. Simple Random Sampling

6

Hypothesis Testing

The focus of this chapter is hypothesis testing in inferential criminal justice research. The methods of hypothesis testing are presented along with a discussion of statistical decision errors. Finally, a distinction is made between statistical and practical significance.

The material in this chapter is at times abstract and challenging to learn. That is because it discusses the theoretical statistics that underlie statistical reasoning and the hypothesis testing process. Future chapters will apply these concepts with data illustrations and you should become more comfortable with the material through these applications. It is recommended that you repeatedly review this chapter whenever necessary as you learn to put these concepts to work through criminal justice applications.

ROLE OF HYPOTHESIS TESTING IN CRIMINAL JUSTICE RESEARCH

In the last chapter you learned how inferential statistics are used to generate interval estimates (confidence intervals) to accompany a point estimate (sample mean). Now you will learn the other primary use of inferential statistics, which is hypothesis testing. **Hypothesis testing** involves breaking a research question down to succinct testable statements (called **hypotheses**) about relationships between variables, testing those relationships, and using inferential statistics to determine the reliability of the test results. Because the study sample would be selected using a probability sampling technique, the results of the hypothesis testing can be generalized back to the population from which is was drawn.

It is through hypothesis testing that the important questions in our discipline get answered. For example, if you wanted to examine whether there are gender differences in recidivism rates for juvenile delinquents completing a six-month boot camp program, you could use hypothesis testing to determine if gender is reliably related to the measure of recidivism. If you wanted to examine whether there are differences between races in stress levels of correctional officers, you could use hypothesis testing to determine if race is reliably related to the measure of stress. If you wanted to examine whether arrest levels one year after release from prison were lower for a sample of male inmates than the arrest levels one year prior to being admitted to prison, you could use hypothesis testing to determine whether incarceration is reliably related to a decrease in arrest activity. There are an infinite number of questions in our discipline that can be addressed using hypothesis testing.

There are two concepts that need to be developed before the methodology of hypothesis testing is presented. First, it should be noted from the examples above that when we ask questions of differences between groups on some criterion (outcome) variable, we are asking whether there is a reliable relationship between the variable measuring group membership and the criterion variable. The question of whether there is reliable group difference on some criterion variable is the flip side of the same coin measuring whether there is a reliable association or relationship between the variable measuring group membership and the criterion variable. Both sides of the coin are addressing the same underlying question: are two variables reliably related to each other? If a variable measuring group membership is reliably related to a criterion variable (the "reliable relationship" side of the coin), then there is a reliable difference between the groups on the criterion variable (the "reliable group differences" side of the coin). So when we ask if there is a reliable difference between male and female juvenile delinquents in their number of police contacts, we also are asking if there is a reliable relationship between the variable measuring gender and the criterion variable measuring police contacts.

The other concept that needs to be developed concerns the meaning of the term **reliable differences**, which in statistical terms is more generally referred to as **statistically significant differences**. Reliable (statistically significant) differences are ones that can be expected to be observed repeatedly across different samples in different studies measuring the same relationship. They are differences that are in fact real, and not simply an artifact of the differences we might expect between groups simply due to the particular sample we drew for our study. Every sample is unique in terms of the individual variations across people comprising the sample. That means that some samples will display group differences on a criterion variable simply due to the unique characteristics of that particular sample. In statistics this is referred to as random sampling variability, a concept you were introduced to when learning about confidence intervals in chapter five. **Random sampling variability** is the part of observed group differences that is due to the unique characteristics of the sample the researcher happened to select for that particular study. It is the job of statistics to distinguish for the researcher which observed group differences (or relationships between variables) are in fact real, reliable, repeatable, and statistically significant, and which observed group differences are simply the result of random sampling variability.

METHODS OF HYPOTHESIS TESTING

The Research Question

We often undertake an area of research because we want to answer some broad research question. For example, we may start out with the following research question: Are female inmates more likely to have completed more years of education than male inmates? It is important that before starting the process of hypothesis testing we have properly measured (operationalized) all of the variables imbedded in the research question. Clearly, gender should be operationalized as a dichotomous (two-category) variable of males and females. The variable "years of education" is straightforward as well since it can be measured at the interval-ratio level and continuously as "number of years of school completed." Now the research question can be refined as follows: Are there reliable (statistically significant) differences across gender groups in the average number of years of school completed? This is an example of a research question that is now amenable to the hypothesis testing process because it clearly indicates what groups are being compared and on what criterion they are being compared.

The Five-Step Model for Hypothesis Testing

There is a **five-step model for hypothesis testing** that is commonly used in inferential statistics. It is useful because it makes the process more systematic, and it keeps us from forgetting important things that should be kept in mind when doing hypothesis testing. This model will be taught in this chapter and then will be demonstrated in applications throughout the rest of the chapters in this section of the book. In brief, the five steps are:

Step 1: Make Assumptions
Step 2: State Hypotheses
Step 3: Select Sampling Distribution and Specify Decision Criteria
Step 4: Compute the Test Statistic
Step 5: Make a Decision

Each of these steps will described now in detail.

Step 1: Make Assumptions

As you have already learned from working with probability sampling, sampling distributions, and confidence intervals, statistics is all about the laws of probability. Theoretical curves (like the normal curve) display areas representing probabilities of events. Each type of statistical test has an underlying theoretical curve as well as a number of assumptions upon which the accuracy of the test is based. When assumptions of statistical tests are violated, there is an increased chance that the statistical tests and their results will be inaccurate. A few of the most common assumptions made when using inferential statistics in hypothesis testing will be discussed here; others will be discussed as they become applicable in future applications and chapters.

You have already learned from the discussion of probability sampling techniques that samples must be randomly selected in order for the laws of probability to kick in, ensuring a sample that is representative of the population and thus allowing for reliable inferences of results from the sample back to the population. This means you are already acquainted with the **assumption of randomization**, where the statistical test assumes the sample was selected using randomized probability sampling techniques. The more that pure randomization (simple random sampling) is involved in the probability sampling method, the more this assumption is upheld and the inferences of results are appropriate. The more the sampling method moves away from pure randomization, the greater the degree to which this assumption is violated and the inferences are inappropriate.

Another common assumption in hypothesis testing is the **assumption of normality**, where the statistical test assumes that the sampling distribution upon which the statistical test is based is normally distributed. The normality requirement is due to the fact that the known areas (probabilities) under the normal curve will be displaced to other unknown areas of the curve to the degree that the sampling distribution is not normal. For example, 68.26% of sample means (and area under the curve) falls between ± 1 standard error of the mean in a normally distributed sampling distribution of means. If the sampling distribution is not normally distributed, then a different (and unknown) percentage of sample means (and area under the curve) falls between ± 1 standard error of the mean, resulting in inaccurate statistical results. We know from the normality and central limit theorems that as long as sample size (N) is large, the sampling distribution will be normally distributed, regardless of the shape of the population distribution from which the sample was drawn. A researcher tries to employ as large a sample as possible so that this assumption can be upheld; small sample sizes increase the likelihood that this assumption will be violated and that the statistical results will be inaccurate.

The third most common assumption in hypothesis testing has to do with the level of measurement of the dependent variable. If the statistical test is testing for reliable gender differences in the number of years of education completed, then the test will assume that the dependent variable, number of years of education completed, is measured at the interval-ratio level of measurement (e.g., actual number of years of schooling completed). If the variable is measured at a lower level, say the ordinal level (e.g., < high school; high school/GED; college degree), then the **assumption of interval-ratio data** would be violated and the test results would be inaccurate. If a statistical test is testing whether there is a reliable relationship between two nominal level variables (e.g., gender and a dichotomous variable measuring completion or noncompletion of high school), then the **assumption of nominal data** would be the appropriate assumption underlying the hypothesis test of that relationship.

Step 2: State Hypotheses

In this step the research question is broken down into two succinct, testable statements about the relationship between the variables. There are two types of hypotheses that are used to capture our research question, "Are there reliable (statistically significant) differences across gender groups in the average number of years of school completed?" The first type of hypothesis is the **null hypothesis** (H_0, pronounced H-sub-not), and it is always a statement of "no difference." It states that there is no difference between the groups on the criterion variable and that any observed difference is simply a result of random sampling variability (the sample we happened to select). The null hypothesis always represents the status quo; at the outset of the study we have no reason to believe that there is a difference between male and female inmates in their education levels, and we must continue to believe that until we have research evidence to indicate otherwise.

The other type of hypothesis is the **alternative hypothesis** (H_1, pronounced H-sub-one), and is always the opposite of the null hypothesis. It states that there is a real, reliable, and statistically significant difference between the groups on the criterion variable. In the case of our example, it states that there is a reliable difference between male and female inmates in their education levels. The alternative hypothesis is sometimes called the research hypothesis because it affirmatively captures the relationship between the variables specified in the research question.

It usually is the hope of the researcher that the conclusion of the statistical results will indicate that the null hypothesis should be rejected and that the data will provide support for the alternative hypothesis. It is important to note that the statistical analysis can rule out (cause us to reject) the null hypothesis, indicating that the statement of "no difference" across the groups on the criterion variable is false. But rejecting the null hypothesis does not necessarily mean that the alternative hypothesis statement of a real, reliable, and statistically significant difference has been proven true. It only means that research data has been uncovered that lends support to the alternative hypothesis. Statistics are all about probabilities, and there is always the chance that our statistics are wrong simply due to sampling and statistical artifacts. It takes other researchers repeating the study on other samples (called **replication**) to demonstrate that the relationship stated in the alternative hypothesis is in fact real and reliable. Remember the scientific inquiry process from chapter 1. It is the job of each researcher to take that wheel around as far as s\he can, and only after many researchers have each taken the wheel around to study the same relationship and have consistently come up with the same conclusions can we feel confident in saying that a reliable difference between groups (or relationship between variables) exists.

Continuing with our "gender differences in education" example, the null hypothesis states that there are no reliable differences between male and female inmates in their average number of years of education completed; symbolically we would write this as: $H_0: \mu_1 = \mu_2$, which states that the population mean education level for group one (males) equals the population mean education level for group two (females).

In similar fashion, the alternative hypothesis states that there are reliable differences between male and female inmates in their average number of years of education completed; symbolically we would write this as: $H_1: \mu_1 \neq \mu_2$, which states that the population mean education level for group one (males) does not equal the population mean education level for group two (females). The process of hypothesis testing results in a conclusion as to which of these hypotheses is most probable.

Hypotheses are always stated using population parameters (e.g., μ) instead of sample estimates (e.g., $\bar{X}$). The reason for using population parameters is that the primary purpose of inferential statistics and probability sampling is to be able to conclude something about a population based on data obtained from a representative sample. Even though the data came from a sample, probability sampling ensures that the sample is representative of the population, so the sample results can be generalized back to the population. We infer things about the population based on evidence obtained from the sample.

Step 3: Select Sampling Distribution and Specify Decision Criteria

Selecting the Sampling Distribution. As stated previously, each statistical test has an underlying sampling distribution upon which it is based. The first thing that takes place in this step is to select the statistical test, hence the sampling distribution, that will be used to test the hypotheses. Each type of research question you ask lends itself to the calculation of a specific statistical test (called the **test statistic**). For example, a research question regarding gender differences in education levels of inmates would lead to one type of statistical test, while a research question regarding the relationship between gender and type of conviction charge of inmates would lead to another type of statistical test. You will learn about many of the possible research questions and their appropriate test statistics throughout the remainder of this textbook.

The sampling distribution for each statistical test maps out the probabilities associated with a true null hypothesis since that is the hypothesis being retained until there is evidence to believe otherwise. As you will soon learn, the conclusion regarding whether the null hypothesis should continue to be retained or whether it should be rejected is based on those probabilities.

It also is in this step that the researcher sets the criteria for determining whether an observed difference between groups (or an observed relationship between variables) is statistically significant (reliable). You will recall when learning about confidence intervals in chapter five that sample estimates ($\bar{X}$) may vary around the true population value (μ) simply due to random sampling variability (unique variation brought to each sample by the individuals comprising the sample) and not due to a reliable difference between the sample mean and the population mean. Any sample mean that fell within the 95% confidence interval (level of confidence typically used in the social sciences) of mean values was considered to be a good estimate of the population mean, meaning that the observed differences across those sample means was due to random sampling variability. Any sample mean that fell outside that 95% confidence interval of mean values was considered to be reliably different from the population mean.

Sampling distributions for test statistics work similarly. The test statistic sampling distribution is based on the assumption that the null hypothesis is true. The center of that sampling distribution is the test statistic value of zero, which represents a population that has no reliable differences between groups on the criterion variable. There is a 95% confidence interval that allows for variations of the test statistic around that population value simply due to random sampling variability. But if a test statistic falls outside that 95% confidence region, it falls into what is called the **critical region**, the area of extreme test statistic values (located in the upper and lower tails of the sampling distribution) that would cause us to reject the null hypothesis since those test statistic values have varied away from the center of the sampling distribution (representing "no group differences") by an amount that we would not consider to be simply the result of random sampling variability. When this happens we conclude that we have detected reliable (statistically significant) group differences.

But if the null hypothesis is really true, and the extreme test statistic values have caused us to incorrectly reject the null hypothesis, then our statistical conclusion is wrong. We know in statistics we can never be 100% certain of our statistical results since they are based on laws of probability; statistics is not an exact science. How often will we incorrectly reject the null hypothesis? The answer depends on the percentage of the test statistic's sampling distribution we designate as the critical region. The specification of this percentage is called **setting alpha**.

Setting Alpha. The Greek letter **alpha** (α) represents the probability of incorrectly rejecting a true null hypothesis. When the researcher sets alpha, he is specifying the risk level he is willing to take for being wrong in his decision to reject a true null hypothesis. It also is the percentage of area under the sampling distribution curve that makes up the critical region, so setting the alpha also defines the critical region. Typically, in social science research this area is set at 5% and is called alpha ($\alpha = .05$).

The area not in the critical region represents our confidence that any variations of the obtained test statistic from the population value of zero (representing no group differences) is simply due to random sampling variability. The noncritical region is similar to a confidence interval in that respect. The noncritical region and its corresponding critical region (set by alpha) always add up to 100% of the area under the curve. If we are willing to risk incorrectly rejecting a true null hypothesis 5% of the time ($\alpha = .05$), then the noncritical region is 95%. If we are willing to risk incorrectly rejecting a null hypothesis only 1% of the time ($\alpha = .01$), then the noncritical region is 99%. And if we are willing to be wrong in our decision to reject the null hypothesis only 0.1% ($\alpha = .001$), then the noncritical region is 99.9%.

Figure 6.1 displays the critical regions for risk levels of .05 and .01. Note that the larger alpha (.05) yields larger critical regions or areas under the curve that will lead to the rejection of the null hypothesis. This means that it is easier to reject the null hypothesis at the higher alpha level, but it simultaneously means that there is an increased probability that the null hypothesis has been incorrectly rejected.

The noncritical regions are the percentages of the time that we will allow fluctuations of the test statistic from the center of the distribution, fluctuations that we will attribute to random sampling variability. But when an obtained test statistic falls inside the critical region we will reject the null hypothesis. Alpha is the probability that we will get

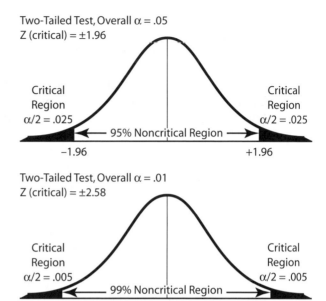

Figure 6.1 Critical Regions for .05 and .01 Alpha Levels

an obtained value of the test statistic that is so extreme (inside the critical region) that we will reject the null hypothesis and conclude that there is a reliable group difference (or relationship), but in reality it really was due to random sampling variability and our statistical conclusion to reject the null hypothesis is wrong.

When we do hypothesis testing and we set alpha at 0.05, we are acknowledging that five out of 100 statistical tests that should cause us to retain the null hypothesis will actually indicate that we should reject it. But we never know if our particular statistical test result is one of the 95 that resulted in the proper decision to retain the null hypothesis, or if it is one of the five that will have us incorrectly reject the null hypothesis. That is the probabilistic nature of statistics and the reason caution should always be exercised when interpreting statistical results.

All researchers must set the criterion of how "wrong" they are willing to be in their statistical decision. In social science research we typically accept a risk level of 5% ($\alpha = .05$), meaning we are willing to be wrong 5% of the time in our statistical decision to reject the null hypothesis. In research that has much more critical and life-impacting consequences, like medical research (e.g., we would not want the statistical test to falsely indicate that a new cancer drug is effective and should replace traditional treatments), more stringent risk levels (e.g., $\alpha = .01$ and $\alpha = .001$) should be employed.

Choosing One-Tailed or Two-Tailed Tests. The final activity that takes place in step 3 of the hypothesis testing model is to choose whether a **one-tailed test** or a **two-tailed test** will be conducted. The most common type of test is two-tailed. A two-tailed test means that alpha (the risk level of incorrectly rejecting a true null hypothesis) will be split evenly into the two tails (lower and upper) of the sampling distribution of the test statistic. Two-tailed tests indicate that we don't know if our error in decision making will occur due to an obtained test statistic that is either too low or too high. Since we rarely have reason to believe that the error would be more likely to occur in one tail more than the other, we typically split alpha between the two tails. For example, if we set alpha at 0.05, then 0.025 would be placed in the lower tail and 0.025 would be placed in the upper tail. Since alpha also sets the critical region, an obtained test statistic would have to fall into the extreme 2.5% of either tail of the sampling distribution in order for us to conclude that the null hypothesis should be rejected and that there is a reliable group difference (or relationship). Two-tailed tests are the default in most statistical software packages, including SPSS.

One-tailed tests occur when all of alpha is placed into only one tail (either lower or upper) of the sampling distribution of the test statistic. The implication is that the error in decision making would only occur in one direction and not the other. For example, if a sample of fourth graders were selected based on low reading scores to participate in a special reading program, and if the program were being evaluated for effectiveness in increasing reading scores after six months in the program, the researcher would only expect that all scores would either stay the same or improve. The researcher would not expect scores to decrease. Thus, there is no need for the statistical test to test for average reading score differences in the lower end of the sampling distribution (the end reflecting lowered reading scores; H_1: $\mu_{post} < \mu_{pre}$). Instead, the researcher could feel fairly confident that if any reliable differences in test scores occurred after exposure to the reading program, they would only occur in the upper end of the sampling distribution (the end reflecting improved reading scores; H_1: $\mu_{post} > \mu_{pre}$). Note that when conducting a one-tailed test, the alternative hypothesis (H_1) is the statement that reflects the change from the more common two-tailed test. The null hypothesis continues to be a statement of no difference (H_0: $\mu_{post} = \mu_{pre}$). Figure 6.2 illustrates two-tailed and upper and lower one-tailed tests when overall alpha = .05.

Great caution should be exercised when using one-tailed tests. If you suspect that the error in decision making would only occur in the upper tail, and it really occurred in the lower tail, it would be missed by the statistical test, and vice versa. So why do researchers ever use one-tailed tests when they know that it is safer to use two-tailed tests? The reason is that it is easier to reject the null hypothesis in a one-tailed test. Remember that alpha sets the critical region for rejecting the null hypothesis. If an obtained test statistic falls into the upper tail of the sampling distribution, it is much harder for it to land in the 2.5% critical region of a two-tailed test. But if all of alpha is placed into the upper tail to begin with (a one-tailed test), then the obtained test statistic only has to make it into the 5% critical region in order for the null hypothesis to be rejected. Simply stated, the one-tailed test makes it easier to reject the null hypothesis.

Most researchers set out to conduct their research with the hopes that the null hypothesis will be rejected and that support will be found for their alternative hypothesis of reliable group differences and relationships. You could say that researchers using one-tailed tests are stacking the probability deck in their favor to find statistically signifi-

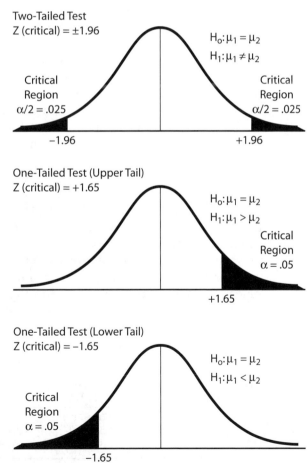

Figure 6.2 Two-Tailed and One-Tailed Tests (Overall α = .05)

cant results. The more conservative approach (and the one that will be demonstrated in this textbook) is to always use the two-tailed test. If the relationship between variables is strong enough to call it reliable, then it should be evident from both the one-tailed and the two-tailed tests. Always be leery of statistical conclusions that can be supported using a one-tailed test but not a two-tailed test.

Table 6.1 presents the placement of alpha in both tails, the upper or lower tails, and the corresponding critical values of z for a 5% alpha level. The critical value of z establishes the critical region of the sampling distribution that will be used to make the ultimate decision regarding statistical significance. Locating $z = 1.96$ in appendix A, which reports the areas under the normal curve, you will discover that there is .4750 or 47.5% of the area under the curve between the z-score of 1.96 and the mean. This means that there is 2.5% in the tail (50% – 47.5%). Because the lower half of the curve mirrors the upper half it is apparent that 5% (2 × 2.5%) of the area under the curve exceeds $z = \pm 1.96$. That corresponds to our 5% alpha level and allows for the identification of the critical region.

If we want to perform a one-tailed test, meaning that all 5% of alpha will be placed in one tail, we need to look for the z-score that leaves 45% between the z-score and the mean. Using appendix A we find that the z-scores 1.64 and 1.65 are each off by .05% so the common practice is to select the most conservative value (the one that pushes the critical value further into the tail and thus makes it harder to reject the null hypothesis), meaning that + or –1.65 is the appropriate critical z-score to use when conducting a one-tailed test. Figure 6.2 demonstrates the use of z-scores to establish the critical regions.

To summarize the third step of the hypothesis testing model, the researcher states the statistical test to be used, the alpha level to be used to make the decision as to whether the null hypothesis should be retained or rejected, and whether the test is one-tailed or two-tailed. If performing the statistical test by hand the researcher would go one step further to identify the critical value of z (using appendix A), which places the specified alpha level into the tails of the sampling distribution thereby establishing the critical regions for the statistical test.

Table 6.1   One-Tailed versus Two-Tailed Tests

Symbol in Alternative Hypothesis (H_1)	Type of Test	Placement of α	z-Score That Marks Off Critical Region
≠	two-tailed	both tails	±1.96
>	one-tailed	upper tail	+1.65
<	one-tailed	lower tail	–1.65

Step 4: Compute the Test Statistic

In this step the actual sample data are processed through formulas to yield an obtained test statistic that can then be used in step 5 to make a decision regarding whether the null hypothesis should be retained or rejected. As stated earlier, each type of research question can be matched to an appropriate statistical test. The appropriateness of specific tests to particular research questions will be discussed and demonstrated throughout the remaining chapters in this book.

Step 5: Make a Decision

Each time a statistical test is computed (step 4), the probability associated with that obtained test statistic (called a ***p-value***) is calculated as well. The researcher compares that p-value with the alpha level that was set in step 3, since alpha is what defines the critical region. If the p-value is greater than alpha, the obtained test statistic falls outside the critical region, the null hypothesis is retained and the observed group difference (or relationship) is concluded to be unreliable, not statistically significant, and the result of random sampling variability. If the p-value is less than alpha, the obtained test statistic falls inside the critical region, the null hypothesis is rejected and the observed difference is concluded to be reliable, repeatable, and statistically significant.

Another way to determine if the obtained test statistic falls in the critical region is to compare the obtained test statistic with the critical value of the test statistic. If the obtained statistic exceeds the critical value that marked off the beginning of the critical region, then it makes sense that the test statistic falls inside the critical region and the null hypothesis should be rejected. If the obtained test statistic does not exceed the critical value then the test statistic necessarily falls outside the critical region and the null hypothesis should be retained.

It bears repeating that the decision is always made with respect to the null hypothesis: either it is retained and the conclusion is that there is no statistically significant (reliable) group difference (or relationship between variables), or it is rejected and the conclusion is that there is some empirical support (but not definitive proof) that there is a statistically significant (reliable) group difference (or relationship between variables). Figure 6.3 illustrates the relationship between p and α in making the decision to retain or reject the null hypothesis.

TYPE I AND TYPE II ERRORS

We have already said that alpha is the probability of falsely rejecting a true null hypothesis. If we falsely reject a true null hypothesis, then we have committed what is called an **alpha error** or a **Type I**

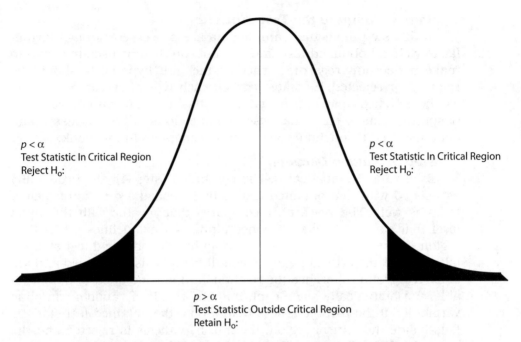

Figure 6.3 Making the Decision to Retain or Reject the Null Hypothesis

error. The probability of making a Type I error is whatever we set alpha to be. If $\alpha = .05$, then there is a 5% chance that we will make a Type I error, which means there is a 5% chance that we will reject the null hypothesis and conclude that a statistically significant group difference (or relationship) exists, when in fact there is no reliable group difference (or relationship). This is why medical researchers often use $\alpha = .01$ so that there is only a 1% chance that they have falsely concluded that a reliable group difference or relationship exists. Lowering alpha makes it harder to reject the null hypothesis so it makes sense that it would result in a lower probability of falsely rejecting a true null hypothesis. The opposite also is true; increasing alpha makes it easier to reject the null hypothesis and the probability is higher that a true null hypothesis will be rejected falsely.

Why wouldn't all researchers use a more conservative alpha level like medical researchers? Wouldn't all researchers like to minimize the risk of falsely rejecting a true null hypothesis? Of course, but minimizing the risk of making a Type I error is linked to the flip side of the probability coin representing the probability of making a Type II error. A **Type II error**, often called a **beta error**, occurs when the researcher fails to reject a null hypothesis that really is false. The Type II error means that the researcher retained the null hypothesis, concluded that there was no statistically significant group difference (or relationship), when in fact a reliable group difference or relationship exists.

While Type I and Type II errors are the opposite of each other, the probability of setting a Type II error is only partially and indirectly determined by the alpha level chosen by the researcher. It is complicated and beyond the scope of this book to delve into how the probability of making a Type II error is determined. What is important to know is that alpha and beta are inversely related to each other; the lower the alpha (probability of making a Type I error) is set by the researcher, the higher the probability of making a Type II error, and vise versa.

Statistics textbooks often present a table like 6.2 to illustrate how Type I and Type II errors relate to hypothesis testing. This table illustrates that there are two possible situations in reality: the null hypothesis can be false, and the null hypothesis can be true. There are two possible decisions that the researcher may make in the process of hypothesis testing: reject the null hypothesis or retain the null hypothesis. If the researcher's statistical results cause him to reject a false null hypothesis then the correct decision was made. If the researcher's statistical results cause him to reject a true null hypothesis then a Type I (alpha) error was made. If the researcher's results cause him to retain a true null hypothesis then the correct decision was made. If the researcher's results cause him to retain a false null hypothesis then a Type II (beta) error was made.

Table 6.2   Type I and Type II Errors in Decision Making

Decision	Reality	
	False Null	True Null
Reject Null	Correct Decision	Type I (alpha) Error
Retain Null	Type II (beta) Error	Correct Decision

The decision that the researcher has to make at the very outset of the study is which type of error is of the most concern for the study results. If the study tests medications that involve the health of human beings, then the researcher is going to want to use a very conservative alpha level, resulting in a lower probability of falsely rejecting a true null hypothesis, i.e., a lower probability of concluding that a medication has an impact that it, in fact, does not. But this researcher must be wary of the fact that by lowering the probability of making a Type I error he has increased the probability of making a Type II error, resulting in a higher probability of failing to reject a false null hypothesis, i.e., a higher probability of concluding that a medication does not have an impact that it, in fact, does.

This dilemma is the main reason why researchers tend to look to their own discipline for guidelines on where to set alpha and the corre-

Table 6.3 Relationship between Alpha and Type I and Type II Errors

Action	Effect on Null Hypothesis
Decrease α	• Makes it harder to reject H_0 • Decreases probability that a true H_0 will be rejected incorrectly (Type I Error) • Increases probability that a false H_0 will be retained incorrectly (Type II Error)
Increase α	• Makes it easier to reject H_0 • Increases probability that a true H_0 will be rejected incorrectly (Type I Error) • Decreases probability that a false H_0 will be retained incorrectly (Type II Error)

sponding Type I error rate. In the social sciences, setting the Type I error rate at α = .05 seems to provide a good balance between Type I and Type II error rates. Researchers in the hard sciences and medicine tend to use a more conservative Type I error rate, such as α = .01 and α = .001, so as to make it harder for them to falsely reject a true null hypothesis, but at the same time making it easier for them to commit the Type II error of failing to reject a false null hypothesis.

STATISTICAL VERSUS PRACTICAL SIGNIFICANCE

We have spent a considerable amount of time on the decision-making process regarding whether a group difference (or relationship between two variables) is statistically significant. Yes, statistical significance is required for us to be able to conclude that a reliable group difference (or relationship) exists. But statistical significance does not guarantee practical significance. **Practical significance** means that the identified group difference or relationship has meaning in practical application. For example, if it is determined that a new reading curriculum for fourth-graders significantly (reliably) improves reading scores by two points on a 100-point reading test, the finding may not have practical significance. If that two-point increase does not translate into anything meaningful in terms of outcomes (e.g., improved grades in other course work) then it is likely that it will not be worth the money it would take to implement the new reading curriculum.

Typically researchers hope that their research findings will result in substantive implications for practice or policy. We know that sample size plays an important role in the statistical outcome of hypothesis testing. We want to employ as large a sample as possible in our study because the central limit theorem tells us that large samples make it easier to get statistically significant findings. If a huge sample of several thousand subjects is employed in a study, it is likely that even tiny differences between groups and slight associations between variables will be determined to be statistically significant. It is the job of the researcher to use caution when interpreting statistical results based on large samples to make sure that any group differences and relationships between variables found to be statistically significant are also practically significant and meaningful before practice and policy implications are addressed.

SUMMARY

This chapter covered many of the key concepts at the heart of statistical hypothesis testing and the role that hypothesis testing plays in answering questions in our discipline. The logic and reasoning of the five steps in the hypothesis testing model were presented. We discussed the role of alpha in determining Type I and Type II error rates. Finally, we distinguished statistical from practical significance. While this chapter was abstract and conceptual, it provides a strong foundation for the more applied half of the course.

KEY TERMS

Hypothesis Testing
Hypothesis
Reliable Differences
Statistically Significant Differences
Random Sampling Variability
Five-Step Model for Hypothesis Testing
Assumption of Randomization
Assumption of Normality
Assumption of Interval-Ratio Data
Assumption of Nominal Data
Null Hypothesis (H_0)
Alternative Hypothesis (H_1)

Replication
Test Statistic
Critical Region
Setting Alpha
alpha (α)
One-Tailed Test
Two-Tailed Test
p-value
Type I (alpha) Error
Type II (beta) Error
Practical Significance

HOMEWORK ASSIGNMENT

Answer each of the following questions by writing a paragraph using your own words:

1. Explain the meaning of the following phrase: "The null hypothesis is always a statement of no difference."

2. Explain what it means to have concluded that a "statistically significant" difference between groups exists on some criterion variable.

3. Explain the effect of increasing alpha on the decision to reject the null hypothesis.

4. Explain how alpha is related to Type I and Type II errors.

5. Explain the importance of replication in research.

MULTIPLE-CHOICE QUESTIONS

1. The point of making the assumption of randomization is to _____.
   A. Make sure that the highest level of measurement is always used
   B. Make sure the correct hypotheses are stated
   C. Make sure the appropriate statistical analyses are performed on the data
   D. Ensure that the laws of probability are invoked

2. Rejecting a null hypothesis that is actually true is called a _____.
   A. Type I Error
   B. Type II Error
   C. Critical Region
   D. Critical Value

3. Performing a two-tailed test instead of a one-tailed test makes it _____.
   A. More difficult to reject the null hypothesis
   B. Less difficult to reject the null hypothesis
   C. More difficult to test the null hypothesis
   D. Less difficult to test the null hypothesis

4. Reliable group differences are also called _____.
   A. Random Sampling Variability
   B. Statistically Significant Differences
   C. Critical Values
   D. Type I Errors

5. A research question can be broken down into succinct testable statements. These statements are called _____.
   A. Assumptions
   B. Critical Phrases
   C. Hypotheses
   D. Paradigms

6. If the *p*-value is greater than alpha, the obtained test statistic falls outside the critical region and the null hypothesis should be _____.
   A. Restated
   B. Retested
   C. Retained
   D. Rejected

7. Increasing alpha makes it _____.
   A. More difficult to reject the null hypothesis
   B. Less difficult to reject the null hypothesis
   C. More difficult to test the null hypothesis
   D. Less difficult to test the null hypothesis

8. If the *p*-value is less than alpha, the obtained test statistic falls inside the critical region and the null hypothesis should be _____.
   A. Restated
   B. Retested
   C. Retained
   D. Rejected

9. Observed group differences that are due to the unique characteristics of the particular samples selected for the study are called _____.
   A. Random Sampling Variability
   B. Statistically Significant Differences
   C. Critical Values
   D. Type I Errors

10. Making assumptions regarding the level of measurement of the dependent variable is done to _____.
    A. Make sure that the highest level of measurement is always used
    B. Make sure the correct hypotheses are stated
    C. Make sure the appropriate statistical analyses are performed on the data
    D. Ensure that the laws of probability are invoked

7

Nonparametric Tests
Chi-Square Tests

This chapter continues to apply concepts learned earlier in the text to hypothetical research situations that are realistic for the field of criminal justice. The two statistical tests in this chapter come from a family of tests called **nonparametric**, which simply means "assumption freeer." Specifically, tests from the nonparametric family typically do not have the requirement that the assumption of normality be made; thus, there is no need to use large sample sizes in order to activate the central limit theorem. The combination of being able to use small sample sizes, along with data that are measured at the lowest levels of measurement, makes **nonparametric tests** desirable for analyzing categorical data obtained from small samples. While there are many statistical tests in the nonparametric family, the two most popular, the chi-square goodness-of-fit test and the chi-square test for independence, will be the only nonparametric tests presented in this chapter. Both chi-square (χ^2, pronounced kī square) tests use the Greek letter chi (χ) as their symbol.

▬ Purpose and Types of Chi-Square Tests

The purpose of this chapter is to present two statistics tests that are used to conduct statistical testing of nominal dependent variables (or ordinal variables that are treated as nominal). Both of these tests involve testing for significant differences between the observed and expected frequency patterns of either one or two categorical variables. In the case of the **chi-square (χ^2) goodness-of-fit test**, **observed frequency counts** across the categories of a single categorical variable will be compared to the **expected frequency counts**. The expected frequencies are usually defined as an equal number of cases occurring in each category of the variable. The test allows the researcher to determine if the observed frequency pattern across the categories of a single categorical variable differs in a statistically significant way from the expected frequency distribution, or if instead, the observed and expected frequency patterns just differ from each other in a way that is due to random sampling variability.

For example, if we wanted to know if any type of crime is reported to the police in one (or more) season of the year more than in the other seasons, this type of test would allow for statistical testing of the research question. The test would compare the observed frequencies (or number of crimes committed) across the four seasons of the year with the expected frequency pattern defined as an equal number of crimes committed in each season of the year. If the observed and expected frequency patterns are determined by the test to be statistically significantly different, then seasonal variation in the crime occurred; however, if the observed and expected frequency patterns are determined to vary from each other simply as a result of random sampling variability, then the conclusion would be that there is no seasonal variation in the occurrence of the specified crime.

In the case of the **chi-square (χ^2) test for independence**, the observed and expected joint-frequency distributions of two categorical variables are compared. (The term joint-frequency will be explained a bit later in the chapter.) In the chi-square test for independence, if statistically significant differences are discovered between the observed and expected joint frequency patterns of the two variables, the conclusion is that the variables are reliably related to each other. If no statistically significant differences between the observed and expected joint frequency patterns of the two variables are discovered, the two variables are unrelated to each other.

Remember from earlier in the textbook that the question of statistically significant differences is the flip side of the statistical significance coin, whereby the other side tests for statistically significant relationships. Each side of the coin asks the research question differently, but regardless of whether a significant difference question or a significant relationship question is being asked of the same data, the answer will be the same. This is because the math used to answer a significant difference question is just an algebraic reworking of the same formula that is used to answer a significant relationship question. In the chi-square test for independence, the research question being tested is whether there is a significant relationship between two categorical variables; however, the statistical test answers this question by testing for significant differences between the observed joint-frequency distribution and the expected joint-frequency distribution.

For example, if we wanted to determine whether support for the death penalty (defined here as Yes or No) is related to (i.e., dependent on) political affiliation (defined here as Democrat, Republican, or Other), then we would analyze the data using the chi-square test for independence. This statistical test would compare the observed and expected joint frequencies for the two variables; if they were determined to be statistically significantly different from each other, we would conclude that the two variables are indeed statistically significantly related to each other (i.e., support for the death penalty was dependent on, or related to, one's political affiliation). However, if the testing determined that the observed and expected joint frequencies only differed as a result of random sampling variability and, thus, were not statistically significantly different from each other, we would conclude that the two variables were not statistically significantly related to each other (i.e., support for the death penalty did not depend on, or was not related to, one's political affiliation).

RESEARCH EXAMPLES

Our research example for the application of the chi-square goodness-of-fit test involves us asking the question whether there is seasonal variation in domestic violence calls in a study city. By seasonal variation we mean that we are testing whether domestic violence calls to police occur more frequently in one (or more) season as opposed to the number of calls in the other seasons. Season of the Domestic Violence Call will be the nominal level dependent variable for this test. Thus, every case in the data set will be comprised of a domestic violence call to the police, and the season that the call was received will be recorded in another variable in the data set. There are four seasons of the year (winter, spring, summer, fall), so there will be four categories on the dependent variable. The observed frequency counts will be obtained by the computer counting how many domestic violence calls came in for each of the four seasons of the year. The particular nonparametric test that will be employed is the chi-square goodness-of-fit test since it is the appropriate test for examining variation in frequency counts across a single nominal variable. Additionally, we will use the five-step model for hypothesis testing to ensure that we follow all of the scientific requirements of the traditional social science method.

Our research example for the chi-square test for independence will address the following research question: Is there a statistically significant relationship between type of sanction (prison or boot camp) and type of offense committed (drug, minor property, or serious property) for our combined prison and boot camp sample? The conclusion of a reliable relationship between the two variables would mean that statistically significant differences were 5 found between the observed and expected joint-frequency patterns of the two variables, meaning that certain types of offenses were more prevalent in one type of sanction than the other. The conclusion of no reliable relationship between the two variables would mean that no statistically significant differences were found between the variables' observed and expected joint-frequency patterns, meaning that certain types of offenses were not more prevalent in one type of sanction than in the other. Note that both of these variables are measured technically at the ordinal level of measurement but will be treated as nominal. Chi-square tests always treat categorical variables as being measured at the lowest level of measurement, even in the event that they truly are measured at the ordinal level.

Now that the logic of the chi-square tests has been explained, applications of the chi-square goodness-of-fit test and the chi-square test for independence will be demonstrated separately through the use of the five-step model for hypothesis testing.

THE CHI-SQUARE (χ^2) GOODNESS-OF-FIT TEST

Purpose of the Chi-Square Goodness-of-Fit Test

The purpose of the chi-square goodness-of-fit test is to answer the following research question: Do the observed frequencies across the categories of a nominal dependent variable differ from the expected distribution of frequencies? The expected distribution typically comes from the expectation that equal numbers of cases will appear in each category of the dependent variable (we will use this most common definition of expected frequencies for our application), but it can also refer to a known distribution of frequencies within some known population. This research question implies that the dependent variable is measured at the nominal level since the number of cases will be counted within each category of the dependent variable. However, ordinal variables and interval-ratio variables that have been collapsed into score interval categories can be submitted to the χ^2 analysis as well.

Using our earlier example of domestic violence calls, the research question is: Do the number of domestic violence calls to police in the study city vary in a statistically significant way across the four seasons of the year?

Five-Step Model For Hypothesis Testing

Step 1: Make Assumptions

There are two assumptions of the chi-square goodness-of-fit test:

1. Use of randomized sampling technique. (This ensures sample representativeness, and kicks in the laws of probability so that sampling distributions are accurate.)

2. The dependent variable is measured at the nominal level. (This allows for the counting of cases within categories of the variable.)

Step 2: State Hypotheses

Remember that hypotheses are always stated in terms of population parameters. However, when using the χ^2 test, the hypothesized relationships are stated in words instead of Greek symbols. The null hypothesis will state that the frequency distribution of the dependent variable fits the expected pattern. If the null hypothesis is retained, the conclusion will be that there are no reliable differences between the observed and expected frequency patterns; any observed differences are simply the result of random sampling variability. The alternative hypothesis will state that the frequency distribution of the dependent variable differs significantly from the expected pattern. If the null hypothesis is rejected, the conclusion will be that the observed frequency pattern is statistically significantly different than the expected frequency pattern. The hypotheses would be:

H_0: observed frequency distribution fits the expected frequency distribution

H_1: observed frequency distribution does not fit the expected frequency distribution

Step 3: Select Sampling Distribution and Specify Decision Criteria

This step specifies the statistical test and decision criteria that will allow us to determine whether to reject or retain the null hypothesis. In our example, we are comparing an observed frequency distribution of domestic violence calls within each of four seasons of the year for the study city to the null case expectation of no seasonal variation in calls. If there are no reliable variations in calls across seasons, then we should see approximately equal numbers of calls within each of the four seasons. Our observed frequency distribution will be compared to an expected frequency distribution that will have approximately equal numbers of domestic violence calls across all four season categories. The appropriate statistical test for this research scenario is the χ^2 goodness-of-fit test.

The chi-square distribution is a new distribution for you since up to now you have only learned the normal (Z) distribution. The chi-square is not normally distributed. In fact it is positively skewed with all values being ≥ 0. Shortly, you will see that the chi-square computations involve squaring all of the numbers in the numerator, so it makes sense that the chi-square statistic will never take on a negative number. Since there is only one tail in the chi-square distribution, there is no need to make a decision as to whether you should conduct a one-tailed or a two-tailed test. Critical values of the chi-square that mark off the critical region that is used to reject the null hypothesis will only occur in positive tail of the distribution.

There actually are a family of chi-square sampling distributions and each time the test statistic is computed, the degrees of freedom need to be computed as well so that the statistical test can determine which sampling distribution to use for that particular application of the test. **Degrees of freedom** has to do with how peaked (or flat) the sampling distribution is for any given statistical test. Generally speaking, the flatter the sampling distribution, the more the area of the curve gets pushed into the tail(s) of the sampling distribution. The more area that gets pushed into the tail(s), the further the critical region gets pushed away from the center of the curve. The further the critical region gets pushed away from the center of the sampling distribution, the harder it is to reject the null hypothesis. Thus, the statistical computation of any test statistic requires the calculation of the degrees of freedom so that the sampling distribution can be adjusted in order for accurate decisions to be made regarding retaining or rejecting the null hypothesis.

The chi-square tests base the degrees of freedom on the number of categories in the variable. The greater the number of categories, the greater the degrees of freedom, the flatter the sampling distribution, the further away is the critical region, and the harder it is to reject the null hypothesis. Conversely, the fewer the number of categories, the smaller the degrees of freedom, the more peaked the sampling distribution, the more the critical region is pulled toward the center, and the easier it is to reject the null hypothesis. It should be noted, however, that in the next chapter the degrees of freedom will be based on sample size. In fact, every statistical test in the remainder of this book will have its own unique way to compute the degrees of freedom. Two of the infinitely possible χ^2 sampling distributions are presented in figure 7.1.

The χ^2 goodness-of-fit sampling distribution is made up of all possible sample outcomes of drawing random samples of a specified

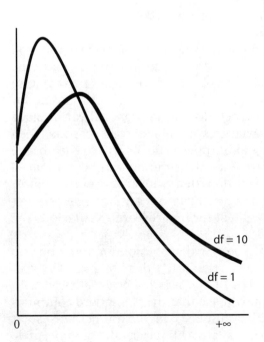

Figure 7.1   Chi-Square Sampling Distributions

sample size, computing the observed frequency pattern for a nominal level variable, and then comparing it to the expected frequency distribution. Slight differences in frequency patterns will cause the test statistic to fall outside the critical regions ($p > \alpha$), will cause the null hypothesis to be retained, and will lead to the conclusion that the observed differences should be attributed to random sampling variability. Large differences between observed and expected frequency patterns will cause the test statistic to fall inside the critical regions ($p < \alpha$), will cause the null hypothesis to be rejected, and the observed differences will be considered real and reliable (i.e., statistically significant and repeatable across other samples from the population).

In our example, the χ^2 goodness-of-fit test will be computed and alpha will be set at .05 (the standard in social science research). The degrees of freedom for this particular test are always computed as k – 1, where k is the number of categories in the test variable. These decision criteria for our example can be summarized as follows:

χ^2 goodness-of-fit test, α = .05, df = k – 1 = 4 – 1 = 3

Step 4: Compute the Test Statistic

In this step the data from the sample are submitted to the chi-square goodness-of-fit analysis in order to compare the frequency distribution across the categories of the test variable (Season of the Domestic Violence Call) to the expected frequency distribution of equal frequencies of cases across the four seasons of the year. Use SPSS Application One at the end of the chapter for the example data set and the SPSS steps to do the calculations.

The formula for the χ^2 goodness-of-fit test is provided in Formula 7.1:

FORMULA 7.1: χ^2 GOODNESS-OF-FIT TEST

$$\chi^2 = \Sigma \frac{(f_o - f_e)^2}{f_e}$$

Where: f_o = observed frequency count for a given category
f_e = expected frequency count for a given category; usually the total number of events divided by the number of categories; this represents the expectation of equal frequencies across categories; however, expected frequencies may also be values of some known (population) distribution.

For our analysis, the following are the values that should be plugged into the formula:

f_o for Winter = 3
f_o for Spring = 4

f_o for Summer = 11
f_o for Fall = 2
f_e = Total # of Events / 4 categories = 20/4 = 5

This indicates that we had a total of 20 domestic violence calls to the police in one year's time. Calculation of the expected frequencies (f_e) tells us to expect 5 domestic violence calls within each of the four seasons if there are no reliable differences between observed and expected frequency patterns. The observed frequency distribution for our domestic calls data set will be compared to this expected frequency pattern. The sigma (Σ) in the formula indicates that we should do these comparisons according to the formula for each category and then add across the categories to obtain the chi-square statistic. The hand calculations are:

$$\chi^2 = \Sigma \frac{(f_o - f_e)^2}{f_e}$$

$$\chi^2 = \frac{(3-5)^2}{5} + \frac{(4-5)^2}{5} + \frac{(11-5)^2}{5} + \frac{(2-5)^2}{5}$$

$$\chi^2 = \frac{(2)^2}{5} + \frac{(-1)^2}{5} + \frac{(6)^2}{5} + \frac{(-3)^2}{5}$$

$$\chi^2 = \frac{4}{5} + \frac{1}{5} + \frac{36}{5} + \frac{9}{5}$$

$$\chi^2 = .80 + .20 + 7.2 + 1.8$$

$$\chi^2 = 10.00$$

The computer printout resulting from using the data set and SPSS steps in application two at the end of the chapter appears below:

NPar Tests
Chi-Square Test
Frequencies

Season of Domestic Violence Call

	Observed N	Expected N	Residual
Winter	3	5.0	-2.0
Spring	4	5.0	-1.0
Summer	11	5.0	6.0
Fall	2	5.0	-3.0
Total	20		

Test Statistics

	Season of Domestic Violence Call
Chi-Square[a]	10.000
df	3
Asymp. Sig.	.019

a. 0 cells (.0%) have expected frequencies less than 5. The minimum expected cell frequency is 5.0.

The top of the printout states that we are running "Npar Tests," which refers to nonparametric tests. Next, the printout indicates that we are running a chi-square test and that frequencies (observed and expected) are provided. The first results box lists the observed and expected frequencies across the categories of the variable. The second results box lists the obtained value for the chi-square goodness-of-fit test (10.00), the associated degrees of freedom (3), and the significance level ($p = .019$). Note that the p-value is labeled "Asymp. Sig.," which means asymptotic significance level, meaning the approximate significance level. SPSS uses a few different variations of this labeling of the p-value, but they all refer to the significance level.

Step 5: Make a Decision

Because the probability (p-value) associated with the statistical result is less than our predetermined alpha level ($p < \alpha$), we reject the null hypothesis (which stated that there were no differences between observed and expected frequency distributions), and we conclude that the test statistic falls inside the critical region of the χ^2 goodness-of-fit sampling distribution. We further conclude that the observed frequency pattern is statistically significantly different than the expected distribution of equal frequencies across the categories. It is a reliable difference that reveals seasonal variation across domestic violence calls to the police in the study city. And a look at the observed frequency pattern reveals that the high number of domestic violence calls that occurred in the summer are what drove the statistical significance of our findings. Furthermore, we can expect to obtain this result again if we repeat the study using another sample from the same population. It is not a difference we would expect to result simply from random sampling variability.

Had the probability associated with the obtained χ^2 test statistic been larger than alpha ($p > \alpha$), we would have concluded that the difference between the observed and expected frequency distributions was not statistically significant, and we would have attributed any observed differences to the sample we happened to draw for our particular study (random sampling variability).

The decision regarding statistical significance could have been made manually (instead of using computer generated p-values) through the use of **critical values tables,** degrees of freedom, and the alpha level. Appendix C contains of the critical values of the χ^2 sampling distributions. In our domestic violence calls example df = 3 and α = .05, thus $\chi^2_{(critical)}$ = 7.81. Since the $\chi^2_{(obtained)}$ = 10.00 exceeds the critical value of the test, indicating that the test statistic falls within the critical region, we reject the null hypothesis and conclude the difference between the observed and expected frequency distributions for the number of domestic violence calls across the four seasons of the year is statistically significant. Again, this is the same conclusion we came to when using the computerized method. The determination of statistical significance using the critical values table for the chi-square sampling distribution is illustrated for the example analysis in figure 7.2.

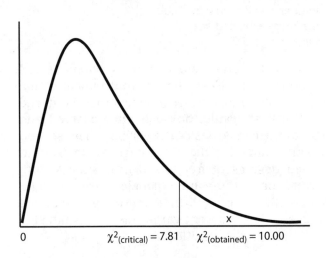

Figure 7.2 Determining Statistical Significance on Chi-Square Distribution (df = 3)

The following is an example of how the results would be stated:

> A study of the 20 domestic violence calls obtained for a city during a one-year period of time revealed that seasonal variation occurred with respect to when the calls were made. A χ^2 goodness-of-fit test was performed in order to determine if the observed frequency pattern of calls across the four seasons of the year differed reliably from the expected distribution representing no seasonal variation in calls. The results indicated that statistically significantly more domestic violence calls occurred during the summer months than during the other three seasons of the year (χ^2_3 = 10.00, p = .019).

The Chi-Square (χ^2) Test for Independence

Purpose and Elements of the Chi-Square Test for Independence

The purpose of the chi-square test for independence is to answer the following research question: Are two nominal level variables (or ordinal variables treated as nominal) reliably related to (or dependent on) each other? This question is answered by performing a χ^2 statistical test that mathematically asks: Do the observed joint-frequencies across the categories of two nominal variables differ from the expected joint-frequencies? The expected joint-frequencies represent the null hypothesis statement of no relationship (or dependency) between the two variables. If the observed joint-frequencies differ from the expected joint frequencies by more than what would be expected from random sampling variability, the test indicates that the two variables are related to (or dependent on) each other. If the observed joint-frequencies differ from the expected joint-frequencies by an amount that could be attributed to random sampling variability, the test indicates that the two variables are unrelated to (independent of) each other.

The term **joint-frequencies** refers to the combined cell frequencies of categories of two variables when they are displayed in a cross-tabulation table. The term **cross-tabulation table** refers to a table comprised of columns that are formed by the categories of one variable, and rows that are formed by the categories of the other variable. Table 7.1 demonstrates a 2 × 2 cross-tabulation table. It is called a 2 × 2 table because there are two rows (meaning 2 categories of variable 1) and two columns (meaning 2 categories of variable 2). If the cross-tabulation table was generated for a variable that had 5 categories and a variable that had 3 categories, it would be called a 5 × 3 cross-tabulation table.

In table 7.1 you can see that the observed frequency (f_o) for the first cell of the cross-tabulation table is the number of cases that fit into the first category of the first variable (Var.1/Cat.1) and the first category of the second variable (Var.2/Cat.1), and so on. The marginal totals are the frequencies of each category of a single variable, regardless of how cases place in categories of the other variable; basically they are the observed frequencies for each variable, without regard to the other variable. The total number of cases in the sample are found in the lower right corner of the table (Total N). Do not worry if this table seems a bit abstract since very shortly we will be putting our application data into the table. The χ^2 test for independence uses the observed joint frequencies in the cross-tabulation table (as mapped out in Table 7.1) in its computation of the χ^2 formula. The χ^2 test sta-

Table 7.1 Example of a 2 × 2 Cross-Tabulation Table

Variable 1	Variable 2		Marginal Totals
	Category 1	Category 2	
Category 1	f_o = # in Var.1/Cat.1 and Var.2/Cat.1	f_o = # in Var.1/Cat.1 and Var.2/Cat.2	Total # in Var.1/Cat.1
Category 2	f_o = # in Var.1/Cat.2 and Var.2/Cat.1	f_o = # in Var.1/Cat.2 and and Var.2/Cat.2	Total # in Var.1/Cat.2
Marginal Totals	Total # in Var.2/Cat.1	Total # in Var.2/Cat.2	Total N

tistic also uses the expected joint frequencies (f_e) that must be computed for each of the cells of the cross-tabulation table. Expected joint frequencies are computed based on the marginal totals of the cross-tabulation table as well as the overall sample size (N), using the following formula:

$$f_e = \frac{(\text{row marginal total})(\text{column marginal total})}{N}$$

This formula would be used for each cell, utilizing their respective marginal totals. Once the expected and observed frequencies are in place, the statistical test can be performed.

An important point that should be made regarding the expected frequencies (for either χ^2 test) is that if they are less than 5 for a substantial number of the cells in the table, the χ^2 statistic may be inaccurate. SPSS will provide the percentage of cells in the cross-tabulation table that have expected frequencies of less than 5 so that the issue can be considered by the researcher. The best ways to prevent this problem are to: (1) Use a large sample size so that there are plenty of cases to distribute throughout the table; and (2) Collapse some of the categories of the variable(s) to get rid of low-frequency cells.

As described earlier in this chapter, our research example for the χ^2 test for independence involves examining the prison and boot camp data set to see if there is a dependency or joint-frequency pattern that suggests that certain types of offenses are more prevalent in either the prison or the boot camp sample. Specifically, our research question asks: Is there a statistically significant relationship between type of sanction (prison or boot camp) an offender received and the type of offense committed (drug, minor property, or serious property) for our combined prison and boot camp sample?

Five-Step Model For Hypothesis Testing

Step 1: Make Assumptions

There are two assumptions of the χ^2 test for independence:

1. Use of randomized sampling technique. (This ensures sample representativeness and invokes the laws of probability so that sampling distributions are accurate.)
2. The dependent variable is measured at the nominal level. (This allows for the counting of cases within categories of the variable.)

Step 2: State Hypotheses

As was the case with the χ^2 goodness-of-fit test, the hypothesized relationships are stated in words instead of Greek symbols. The null hypothesis will state that the two variables are independent of each other. If the observed and expected joint-frequencies differ only slightly, the null hypothesis will be retained, and the conclusion will be that there is not a reliable relationship between the two variables. The alternative hypothesis will state that the two variables are dependent on each other. If the observed and expected joint frequencies differ significantly, the null hypothesis will be rejected, and the conclusion will be that there is a reliable relationship between the two variables. The hypotheses would be:

H_0: the two variables are independent of each other
H_1: the two variables are dependent on each other

Step 3: Select Sampling Distribution and Specify Decision Criteria

The chi-square distribution you will be using for the χ^2 test for independence is the same positively skewed chi-square sampling distribution you used for the χ^2 goodness-of-fit test. As before, the obtained chi-square statistic will always be positive in value since its computations involve squaring all of the numbers in the numerator. Since there is only one tail in the chi-square distribution, there is no need to make a decision as to whether you should conduct a one-tailed or a two-tailed test. Critical values of the chi-square that mark off the critical region that is used to reject the null hypothesis will only occur in the positive tail of the distribution.

Use the boot camp data set in the second SPSS application at the end of the chapter to generate the cross-tabulation table displaying the example data. The 2 × 3 table will look like the one presented in Table 7.2:

Table 7.2 Cross-Tabulation Table Using Data from Boot Camp Example

	Type of Offense			
Type of Sanction	**Drug**	**Minor Property**	**Serious Property**	**Marginal Totals**
Prison	$f_o = 2; f_e = 4$	$f_o = 1; f_e = 2$	$f_o = 7; f_e = 4$	10
Boot Camp	$f_o = 6; f_e = 4$	$f_o = 3; f_e = 2$	$f_o = 1; f_e = 4$	10
Marginal Totals	8	4	8	20

The observed frequencies (f_o) were generated by counting the number of cases that fell into each cell of the cross-tabulation table. For example, the observed frequency (f_o) for the Var.1/Cat.1 and Var.2/Cat.1 cell of the cross-tabulation table equals two, meaning that two of the 20 subjects were drug offenders from the prison inmate sample. The expected frequencies (f_e) were computed using the formula presented earlier. The following are those calculations:

$$f_e = \frac{(\text{row marginal})(\text{column marginal})}{N}$$

$$= \frac{(10)(8)}{20} = \frac{80}{20} = 4 \quad \text{[Prison/Drug Cell]}$$

$$f_e = \frac{(\text{row marginal})(\text{column marginal})}{N}$$

$$= \frac{(10)(4)}{20} = \frac{40}{20} = 2 \quad \text{[Prison/Minor Property Cell]}$$

$$f_e = \frac{(\text{row marginal})(\text{column marginal})}{N}$$

$$= \frac{(10)(8)}{20} = \frac{80}{20} = 4 \quad \text{[Prison/Serious Property Cell]}$$

$$f_e = \frac{(\text{row marginal})(\text{column marginal})}{N}$$

$$= \frac{(10)(8)}{20} = \frac{80}{20} = 4 \quad \text{[Boot Camp/Drug Cell]}$$

$$f_e = \frac{(\text{row marginal})(\text{column marginal})}{N}$$

$$= \frac{(10)(4)}{20} = \frac{40}{20} = 2 \quad \text{[Boot Camp/Minor Property Cell]}$$

$$f_e = \frac{(\text{row marginal})(\text{column marginal})}{N}$$

$$= \frac{(10)(8)}{20} = \frac{80}{20} = 4 \quad \text{[Boot Camp/Serious Property Cell]}$$

Since all of these expected frequencies are less than five, we definitely would want to increase sample size to fix the inaccuracy problems likely to affect our χ^2 test. We do not have many categories in each variable, so it would not be necessary to try to address the problem by collapsing categories of either variable. But we will continue with the small sample size for illustration purposes.

For our example, the χ^2 test for independence statistic will be computed and alpha will be set at .05. The degrees of freedom for this type of χ^2 test are computed as df = $(r - 1)(c - 1)$, where r is the number of rows in the cross-tabulation table, and c is the number of columns in the cross-tabulation table. These decision criteria for our example can be summarized as follows:

$$\chi^2 \text{ test for independence, } \alpha = .05,$$
$$\text{df} = (r - 1)(c - 1) = (2 - 1)(3 - 1) = (1)(2) = 2$$

Step 4: Compute the Test Statistic

In this step the data from the cross-tabulation table are submitted to the χ^2 test for independence analysis in order to compare the observed and expected joint-frequency distributions. Use the SPSS application at the end of the chapter for the boot camp example data set and the SPSS steps to do the calculations.

The formula for the χ^2 test for independence is provided in formula 7.2. Note that it is identical to the χ^2 goodness-of-fit test formula. The elements that are different come from the way that the observed and expected frequencies are generated in the cross-tabulation table.

FORMULA 7.2: χ^2 TEST FOR INDEPENDENCE

$$\chi^2 = \Sigma \frac{(f_o - f_e)^2}{f_e}$$

Where: f_o = observed joint-frequency count for a given cell in the cross-tabulation table
f_e = expected joint-frequency count for a given cell in the cross-tabulation table

For our example analysis, the values from the cross-tabulation table should be plugged into the formula to compute the obtained χ^2 statistic. SPSS generates the cross-tabulation table and the χ^2 analysis at the same time. The hand-calculations are:

$$\chi^2 = \sum \frac{(f_o - f_e)^2}{f_e}$$

$$\chi^2 = \frac{(2-4)^2}{4} + \frac{(1-2)^2}{2} + \frac{(7-4)^2}{4} + \frac{(6-4)^2}{4} + \frac{(3-2)^2}{2} + \frac{(1-4)^2}{4}$$

$$\chi^2 = \frac{(-2)^2}{4} + \frac{(-1)^2}{2} + \frac{(3)^2}{4} + \frac{(2)^2}{4} + \frac{(1)^2}{2} + \frac{(-3)^2}{4}$$

$$\chi^2 = \frac{4}{4} + \frac{1}{2} + \frac{9}{4} + \frac{4}{4} + \frac{1}{2} + \frac{9}{4}$$

$$\chi^2 = 1.00 + .50 + 2.25 + 1.00 + .50 + 2.25$$

$$\chi^2 = 7.50$$

The computer printout resulting from using the data set and SPSS steps at the end of the chapter appears below:

Crosstabs

Case Processing Summary

	Cases					
	Valid		Missing		Total	
	N	Percent	N	Percent	N	Percent
Type of Sanction * Most Serious Conviction Charge	20	100.0%	0	.0%	20	100.0%

Type of Sanction * Most Serious Conviction Charge Crosstabulation

			Most Serious Conviction Charge			Total
			Drug Offense	Minor Property Offense	Serious Property Offense	
Type of Sanction	Prison	Count	2	1	7	10
		Expected Count	4.0	2.0	4.0	10.0
	Boot Camp	Count	6	3	1	10
		Expected Count	4.0	2.0	4.0	10.0
Total		Count	8	4	8	20
		Expected Count	8.0	4.0	8.0	20.0

Chi-Square Tests

	Value	df	Asymp. Sig. (2-sided)
Pearson Chi-Square	7.500[a]	2	.024
Likelihood Ratio	8.202	2	.017
Linear-by-Linear Association	5.938	1	.015
N of Valid Cases	20		

a. 6 cells (100.0%) have expected count less than 5. The minimum expected count is 2.00.

The top of the printout states that we are running "Crosstabs," which refers to the generation of the cross-tabulation table. You will soon see that while in that SPSS menu option, the chi-square statistical test is not automatically computed and must be requested.

The first results box lists the "Case Processing Summary" that indicates the numbers of valid, missing, and total cases used in the analysis. The second results box displays the cross-tabulation table containing observed joint-frequencies ("Count"), expected joint-frequencies ("Expected Count"), and marginal and overall sample size totals ("Total"). The last results box displays the chi-square statistical tests. The one that should be interpreted as the χ^2 test for independence is the one labeled "Pearson chi-square," named for the person who developed the test. The other tests (Likelihood Ratio and Linear-by-Linear Association) will not be covered in this text. Note that the results box provides the obtained value for the χ^2 test for independence (7.500), the associated degrees of freedom (2), and the asymptotic (or approximate) significance level ($p = .024$). Take time to verify that the computer-generated results match the hand calculations.

Step 5: Make a Decision

Because the probability (p-value) associated with the statistical result is less than our pre-determined alpha level ($p < \alpha$), we reject the null hypothesis that states that the two variables are independent of (unrelated to) each other, and we conclude that the test statistic falls inside the critical region of the χ^2 test for independence sampling distribution. We further conclude that the two variables (Type of Sanction and Most Serious Conviction Charge) are statistically significantly dependent on (related to) each other. It is a reliable relationship that reveals that the observed frequency pattern for one variable depends on the observed frequency pattern for the other variable. Close examination of the observed frequencies suggests that the statistically significant relationship between the two variables is likely being driven by the fact that the vast majority (7 of 8) of serious property offenders were in the prison sample, while the majority of drug offenders (6 of 8) and minor property offenders (3 of 4) were in the boot camp sample.

Had the probability associated with the obtained χ^2 test statistic been larger than alpha ($p > \alpha$), we would have concluded that the two variables were independent of each other. We also would have attributed any observed differences between observed and expected joint-frequencies to the unique characteristics of the samples we happened to draw for our particular study (random sampling variability).

In terms of making the decision regarding statistical significance manually through the use of critical values tables, degrees of freedom and alpha level are required. Appendix C contains the critical values of

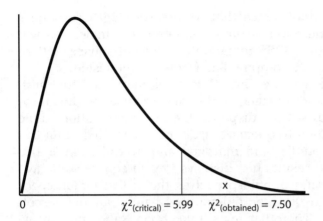

Figure 7.3 Determining Statistical Significance on the Chi-Square Distribution (df = 2)

the χ^2 test for independence sampling distribution. In our sanctions and offenses example df = 2 and α = .05, thus $\chi^2_{(critical)}$ = 5.991. Since the $\chi^2_{(obtained)}$ = 7.500, which exceeds the critical value of the test, we reject the null hypothesis and conclude that the relationship between the type of sanction and the type of offense is statistically significant. Again, this is the same conclusion we came to when using the computerized method. The determination of statistical significance using the critical values table for the chi-square sampling distribution is illustrated for the example analysis in figure 7.3.

The following is an example of how the results would be stated:

> A study of a random sample of 10 nonviolent prison inmates and a random sample of 10 boot camp participants was conducted to test whether type of conviction charge (drug offense, minor property offense, serious property offense) was reliably related to the type of sanction (prison or boot camp) received. A χ^2 test for independence was performed in order to test the relationship between the two categorical variables. The results indicated that statistically significantly more drug offenders and minor property offenders received the boot camp sanction, while statistically significantly more serious property offenders received the prison sanction (χ^2_2 = 7.50, p = .024).

SUMMARY

This chapter began the applications portion of the textbook intended to put foundational knowledge learned earlier in the textbook to work. In this chapter you have learned the purpose of conducting two chi-square tests and the types of research questions they can be used to answer. Specifically, you have learned the two most commonly used nonparametric tests, the chi-square goodness-of-fit test and the chi-square test for independence. You also learned how to determine statistical significance using both the computer and critical values tables. All of these concepts were demonstrated through SPSS applications that employed realistic, hypothetical research scenarios in the field of criminal justice.

KEY TERMS

Nonparametric
Nonparametric Tests
Chi-Square (χ^2) Goodness-of-Fit Test
Observed Frequency Counts
Expected Frequency Counts
Chi-Square (χ^2) Test for Independence

Degrees of Freedom
Critical Values Tables
$\chi^2_{\text{(critical)}}$
$\chi^2_{\text{(obtained)}}$
Joint-Frequencies
Cross-Tabulation Table

SPSS APPLICATION ONE: CHI-SQUARE GOODNESS-OF-FIT TEST

1. Create the following "Domestic Violence Calls" data set. The cases (rows) represent 20 domestic violence calls. The nominal variable "Season" indicates in which season each call occurred.

"Domestic Violence Calls" Data Set:

Call ID #	Season
1	1
2	1
3	1
4	1
5	2
6	2
7	2
8	2
9	2
10	2
11	2
12	2
13	2
14	2
15	2
16	3
17	3
18	4
19	4
20	4

Section Two: Inferential Statistics—Tests of Group Differences

2. Label the variable "Season":
   1 = Spring
   2 = Summer
   3 = Fall
   4 = Winter

3. Perform the χ^2 goodness-of-fit test on the variable "Season":
   i. Analyze
      ii. Nonparametric Tests
   iii. Legacy Dialogs
   iv. Chi-Square
      v. Move "Season" variable to the "Test Variable List"
   vi. Click on the "OK" button

SPSS Application Two: Chi-Square Test for Independence

1. Create the following "Boot Camp" data set.

ID #	Type of Sanction (Sanction) (0 = Prison; 1 = Boot Camp)	Conviction Charge (Offense) (1 = Drug Offense; 2 = Minor Property Offense; 3 = Serious Property Offense)
1	0	3
2	0	3
3	0	1
4	0	3
5	0	2
6	0	3
7	0	3
8	0	1
9	0	3
10	0	3
11	1	1
12	1	2
13	1	1
14	1	1
15	1	1
16	1	2
17	1	3
18	1	1
19	1	2
20	1	1

2. Perform the χ^2 test for independence:
   i. Analyze
      ii. Descriptive Statistics
      iii. Crosstabs
         iv. Arrow "Sanction" variable into the "Rows" box
         v. Arrow "Offense" variable into the "Columns" box
         vi. Click on the "Statistics" button
            vii. Click on "Chi-Square"
            viii. Click on "Continue"
         ix. Click on the "Cells" button
            x. Click on "Expected" under "Counts"
            xi. Click on "Continue"
         xii. Click on "OK"

SPSS ASSIGNMENT

1. Create the "Parolees" data set below. This fictitious data set contains a random sample of 15 parolees released from prison six months ago. The data set includes the variables "Gender" (1 = Male; 2 = Female) and "Crime Type," which shows what type of crime each individual committed that resulted in incarceration. This variable should be coded as: 1 = Violent Crime; 2 = Property Crime; 3 = Drug/Vice Crime.

2. Use the five-step model for hypothesis testing and perform a chi-square goodness-of-fit test to answer the following research question: Is there statistically significant variation in the number of individuals that committed each of the three types of crime? The expected frequency distribution is that there will be an equal number of people that fall into each of the three crimes types. Do the computations using SPSS.

3. Perform a chi-square test for independence to find out whether the parolees crime types were dependent on their gender. Use the five-step model for hypothesis testing and do the computations using SPSS.

4. Write a couple of paragraphs summarizing the results of the analyses performed in steps two and three.

"Parolees" Data Set

Parolee ID	Gender	Crime Type
01	Male	Violent
02	Male	Property
03	Female	Drug/Vice
04	Male	Violent
05	Male	Violent
06	Male	Property
07	Male	Property
08	Female	Drug/Vice
09	Female	Drug/Vice
10	Male	Drug/Vice
11	Female	Drug/Vice
12	Male	Violent
13	Female	Drug/Vice
14	Male	Property
15	Female	Property

Multiple Choice Questions

1. If a researcher wants to determine if the number of inmates in a jail differ significantly based on race (white, black, Hispanic, other), the researcher should _____.
    A. Perform a χ^2 goodness-of-fit test
    B. Perform a χ^2 test for independence
    C. Compute a 95% confidence interval
    D. Create a bar chart

2. If $\chi^2_{(obtained)}$ does not exceed $\chi^2_{(critical)}$ the null hypothesis should be _____.
    A. Rejected
    B. Retained
    C. Restated
    D. Ignored

3. We should reject the null hypothesis when _____.
    A. $p < \alpha$
    B. $p > \alpha$
    C. $\alpha < p$
    D. $\alpha = .04$

4. The chi-square test for independence compares _____.
   A. Expected row totals and observed column totals
   B. Expected column totals and observed row totals
   C. Expected means and observed means
   D. Expected joint-frequencies and observed joint-frequencies

5. If we run a chi-square test for independence and get a *p*-value of .059. What decision should we make regarding the null hypothesis?
   A. Reject the null hypothesis
   B. Retain the null hypothesis
   C. Change the null hypothesis
   D. More information is needed before making a decision regarding the null hypothesis

6. A researcher wants to test if gender is related to home ownership (0 = no, 1 = yes). The χ^2 test for this analysis has _____ degrees of freedom.
   A. 4
   B. 3
   C. 2
   D. 1

7. We will reject the null hypothesis in a chi-square test for independence if _____.
   A. There are small differences between observed and expected joint-frequencies
   B. There are any differences between observed and expected joint-frequencies
   C. There are large differences between observed and expected joint-frequencies
   D. There are no differences between observed and expected joint-frequencies

8. For the chi-square goodness-of-fit test, the _____ states that the observed frequency distribution of the variable fits the expected frequency distribution of the variable.
   A. Null hypothesis
   B. Alternate hypothesis
   C. Research hypothesis
   D. Addition theorem

9. If a researcher wants to see if two nominal level variables are reliably related to one another, the researcher should _____.
   A. Perform a χ^2 goodness-of-fit test
   B. Perform a χ^2 test for independence
   C. Compute a 95% confidence interval
   D. Create a line graph

10. Joint-frequencies are _____.
    A. Compared in a chi-square goodness-of-fit test
    B. The combined cell frequencies of categories of two variables
    C. The individual cell frequencies of categories of one variable
    D. The individual residuals of categories of two variables

8

Mean Difference Tests
t-Tests

This chapter, like the previous chapter and the remaining chapters of this textbook, is very applied and will look at the statistics generated to analyze the types of data often found in criminal justice research. This chapter presents three methods of conducting *t*-tests, which are three different tests of comparisons between two means.

■ PURPOSE OF *t*-TESTS

There are three types of *t*-tests: the **one-sample *t*-test**; the **independent samples *t*-test**; and the **dependent samples *t*-test**. All of the *t*-tests are used to test for statistically significant differences between two means. The one-sample *t*-test is used when the researcher wants to compare a sample mean to a known population mean. For example, if we wanted to know if the average number of days served by a sample of inmates from one jail ($\bar{X}$) is reliably different from the average number of days served in jails nationwide (μ), then we would want to conduct a one-sample test of means. More specifically, we would use the one-sample *t*-test, since it compares a mean that was generated from a sample to a mean that was generated from a population, and the dependent variable (i.e., number of days served) was measured at the interval-ratio level.

The independent samples *t*-test is used when the researcher wants to compare two means that were generated from two independent samples (a detailed explanation of independent sampling will soon follow). For example, if we wanted to compare the average number of technical violations incurred during a one-year period of time by a random sample of offenders on intensive supervision probation ($\bar{X}_1$)

with a random sample of offenders on regular probation ($\bar{X}_2$), then we would want to conduct an independent samples t-test. More specifically, we would use the independent samples t-test, since it compares two means that were generated from independently obtained samples, and the dependent variable (i.e., number of technical violations) was measured at the interval-ratio level.

Finally, the dependent samples t-test is used when the researcher wants to compare two means that were generated from two related samples (again, an explanation of how two samples could be related will soon follow). For example, if we wanted to test whether there is a difference in the average number of arrests one year prior to incarceration and the average number of arrests one year postincarceration for a random sample of prison inmates, then we would want to conduct a dependent samples t-test. More specifically, we would use the dependent samples t-test because the same sample of inmates would be used to generate both their preincarceration mean ($\bar{X}_1$) and their postincarceration mean ($\bar{X}_2$), thus the two sample means have a dependency in the way that they were generated. Also, we have interval-ratio data from which to generate those two means.

More detailed explanations of these three distinctly different t-tests will now be described. Furthermore, the five-step model for hypothesis testing will be used for each test to ensure that we conduct our research in a scientific manner.

■ THE ONE-SAMPLE t-TEST

Purpose of the One-Sample t-Test

The purpose of the one-sample t-test is to answer the following research question: Is the mean from one sample statistically significantly different from the known population mean? This question implies that the dependent variable is measured at the interval-ratio level since a mean is being computed. Returning to the average number of days served in jail example, the research question is: Is the average number of days served in the jail sample statistically significantly different from the known average for jail inmates nationwide?

Five-Step Model For Hypothesis Testing

Step 1: Make Assumptions
There are three assumptions of the one-sample t-test:
1. Use of randomized sampling technique. (This ensures sample representativeness and invokes the laws of probability so that sampling distributions are accurate.)

2. The dependent variable is measured at the interval-ratio level. (This allows for the calculation of a mean.)
3. The sampling distribution is normally distributed. (This ensures that areas under the curve are accurate and will lead to a proper decision regarding statistical significance.)

Step 2: State Hypotheses

Remember that hypotheses are always stated in terms of population parameters. In the one-sample *t*-test the null hypothesis indicates that the sample mean is equal to the population mean. This known value often comes from census data or other published data sources that report a mean on some interval-ratio variable for a specified population. If the null hypothesis is supported, we will continue to believe that the jail sample's average time served is approximately equal (differing only by an amount that can be attributed to random sampling variability) to the average time served in the rest of the nation, meaning that the jail sample is really just a subsample of the full population. The alternative hypothesis indicates that the jail sample's mean is not equal to the known population mean, and if the null hypothesis is rejected, we will have support for the alternative hypothesis. In other words, we would have statistical evidence to support the belief that our jail sample is different from the population in a reliable way with respect to the average number of days served at that jail (either serving more or less days than jails nationwide). Let's say that in our example the population average is 210 days and the sample mean is 280.2 days. The hypotheses would be:

$$H_o: \mu = 210$$
$$H_1: \mu \neq 210$$

Remember that hypotheses are always stated in terms of the population parameters, reflecting the status quo of believing the null hypothesis to be true until there is evidence to reject the null hypothesis and believe something different. Our hypotheses make testable statements about whether the sample comes from the population that is known to serve an average of 210 days in jail.

Step 3: Select Sampling Distribution and Specify Decision Criteria

It is in this step that we specify the statistical test and other things (one-tailed or two-tailed, degrees of freedom, and alpha) we will be using to determine whether to reject the null hypothesis. In our jail-time-served example we are comparing a sample mean to a population mean ($\bar{X} - \mu$), so we are using the one-sample *t*-distribution. The one-sample *t*-test sampling distribution is presented in figure 8.1 This

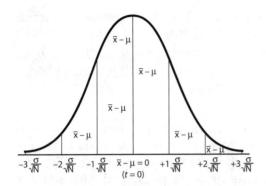

Figure 8.1 One-Sample *t*-Test Sampling Distribution

sampling distribution is made up of all possible outcomes of drawing a jail sample, computing the average number of days served, and comparing those sample means to the known population value (i.e., subtracting the population mean from each sample mean). Slight differences in means will cause the test statistic to fall outside the critical regions and close to the central tendency point of the *t*-test sampling distribution ($p > \alpha$), causing the null hypothesis to be retained, and causing us to conclude that any observed differences between the sample mean and the population mean will be attributed to random sampling variability. Large differences in the sample and population means will cause the test statistic to fall inside the critical regions located in the tails of the sampling distribution ($p < \alpha$), will cause the null hypothesis to be rejected, and will cause us to conclude that any observed differences between the sample and population means will be considered statistically significant (i.e., real, reliable and repeatable across other samples from the population).

Actually, there are many *t*-test sampling distributions corresponding to every possible sample size. The *t*-distribution is normal in shape, but for combined sample sizes below 120 the *t*-distributions become flatter (less peaked) in the center and thicker in the tails as the combined sample size decreases. The smaller the sample size, the flatter and thicker-tailed the *t*-distribution. The greater the sample size, the more center-peaked and thinner-tailed the *t*-distribution. For all sample sizes above 120, the *t*-distribution superimposes itself on the normal curve, meaning the areas under the normal curve and the *t*-distribution become indistinguishable. However, even the normal curve obeys the central limit theorem, becoming more peaked and thinner tailed as sample size increases. Thus, *t*-distributions corresponding to smaller sample sizes are flatter than the normal curve; the curve adjusts its areas under the curve in a conservative way, making it harder to reject the null hypothesis. Figure 8.2 illustrates the family of *t*-distributions.

How does the statistical test know which *t*-distribution to employ? **Degrees of freedom (df)** is primarily a function of sample size but is also affected by how many categories exist within a categorical variable, or how many variables are used in analyses employing multiple continuous variables. You were introduced to degrees of freedom in the last chapter; however, a more detailed description of its function will now be given. Degrees of freedom is a rather abstract concept that has to do with how many values are free to vary (take on other values) in a mathematical computation. For example, if you were calculating a mean for five raw scores and you knew the mean and one of the five scores, there would be four values free to vary in order to derive the specified mean.

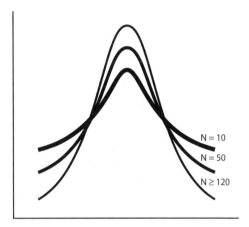

Figure 8.2   Family of *t*-Distributions

Conversely, if you knew the mean and four of the five scores, there would be no scores free to vary, since locking in four of the values leaves only one possible other score to get the specified mean. This amount of freedom to vary has an impact on how the area under the sampling distribution gets disbursed. Basically, the degrees of freedom of any statistical test, along with the alpha level, is what defines areas (or probabilities) under the sampling distribution curve. Since we use the sampling distribution to make decisions about statistical significance, it is important that the sampling distributions are accurately compiled. For the one-sample *t*-test the degrees of freedom are computed as N – 1. If we have a sample of five scores, the degrees of freedom would be N – 1, or 5 – 1, and would equal four. The *t*-test involving that data would be a 4 degree of freedom test. For all three *t*-tests, the greater the degrees of freedom, the more peaked the sampling distribution, and the easier it is to reject the null hypothesis.

In our time served example, the one-sample *t*-test will be computed, the test will be two-tailed since we have no reason to believe that the jail sample mean would be either higher or lower than the population mean. If we did have a reason to believe that the observed difference would indicate that the sample mean would be only greater than (or only less than) the population mean, then we would run a one-tailed test. While running one-tailed tests does make it easier to reject the null hypothesis, you shouldn't need to stack the probability deck in your favor to get statistical significance. If a truly reliable difference exists between your means, you will see it whether you run a **one-tailed test** or a **two-tailed test;** thus, we recommend that you always run a two tailed *t*-test. In addition to the decision about one-tailed or two-tailed sampling distributions, the researcher must set alpha, which we will set at .05 (the standard in social science research). Furthermore, df = N – 1 and since we have 15 subjects in our example, we will have a 14 df t-test. These Step 3 decision criteria can be summarized for our example as follows:

one-sample t-test, two-tailed,
$\alpha = .05$, df = N – 1 = 15 – 1 = 14

Step 4: Compute the Test Statistic

In this step the data from the sample are used to compute a mean on the dependent variable (days served). The one-sample t-test is then computed to compare the sample mean to the population mean. Use SPSS Application One at the end of the chapter for the example data set and the SPSS steps to do the calculations. The formula for computing this t-test by hand is demonstrated below.

The formula for the one-sample t-test is provided in Formula 8.1:

FORMULA 8.1: ONE-SAMPLE t-TEST

$$t = \frac{\bar{X} - \mu}{\frac{s}{\sqrt{N}}}$$

Where: $\bar{X}$ = sample mean
μ = population mean
s = sample standard deviation
N = sample size

For our analysis, the following are the values that should be plugged into the formula:

$\bar{X} = 280.2$
$\mu = 210$
$s = 75.14$
$N = 15$

The hand calculations are:

$$t = \frac{\bar{X} - \mu}{\frac{s}{\sqrt{N}}}$$

$$t = \frac{280.2 - 210}{\frac{75.14}{\sqrt{15}}}$$

$$t = \frac{70.2}{\frac{75.14}{3.873}}$$

$$t = \frac{70.2}{19.40}$$

$$t = 3.619$$

The computer printout resulting from using the data set and SPSS steps in Application One at the end of the chapter is listed below:

One-Sample Statistics

	N	Mean	Std. Deviation	Std. Error Mean
Days Served	15	280.20	75.136	19.400

One-Sample Test

	Test Value = 210					
	t	df	Sig. (2-tailed)	Mean Difference	95% Confidence Interval of the Difference	
					Lower	Upper
Days Served	3.619	14	.003	70.200	28.59	111.81

The first results box provides descriptive statistics on the sample indicating sample size (N), mean ($\bar{X}$), standard deviation (s), and standard error of the mean ($s / \sqrt{N}$). The second results box presents the obtained value of the t-test (t), its degrees of freedom (df), the two-tailed p-value—listed as Sig. (2-tailed)—the difference between the means ($\bar{X} - \mu$), and the 95% confidence interval containing values of mean differences that would occur from similar analysis of 95% of all possible samples of size 15 drawn from the population.

Step 5: Make a Decision

Because the probability (p-value) associated with the statistical result is less than our prespecified alpha level ($p < \alpha$), we reject the null hypothesis (the statement of no differences between the sample and population means), and we conclude that the test statistic falls inside the critical region of the one-sample t-test sampling distribution. We further conclude that the difference observed between the sample mean (280.2) and the population mean (210) is statistically significant. It is a reliable difference. We can expect to find it again if we repeat the study using another sample from the same population. It is not a difference we would expect simply due to random sampling variability.

Had the probability associated with the obtained t-test statistic been larger than alpha ($p > \alpha$), we would have concluded that the difference between the sample mean and the population mean was not statistically significant, and we would have attributed any observed differences between the means to be an artifact of the sample we happened to draw for our particular study (random sampling variability).

As discussed in the last chapter, while this text relies heavily on the expectation that analyses will be conducted through the use of a statistical analysis package like SPSS, it is important to note that the determination of statistical significance can also be made manually through the use of critical values tables found in the appendices in the back of the book. **Critical values tables** work just the opposite of computer output that provides the statistical significance (p-value) of the obtained test statistic. The computer output tells us whether the p-value is *less than* the alpha level, in which case we would reject the null hypothesis. With critical values tables, a critical value of the test statistic is provided, based on the alpha level, degrees of freedom, and the one-tailed or two-tailed direction of the test. This critical value marks off the critical regions on the statistic's sampling distribution. Only positive values are presented, marking off the positive tail of the sampling distribution; the negative tail is determined by assigning a negative sign to the critical value since one side of the sampling distribution curve is a mirror image of the other side. If the obtained test statistic is *greater than* the critical value of the test statistic, the obtained statistic falls in the critical region, and the null hypothesis is rejected. The relationship between p-values and critical values is summarized in Table 8.1.

Appendix B contains the critical values of the t-distribution and should be used by locating the relevant degrees of freedom and alpha level for the specific analysis. For our example data the df = 14 and $\alpha = .05$, thus $t_{\text{(critical)}} = \pm 2.145$. Since the $t_{\text{(obtained)}} = 3.619$, we reject the null hypothesis and conclude the difference between the sample and population means is statistically significant, which is the same conclusion we came to when using the computerized method. Whether the decision is made in a computerized way or a manual way, the results will always be the same. Figure 8.3 illustrates the use of the critical value of t in determining the statistical significance of the example analysis.

Table 8.1 Determining Statistical Significance Manually versus Computerized

Method	Criterion for Rejecting Null Hypothesis
Critical values table	$t_{\text{(obtained)}} > t_{\text{(critical)}}$
Computer Generated Significance Level (p-value)	($p < \alpha$)

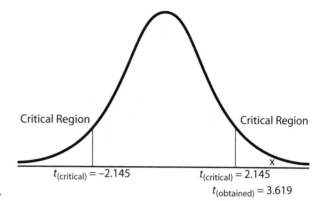

**Figure 8.3
Determining Statistical Significance on t-Distribution**

The following is an example of how the results of the analysis of our example data would be stated:

> A study of a random sample of 15 inmates from a county jail served an average of 280.20 (SD = 75.14) days. A one-sample t-test was performed in order to determine if the average number of days served in this county jail differed reliably from the national average of 210 days. The results indicated that inmates in this county jail serve on average, statistically significantly more days than jail inmates nationwide ($t_{14} = 3.62$, $p = .003$).

Note that the degrees of freedom of the test are listed in subscript beside the test statistic. Note that p-values are carried out at least three decimals. Also note that the final statement of the research results claims that the county jail sample served "on average, statistically significantly more days." Even though the alternative hypothesis was two-tailed and stated that the sample average would be "statistically significantly different" from the population average, the fact that the sample mean was higher in value than the population mean allows us to make our directional statement once the statistical test has completed testing for differences in both directions.

▰ IMPORTANT CONCEPTS RELATED TO INDEPENDENT AND DEPENDENT SAMPLES t-TESTS

We are now moving into the portions of this chapter that cover t-tests where two sample means are being compared to each other, rather than a single sample mean being compared to a population mean (as was the case with the one-sample t-test). There are two concepts that need to be discussed before we move on to the independent and dependent samples t-tests. These concepts do not apply to the one-sample t-test that you just learned. However, when we want to compare two sample means, as the remainder of this chapter entails, we have to be concerned about whether the two means being compared came from samples that were selected independently or dependently, because this is what determines whether we will employ an independent samples t-test or a dependent samples t-test to address our research question. Additionally, in the case where we are comparing means from two independently selected samples, we also have to give special attention to whether the samples have homogeneity of variance or heterogeneity of variance. These concepts will now be discussed before we go on to learn how to conduct the two remaining t-tests in this chapter.

Independent and Dependent Sampling

The particular two-sample test that will be employed to address our research example, comparing intensive supervision probation offenders versus regular probation offenders on their average number of technical violations incurred during a one-year period, is the independent samples t-test (sometimes called a **between-subjects t-test**). It compares means that were generated from data obtained on an interval-ratio dependent variable for two independent random samples. The term **independent random samples** refers to the sampling design and indicates that the way that subjects were randomly selected to be in one sample had no impact on the way that subjects were randomly selected for the second sample.

The ideal way to obtain independent random samples in our intensive supervision probation versus regular probation example is to randomly select the desired number of study participants from each population separately. Sometimes in criminal justice research it is not possible to obtain random samples of offenders and we end up using intact samples instead. This methodological problem of not being able to use independent random samples leads to what is called **selection bias**, which means there is uncertainty about the equivalency of the groups being compared at the beginning of the study. Selection bias is a problem that leaves the researcher wondering if any observed mean differences identified by the t-test were due to real differences between the two groups on the dependent variable, or whether any observed mean differences simply reflect the fact that the two comparison groups were very different before the study began. Importantly, selection bias is a problem that plagues much criminal justice research since we frequently have to study intact groups of offenders. Selection bias is a primary reason that the equivalency between intact samples at the outset of a study should be established by statistically comparing important characteristics (e.g., age, race, gender, and prior criminal histories) of the intact comparison samples.

For our example research scenario, we will say that we have randomly selected the two types of probation samples from their respective populations. Because the two samples will be selected separately using random sampling techniques, the two samples will be considered independent random samples suitable for independent samples *t*-testing.

Had these two samples been related to each other in terms of sampling design, we would use a different *t*-test, the dependent samples *t*-test (sometimes called a **within-subjects *t*-test** or a **repeated-measures *t*-test**), to answer the same research question. The dependency refers to the fact that the composition of the second sample is determined to some degree by which subjects were selected for the first sample, meaning the research scenario involves two **dependent samples**. There are many different types of dependent sampling strategies, and those will be discussed next. Ultimately, it depends on the research question as to which type of dependent samples a researcher might decide to obtain.

One of the variations on a dependent sampling strategy is to use "matched" samples, whereby subjects in one randomly selected sample are matched to their equivalent subjects (based on a few prespecified characteristics) in the other population in order to determine who will be in the comparison sample. Our best choice of a sampling design when we are unable to randomly select two separate samples from two populations is to use a **matched samples** design, whereby a random sample of the intensive supervision probation offenders would be selected, and then the regular probation sample would be generated by matching offenders to their intensive probation counterparts on a few selected traits. We also might want to use this technique if we feared that the intensive supervision probation population was comprised of more seasoned criminals than the regular probation group, thus leaving us with quite different samples for comparison if we randomly selected from each population. Fear of this likely scenario should make the researcher think hard about randomly selecting the first sample from the intensive supervision probation population and then finding suitable matches for each subject in that sample (based on age, race, gender, and criminal history) from the regular probation sample. Had we used this sampling technique, our two comparison groups would have been equivalent on our specified criteria (but not on any unspecified matching criteria), and we would need to address our research question comparing the average number of technical violations in a one-year time period for the two matched samples using the dependent samples *t*-test.

Another variation of the dependent sampling strategy involves repeatedly studying the same sample over time, whereby data is collected on the dependent variable from the same sample, but at two different points in time. Thus, the dependent samples *t*-test will be comparing two sample means; however, the means come from dependent samples since it is really one sample being used at two data collection times. Statistical tests based on dependent random samples derived from repeatedly measuring the same sample at each data collection point are sometimes desirable since they eliminate the problems of individual characteristic differences (another potential source of error variation in data analysis) that will exist between subjects from two separate samples. We will use this repeated-measures research design in our textbook example when we test whether the average number of presentence arrests differs significantly from the average number of postrelease arrests for a sample of offenders. We will test this pre-to-post difference for the prison sample using the dependent-samples *t*-test. The fact that both the preincarceration and postincarceration means are being generated from the same sample makes the two "samples" related and thus indicates that the dependent samples *t*-test is the appropriate test to use in this research scenario.

The final variation of a dependent sampling strategy covered by this textbook pertains to the use of samples that are logically related. For example, if a therapist wanted to test whether his marriage counseling technique works better with wives than with husbands, he could draw a random sample from his patient population of wives (sample 1) and then the husbands of the selected wives would automatically constitute the other dependent random sample (sample 2). The therapist could then have each sample fill out a survey that generated scores on how satisfied the respondent was with the counseling. Next, average scores for the sample of wives and for the sample of husbands would be generated. Lastly, the two means would be statistically tested for differences using the dependent samples *t*-test, since the data came from two samples that were dependent on each other (meaning that once one sample was selected, the other sample was automatically selected).

Homogeneity of Variance

A point that needs to be made regarding the independent samples *t*-test is that there is an additional statistical test assumption called homogeneity of variance. **Homogeneity of variance** means that the dispersion of scores on the dependent variable is approximately equal in the two groups. This is an important requirement in order for the areas under the sampling distribution to be accurate. Statistical errors can occur if one sample is tightly dispersed around its mean, while the other sample is widely dispersed around its mean. In fact, the requirement is so important that most statistical software packages (like SPSS) test for the assumption and make necessary adjustments to the computations when the assumption is violated.

SPSS uses Levene's Test for Equality of Variances, which works by computing an F statistic (you will learn much about the F statistic in the next chapter) to test the null hypothesis of homogeneity of variance. If the significance level (p-value) associated with this F-test is less than alpha = .05, the null hypothesis of homogeneity of variance is rejected, and the researcher should interpret the independent samples t-test results in the "Equal variances not assumed" row of the computer printout. If the p-value associated with the F-test is greater than .05, the null hypothesis of homogeneity of variance is retained, and the researcher should interpret the t-test results in the "Equal variances assumed" row of the computer printout. This will be demonstrated shortly.

Now that the concepts of independent and dependent sampling, as well as homogeneity of variance, have been explained, applications of the independent samples t-test, and the dependent samples t-test, will be demonstrated through the use of the five-step model for hypothesis testing.

The Independent Samples t-Test

Purpose of the Independent Samples t-Test

The purpose of the independent samples t-test is to answer the following research question: Is the mean from one independent random sample statistically significantly different from the mean from another independent random sample? This question implies that the dependent variable is measured at the interval-ratio level since a mean is being computed. The test is an independent samples t-test because it utilizes data obtained from two independent random samples.

In our intensive supervision probation versus regular probation example, the research question is: Is the average number of technical violations incurred during a one-year period for a random sample of intensive supervision probationers ($\bar{X}_1$) significantly different from the average number of technical violations incurred during the same time period for a random sample of regular probationers ($\bar{X}_2$)?

Five-Step Model for Hypothesis Testing

Step 1: Make Assumptions
There are four assumptions of the independent samples t-test:
1. Use of independent random samples. (This ensures sample representativeness and informs the statistical test to account for between-group differences.)

2. The dependent variable is measured at the interval-ratio level. (This allows for the calculation of a mean.)
3. The sampling distribution is normally distributed. (This ensures that areas under the curve are accurate and will lead to a proper decision regarding statistical significance.)
4. Homogeneity of variance. (Prevents errors in the statistical test due to differences in dispersion around the point of central tendency across the two samples.)

Step 2: State Hypotheses

Remember that hypotheses are always stated in terms of population parameters. In the independent samples *t*-test, the null hypothesis indicates that the population mean of the first sample is equal to the population mean of the second sample. For our research question the null hypothesis states that the average number of technical violations is equal for both the intensive supervision probation and the regular probation populations. The alternative hypothesis states that the intensive supervision probation population's average number of technical violations is not equal to the regular probation population's average number of technical violations. Symbolically, the hypotheses would be:

$$H_o: \mu_1 = \mu_2$$
$$H_1: \mu_1 \neq \mu_2$$

Again, both of these hypotheses are stated in terms of population parameters and are anchored in the hypothesis-testing logic of continuing to believe the null hypothesis (i.e., there are no significant differences between the two groups' means on the dependent variable) to be true until there is evidence (determined in the fifth step of the five-step model) to reject the null hypothesis and believe there is support for the alternative hypothesis (i.e., that significant differences do exist between the two samples on their means of the dependent variable).

Step 3: Select Sampling Distribution and Specify Decision Criteria

It is in this step that we specify the statistical test and other things (one-tailed or two-tailed, degrees of freedom, and alpha) we will be using to determine whether to reject the null hypothesis. In our intensive supervision probation versus regular probation example we are comparing the intensive supervision probation random sample mean to the regular probation random sample mean ($\bar{X}_1 - \bar{X}_2$), thus, it is appropriate to use the independent samples *t*-test sampling distribution to answer our research question.

The independent samples *t*-test sampling distribution is presented in figure 8.4. This sampling distribution is made up of all possible out-

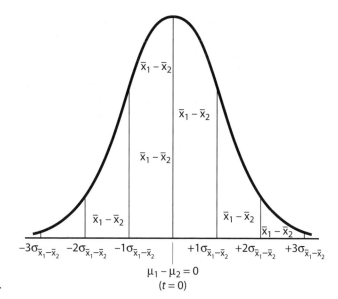

**Figure 8.4
Independent Samples *t*-Test Sampling Distribution**

comes of randomly drawing an intensive supervision probation sample and computing the average number of technical violations, then randomly drawing a regular probation sample and computing the average number of technical violations, and then subtracting the two means. Slight differences in means will cause the test statistic to fall outside the critical regions and close to the central tendency point ($p > \alpha$), will cause the null hypothesis to be retained, and the observed differences will be attributed to random sampling variability. Large differences in means will cause the test statistic to fall inside the critical regions located in the tails of the sampling distribution ($p < \alpha$), will cause the null hypothesis to be rejected, and the observed differences will be considered statistically significant (real, reliable, and repeatable across other samples from the population).

As was the case with the one-sample *t*-test, there are many *t*-test sampling distributions corresponding to every possible sample size. As before, the *t*-distribution is normal in shape but for sample sizes below 120 the *t*-distributions become flatter (less peaked) in the center, thicker in the tails, wider, and more conservative in terms of allowing a rejection of the null hypothesis. The general rule is: The smaller the sample size, the flatter and thicker-tailed the *t*-distribution, the harder to reject the null hypothesis; the greater the sample size, the more peaked, thinner-tailed, and narrower the *t*-distribution, the easier to reject the null hypothesis. For combined sample sizes above 120 the *t*-distribution superimposes itself on the normal curve, meaning the areas under the normal curve and the *t*-distribution become indistinguishable.

As was the case with the one-sample *t*-test, the decision of which *t*-distribution to apply to the particular research situation is based on the degrees of freedom (df), which for the *t*-test is based primarily on sample size. Another factor affecting this decision is that independent samples *t*-distributions are less peaked and wider than dependent samples *t*-distributions, making it harder to reject the null hypothesis when employing independent random samples. As discussed earlier, the control of many individual characteristic differences between the comparison groups is the primary reason that the sampling distribution is narrower (thus, easier to reject the null hypothesis) when using dependent random samples. Figure 8.5 demonstrates this feature.

In our intensive supervision probation versus regular probation example, we will randomly select 10 intensive supervision probation offenders and 10 regular probation offenders. An independent samples *t*-test will be computed, alpha will be set at .05, the tests will be two-tailed (a more conservative approach, even though we likely have reason to believe that the significant difference would only be in the positive tail reflecting the intensive supervision probation sample averages being higher than the regular probation sample averages). For the independent samples *t*-test degrees of freedom are computed as df = $N_1 + N_2 - 2$. These decision criteria can be summarized for our example as follows:

Independent samples *t*-test, two-tailed,
$\alpha = .05$, df = $N_1 + N_2 - 2 = 10 + 10 - 2 = 18$

Step 4: Compute the Test Statistic

In this step the data from the two samples are used to compute their respective means on the interval-ratio dependent variable (num-

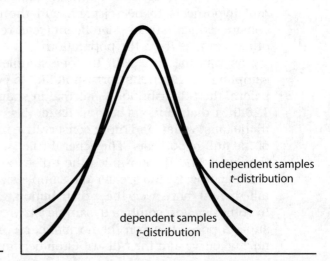

**Figure 8.5
Independent versus Dependent Samples *t*-Test Sampling Distribution**

independent samples *t*-distribution

dependent samples *t*-distribution

ber of technical violations). The independent samples *t*-test is then computed to compare the intensive supervision probation sample mean to the regular probation sample mean. Use SPSS Application Two at the end of the chapter for the example data set and the SPSS steps to do the calculations. Formula 8.2 below allows for the computation of the independent samples *t*-test by hand:

FORMULA 8.2: INDEPENDENT SAMPLES *t*-TEST

$$t = \frac{\bar{X}_1 - \bar{X}_2}{\sigma_{\bar{X}_1 - \bar{X}_2}}$$

Where $\bar{X}_1$ = intensive supervision probation sample mean
$\bar{X}_2$ = regular probation sample mean
$\sigma_{\bar{X}_1 - \bar{X}_2}$ = standard error of the difference

The **standard error of the difference** ($\sigma_{\bar{X}_1 - \bar{X}_2}$; sometimes called a **pooled variance** or simply the standard error) is an algebraic combination of the squared standard deviations (variances) for the two samples and should be computed before computing the *t*-test statistic so that it can be plugged into the *t*-test formula. The formula for the standard error is:

$$\sigma_{\bar{X}_1 - \bar{X}_2} = \sqrt{\frac{s_1^2}{N_1} + \frac{s_2^2}{N_2}}$$

Where: N_1 = sample size for intensive supervision probation sample
N_2 = sample size for regular probation sample
s_1^2 = variance for intensive supervision probation sample
s_2^2 = variance for regular probation sample

For our research question testing the difference between the intensive supervision probation offenders (sample 1) and regular probation offenders (sample 2) on their average number of technical violations, the following are the values that should be plugged into the formulas:

$\bar{X}_1 = 7.4$
$\bar{X}_2 = 2.7$
$N_1 = 10$
$N_2 = 10$
$s_1^2 = 6.713$
$s_2^2 = 2.232$

The hand calculations for the standard error are:

$$\sigma_{\bar{X}_1-\bar{X}_2} = \sqrt{\frac{s_1^2}{N_1} + \frac{s_2^2}{N_2}}$$

$$\sigma_{\bar{X}_1-\bar{X}_2} = \sqrt{\frac{6.713}{10} + \frac{2.232}{10}}$$

$$\sigma_{\bar{X}_1-\bar{X}_2} = \sqrt{.6713 + .2232}$$

$$\sigma_{\bar{X}_1-\bar{X}_2} = \sqrt{.8945}$$

$$\sigma_{\bar{X}_1-\bar{X}_2} = .946$$

The hand calculations for the independent samples t-test are:

$$t = \frac{\bar{X}_1 - \bar{X}_2}{\sigma_{\bar{X}_1-\bar{X}_2}} = \frac{(7.4 - 2.7)}{.946} = \frac{4.7}{.946} = 4.97$$

The computer printout resulting from using the data set and SPSS steps at the end of the chapter is listed below:

Group Statistics

	Type of Probation	N	Mean	Std. Deviation	Std. Error Mean
# of Technical Violations	ISP	10	7.40	2.591	.819
	Regular Probation	10	2.70	1.494	.473

Independent Samples Test

		Levene's Test for Equality of Variances		t-test for Equality of Means						
									95% Confidence Interval of the Difference	
		F	Sig.	t	df	Sig. (2-tailed)	Mean Difference	Std. Error Difference	Lower	Upper
# of Technical Violations	Equal variances assumed	4.414	.050	4.970	18	.000	4.700	.946	2.713	6.687
	Equal variances not assumed			4.970	14.393	.000	4.700	.946	2.677	6.723

The first results box provides descriptive statistics on the two samples indicating sample size (N), mean ($\bar{X}$), standard deviation (s), and standard error of the mean. The second results box presents the information used to conduct the independent samples t-test including the Levene's Test for Homogeneity of Variance (F statistic and significance value), the value of the t-test (t), its degrees of freedom (df), the two-tailed p-value—listed as Sig. (2-tailed), the difference between the means ($\bar{X}_1 - \bar{X}_2$), the standard error of the difference between the means ($\sigma_{\bar{X}_1 - \bar{X}_2}$), and the 95% confidence interval surrounding the standard error. Note that in the Levene's Test for Homogeneity of Variance, $p \geq .05$ so the null hypotheses should be retained and equal variances assumed. This means that the t-test results should be read only from the "equal variances assumed" row. Had the Levene's Test yielded $p < .05$, we would have read the t-test results from the "equal variances not assumed" row.

Step 5: Make a Decision

For our hypothesis test comparing the average number of technical violations for the two samples over a one-year period, the p-value associated with the statistical result is less than our prespecified alpha level ($p < \alpha$). This means that we should reject the null hypothesis and conclude that the test statistic falls inside the critical region of the independent samples t-test sampling distribution. We further conclude that the difference observed between the intensive supervision probation sample's average number of technical violations (7.4) and the regular probation sample's average number of technical violations (2.7) is statistically significant. Since we know that the difference in the averages is reliable, we can go a step further and examine the two samples' means, and say that the intensive supervision probation sample had statistically significantly more technical violations, on average, than did the regular probation sample. Furthermore, we can expect to find this pattern of mean differences again if we repeated the study using new random samples from the two populations.

As was the case in the last chapter, determination of statistical significance can also be made manually through the use of critical values tables found in the appendices in the back of the book. Remember that while computer output tells us whether the p-value is *less than* the alpha level, which would cause us to reject the null hypothesis, critical values tables provide the critical value of the test statistic that needs to be exceeded by the obtained test statistic in order for the test statistic to fall into the critical region causing rejection of the null hypothesis. The critical values table for the independent samples t-test (as well as the dependent samples t-test) is the same as the one used for the one-sample t-test.

Appendix B contains the critical values of the t-distribution and should be used by locating the relevant degrees of freedom and alpha level for the specific analysis. For our example data the critical t-value will be based on the degrees of freedom (df = 18), alpha (α = .05), and direction of the tests (two-tailed). Thus, $t_{(critical)} = \pm 2.101$. For our research question comparing the two types of probation in terms of technical violations, $t_{(obtained)} = 4.97$. This obtained test statistic does exceed the critical value, meaning that it falls inside the critical region, indicating that we should reject the null hypothesis and conclude that the two samples do differ significantly in their average number of technical violations.

The following is an example of how the results of the analysis of our example data would be stated:

> A study of a random sample of 10 intensive supervision probation offenders and a random sample of 10 regular probation offenders was conducted to determine if differences in their average number of technical violations incurred over a one-year period of time could be detected. An independent samples t-test was performed in order to determine if the average number of technical violations over a one-year time period was significantly different across the two samples. The intensive supervision probation sample had significantly more technical violations (M = 7.4, SD = 2.59) on average than the regular probation sample (M = 2.7, SD = 1.49), and the difference was determined to be statistically significant ($t_{18} = 4.97, p = .000$). The results provide some evidence that intensive supervision probation may result in higher levels of technical violations as compared to regular probation simply due to the increased level of supervision. However, the results should be inferred with caution due to the low sample sizes employed in this study.

■ THE DEPENDENT SAMPLES t-TEST

Purpose of the Dependent Samples t-Test

The purpose of the dependent samples t-test is to answer the following research question: Is the mean from one dependent sample statistically significantly different from the mean from another dependent sample? This question implies that the dependent variable is measured at the interval-ratio level since a mean is being computed. The test that should be used to answer the research question is the dependent samples t-test since the data for the two sample means are related in one of the ways described earlier. Specifically, the repeated measures form of dependent sampling will be demonstrated here, whereby data were collected on the same variable at two different data collection points using the same sample.

The pre-to-post change in arrests one year before and one year after incarceration for our prison sample will serve as the focus of our application. Specifically, the research question is: Is there a significant difference in the average number of arrests (one year preincarceration) and the average number of arrests (one year postrelease) for the randomly selected prison sample?

Five-Step Model for Hypothesis Testing

Step 1: Make Assumptions
There are three assumptions of the dependent samples t-test:

1. Use of dependent samples. (This informs the statistical test to account for within-group differences, thus reducing a source of error in the analysis.)
2. The dependent variable is measured at the interval-ratio level. (This allows for the calculation of a mean.)
3. The sampling distribution is normally distributed. (This ensures that areas under the curve are accurate and will lead to a proper decision regarding statistical significance.)

Step 2: State Hypotheses
In the dependent samples t-test the null hypothesis indicates that the difference between the means of the related populations (or repeated measures from one population) is equal to zero. For our research question the null hypothesis states that the difference between the preincarceration average number of arrests and postincarceration average number of arrests is equal to zero for the prison population. The alternative hypothesis for states that the difference between the preincarceration average number of arrests and postincarceration average number of arrests is not zero for the prison population. It is our hope that we will end up rejecting the null hypothesis since it is desirable to see some positive impact of sentencing on recidivism. Symbolically, the hypotheses for our research question is:

$$H_o: \mu_D = 0$$
$$H_1: \mu_D \neq 0$$

Step 3: Select Sampling Distribution and Specify Decision Criteria
It is in this step that we specify the statistical test and other things (one-tailed or two-tailed, degrees of freedom, and alpha) we will be using to determine whether to reject the null hypothesis. Because our research question involves examining pre-to-post changes in the average number of arrests for the prison sample, we are employing a repeated measures research design, meaning that both sample means being compared were generated from data that came from a single sample; thus, it is appropriate to use the dependent samples t-test sampling distribution to answer our research question.

The dependent samples *t*-test sampling distribution is presented in figure 8.6. This sampling distribution is made up all of possible outcomes of randomly drawing a prison sample and computing the average number of presentence arrests and the average number of postrelease arrests, then subtracting the two means. Slight differences in the two means will cause the test statistic to fall outside the critical regions and close to the central tendency point ($p > \alpha$), will cause the null hypothesis to be retained, and any observed mean differences will be attributed to random sampling variability. Large differences in the two means will cause the test statistic to fall inside the critical regions located in the tails of the sampling distribution ($p < \alpha$), will cause the null hypothesis to be rejected, and any observed mean differences will be considered statistically significant (i.e., real, reliable, and repeatable across other samples from the population).

As was the case with the one-sample *t*-test and the independent samples *t*-test, there are many *t*-test sampling distributions corresponding to every possible sample size. Thus, the decision of which *t*-distribution to apply to the particular research situation is based on the degrees of freedom, which for the *t*-test is based primarily on sample size. It should be reiterated from step three of the independent samples hypothesis test that dependent samples *t*-distributions are more peaked and narrower than independent samples *t*-distributions, making it easier to reject the null hypothesis when employing dependent random samples. The control of many individual characteristic differences by having only one sample being observed at two different points in time, rather than two distinctly different comparison groups being observed at only one point in time, is the primary reason that the sampling distribution is narrower (thus, easier to reject the null hypothesis) when using dependent random samples.

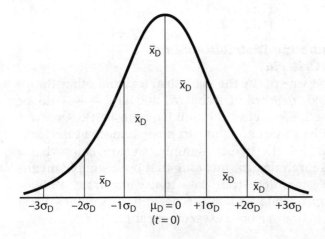

Figure 8.6 Dependent Samples *t*-Test Sampling Distribution

In our prison example, we have randomly selected 10 prison inmates. We have used a repeated measures design where we have measured the average number of arrests at two points in time: (1) the one year prior to serving a six-month sentence; and (2) the one year following completion of the six-month sentence. A single dependent samples *t*-test will be computed to compare the means at these two points in time; alpha will be set at .05, the *t*-test will be two-tailed. In the dependent samples *t*-test the degrees of freedom are computed as df = N − 1, where N equals the number of paired observations. For our prison sample there are 10 presentence and postrelease paired observations for the number of arrests. These decision criteria for our research example can be summarized as follows:

Dependent samples *t*-test, two-tailed,
α = .05, df = N − 1 = 10 − 1 = 9

Step 4: Compute the Test Statistic

In this step the data from the repeated measures (pre and post) of number of arrests are submitted to the dependent samples *t*-test analysis. This is done to test for changes in arrest activity in the prison between one year prior to incarceration and one year postrelease. Use the SPSS "Prison" Application at the end of the chapter for the example data set and the SPSS steps to do the calculations. Formula 8.3 allows for the computation of the dependent samples *t*-test by hand as indicated below:

FORMULA 8.3: DEPENDENT SAMPLES *t*-TEST

$$t = \frac{\bar{X}_D}{\sigma_D}$$

Where: $\bar{X}_D$ = mean of the differences between the paired scores

σ_D = standard error of the mean of the differences

Computation of the **mean of the differences between the paired scores ($\bar{X}_D$)** involves setting up columns where each score is subtracted from its paired score to create **difference scores (D)**, then those difference scores are totaled and divided by sample size (total number of pairs):

$$\bar{X}_D = \frac{\Sigma D}{N}$$

Computation of the **standard error of the mean of the differences (σ_D)**, which is the standard deviation of the sampling distribution for the dependent samples *t*-test, involves creating a column of squared difference scores (D^2), then computing the standard error of the mean of the differences (σ_D) using the following formula (work from top of formula to the bottom):

$$\sigma_D = \frac{\sqrt{\frac{\Sigma D^2 - \frac{(\Sigma D)^2}{N}}{N}}}{\sqrt{N-1}}$$

For our research question testing the difference between preincarceration and postrelease average number of arrests for the prison sample, the following are the columns of information necessary for the hand calculations of the dependent samples *t*-test:

Presanction # of Arrests	Postrelease # of Arrests	D	D^2
8	7	1	1
12	10	2	4
7	6	1	1
6	5	1	1
4	5	−1	1
4	6	−2	4
13	12	1	1
5	6	−1	1
16	11	5	25
8	6	2	4
		9	43

The hand calculations of the mean of the paired score differences are:

$$\bar{X}_D = \frac{\Sigma D}{N}$$

$$\bar{X}_D = \frac{9}{10} = .90$$

The hand calculations for the standard error of the mean of the paired score differences:

$$\sigma_D = \frac{\sqrt{\frac{\Sigma D^2 - \frac{(\Sigma D)^2}{N}}{N}}}{\sqrt{N-1}} = \frac{\sqrt{\frac{43 - \frac{(9)^2}{10}}{10}}}{\sqrt{10-1}} = \frac{\sqrt{\frac{43 - \frac{(81)}{10}}{10}}}{\sqrt{9}}$$

$$= \frac{\sqrt{\frac{43 - 8.1}{10}}}{3} = \frac{\sqrt{\frac{34.9}{10}}}{3} = \frac{\sqrt{3.49}}{3} = \frac{1.868}{3} = .6227$$

The hand calculations for the dependent samples t-test are:

$$t = \frac{\bar{X}_D}{\sigma_D}$$

$$t = \frac{.9}{.6227}$$

$$t = 1.445$$

The computer printout resulting from using the data set and SPSS steps at the end of the chapter is listed below:

Paired Samples Statistics

		Mean	N	Std. Deviation	Std. Error Mean
Pair 1	Number of Pre-Sanction Arrests	8.30	10	4.084	1.291
	Number of Post-Release Arrests	7.40	10	2.591	.819

Paired Samples Correlations

		N	Correlation	Sig.
Pair 1	Number of Pre-Sanction Arrests & Number of Post-Release Arrests	10	.922	.000

Paired Samples Test

		Paired Differences							
		Mean	Std. Deviation	Std. Error Mean	95% Confidence Interval of the Difference		t	df	Sig. (2-tailed)
					Lower	Upper			
Pair 1	Number of Pre-Sanction Arrests - Number of Post-Release Arrests	.900	1.969	.623	-.509	2.309	1.445	9	.182

The first results box contains the descriptive statistics for the two paired variables (presanction and postrelease number of arrests), including the mean, sample size, standard deviation and standard error of the mean for each variable. The second results box contains the correlation between the two variables (you will learn about correlations in chapter 10). The third results box contains the results of the dependent samples t-test (called paired samples t-test in SPSS), including the average difference between the paired scores ($\bar{X}_D = .90$), the standard deviation of the difference scores, the standard error of the mean of the difference scores (σ_D = .623), the 95% confidence interval of the mean of the difference scores, the obtained *t*-test statistic (t = 1.445), the degrees of freedom (df = 9), and the significance level (p = .182). You can observe where the values resulting from the hand calculations appear on the printout.

Step 5: Make a Decision

For our hypothesis test, which examines changes in arrest activity from one year prior to serving a six-month prison sentence to one year after release from custody, the probability (*p*-value) associated with the obtained *t*-test statistic is greater than our prespecified alpha level ($p > \alpha$). This means that we should retain the null hypothesis and conclude that the test statistic falls outside the critical region of the dependent samples *t*-test sampling distribution. We further conclude that the difference observed between the prison sample's average number of presanction arrests (8.3) and the prison sample's average number of postrelease arrests (7.4) is not statistically significant. Any observed difference between the means is likely to be the result of random sampling variability. Thus, it does not appear that having served six months in prison had a positive impact on reducing recidivism for the prison inmate sample.

As before, determination of statistical significance can also be made manually through the use of critical values tables found in the appendices in the back of the book. Appendix B contains the critical values of the *t*-distribution and should be used by locating the relevant degrees of freedom and alpha level for the specific analysis. For our example data the critical *t*-value will be determined based on the degrees of freedom (df = 9), alpha (α = .05), and direction of the tests (two-tailed). Thus, $t_{(critical)}$ = ± 2.262. Since $t_{(obtained)}$ = 1.445, the obtained test statistic does not exceed the critical value. This means that the obtained statistic falls outside the critical region, indicating that we should retain the null hypothesis and conclude that there was not a significant change in arrest activity presanction to postrelease for the prison sample.

The following is an example of how the results of the analysis of our example data would be stated:

> A study of a random sample of 10 prison inmates was conducted to determine if the sample experienced significant changes in its average arrest activity one year postrelease from a six-month incarceration, as compared to its one-year preincarceration average arrest level. A dependent samples *t*-test was performed on the arrest data from the prison sample at the two specified points in time. Among the prison sample, the average number of arrests

during the presanction time period was 8.3 (SD=4.08), and for the postrelease time period the average was 7.4 (SD=2.59). This slight decrease in arrest activity from pre-to-post time periods was not determined to be statistically significant (t_9 = 1.46, p=.182). The results indicate that there is no evidence that a six-month incarceration has any positive impact on recidivism for inmates. However, the results should be inferred with caution due to the low sample size employed in this study.

Summary

In this chapter you have learned the purposes and the appropriate research contexts for conducting three different types of t-tests. You have received instructions and been given demonstrations on how to perform the one sample t-test, the independent samples t-test, and the dependent (paired) samples t-test. You also learned how to determine statistical significance using both the computer and critical values tables. All of these concepts were demonstrated through SPSS applications that employed realistic, hypothetical research scenarios in the field of criminal justice.

Key Terms

One-Sample t-test (t)
Independent Samples t-test (t)
Dependent Samples t-test (t)
Degrees of Freedom (df)
One-Tailed t-test
Two-Tailed t-test
Critical Values Tables
$t_{(obtained)}$
$t_{(critical)}$
Between-Subjects t-test
Independent Random Samples
Selection Bias
Within-Subjects t-test

Repeated Measures t-test
Dependent Samples
Matched Samples
Homogeneity of Variance
Pooled Variance
Standard Error of
 the Difference ($\sigma_{\bar{X}_1-\bar{X}_2}$)
Mean of the Differences between
 the Paired Scores ($\bar{X}_D$)
Difference Scores (D)
Standard Error of the
 Mean of the Differences (σ_D)

SPSS Application One: One-Sample *t*-Test

1. Create the following "Jail Inmates" data set.

ID#	Days Served
16222	317
25888	219
99589	142
12989	418
40125	217
21296	245
23310	274
87554	389
33598	342
10999	245
33333	211
88589	241
66359	345
22585	334
23681	264

2. Perform the One-Sample *t*-test:
    i. Analyze
        ii. Compare Means
        iii. One-Sample *t*-test
            iv. Move "Days Served" variable to the "Test Variable List"
            v. Type the number "210" (the population mean) in the "Test Value" box
            vi. Click on the "OK" button

SPSS APPLICATION TWO: INDEPENDENT SAMPLES t-TEST

1. Create the following "Probation" data set.

ID #	Type of Probation (Probation) (0 = Intensive Supervision Probation; 1 = Regular Probation)	# of Technical Violations (Violations)
01	0	7
02	0	10
03	0	6
04	0	5
05	0	5
06	0	6
07	0	12
08	0	6
09	0	11
10	0	6
11	1	3
12	1	1
13	1	0
14	1	4
15	1	2
16	1	5
17	1	3
18	1	2
19	1	3
20	1	4

2. Perform the Independent Samples t-test:
    i. Analyze
        ii. Compare Means
        iii. Independent Samples t-test
            iv. Move "Violations" variable to the "Test Variable(s) List"
            v. Move "Probation" variable to the "Grouping Variable" Box
            vi. Click on "Define Groups" Button
                vii. Put the value labels for the two groups in their respective boxes (Group 1 = 0; Group 2 = 1).
            viii. Click on "Continue"
            ix. Click on "OK"

SPSS Application Three: Dependent Samples t-Test

1. Create the following "Prison" data set.

ID#	# of Prior Arrests (PreArrests)	# of Postrelease Arrests (PstArrests)
01	8	7
02	12	10
03	7	6
04	6	5
05	4	5
06	4	6
07	13	12
08	5	6
09	16	11
10	8	6

2. Perform the Dependent Samples t-test:
   i. Analyze
      ii. Compare Means
      iii. Paired-Samples t-test
         iv. Click on "PreArrests"
         v. Click on "PstArrests"
         vi. Click on arrow to move the pair of variables into the "Paired Variables" List
         vii. Click on "OK"

SPSS Assignment

1. Open the "Parolees" data set you created for Chapter 7 (see below). This fictitious data set contains a random sample of 15 parolees released from prison six months ago. The data set includes the variables "Gender" (1 = male; 2 = female) and "Crimetype," which shows what type of crime each individual committed that resulted in incarceration. This variable should be coded as: 1 = violent crime, 2 = property crime; 3 = drug/vice crime. Two additional variables were collected for these parolees and should be added to the data set. The variables measure the reading levels of these parolees before and after they completed a basic education course. The variable "Preread" is the reading score before the course, and the variable "Postread" is the reading score after completion of the course. Both of these variables have

possible scores ranging from 0 to 100, with higher scores indicating higher reading levels. Using the values presented in the data set below, add these two variables to the data set and use the full data set to complete the following exercises.

2. Use the five-step model for hypothesis testing to answer the following research question: Does the average postcourse reading level for these parolees differ statistically significantly from the national adult reading level of 79?

3. Perform an independent samples t-test to find out whether males and females differed in their reading levels after the basic education course. Use the five-step model for hypothesis testing for the t-test, but do the computations using SPSS.

4. Perform a dependent samples t-test to find out whether reading levels changed significantly from before to after the basic education course. Use the five-step model for hypothesis testing and do the computations using SPSS.

5. Write a few paragraphs summarizing the results of the analyses performed in steps two through four.

"Parolees" Data Set

Parolee ID	Gender	Crimetype	Preread	Postread
01	Male	Violent	42	51
02	Male	Property	75	80
03	Female	Drug/Vice	72	81
04	Male	Violent	50	55
05	Male	Violent	56	59
06	Male	Property	59	60
07	Male	Property	62	65
08	Female	Drug/Vice	69	69
09	Female	Drug/Vice	55	70
10	Male	Drug/Vice	63	72
11	Female	Drug/Vice	70	78
12	Male	Violent	68	75
13	Female	Drug/Vice	70	74
14	Male	Property	47	55
15	Female	Property	63	67

Multiple Choice Questions

1. _____ will cause the obtained *t*-test statistic to fall inside the critical region.
   A. No differences in means
   B. Small differences in means
   C. Large differences in means
   D. Any differences in means

2. A researcher runs a dependent samples *t*-test with α = .05 and gets a *p*-value of .026. What decision should the researcher make regarding the null hypothesis?
   A. Reject the null hypothesis
   B. Retain the null hypothesis
   C. Change the null hypothesis
   D. More information is needed before making a decision regarding the null hypothesis

3. A researcher should use a(n) _____ to compare sample means if the two selected samples are related to each other.
   A. Dependent samples *t*-test
   B. Independent samples *t*-test
   C. One-sample *t*-test
   D. Null sample *t*-test

4. A one-sample *t*-test sampling distribution is comprised of _____.
   A. All possible sample means for a given sample size
   B. All possible differences between the sample mean and the population mean for a given sample size
   C. All possible population means for a given sample size
   D. All possible raw scores

5. A researcher is interested in comparing mean risk scores among a sample of inmates before and after they complete a treatment program. The researcher should perform a(n) _____.
   A. Dependent samples *t*-test
   B. One-sample *t*-test
   C. Independent samples *t*-test
   D. Chi-square test

6. The *t*-test sampling distribution is identical to the normal distribution once the combined sample size is greater than _____ _____.
   A. 120
   B. 80
   C. 60
   D. 0

7. _____ is a test of homogeneity of dispersion across two samples.
   A. Dependent samples *t*-test
   B. Correlation
   C. Levene's Test of Equality of Variance
   D. Independent samples *t*-test

8. A researcher wants to see if there are significant differences in the average scores received in a class between males and females. The researcher should perform a(n) _____.
   A. Dependent samples *t*-test
   B. One-sample *t*-test
   C. Independent samples *t*-test
   D. Chi-square test

9. A researcher selects a random sample of parolees and asks sample members how many times they have been arrested. The researcher wants to know if the sample's average number of arrests is significantly higher or lower than 4. What analysis should the researcher perform?
   A. Dependent samples *t*-test
   B. One-sample *t*-test
   C. Independent samples *t*-test
   D. Chi-square test

10. A researcher conducts an independent samples *t*-test and gets a *t*-value of 1.263. What decision should the researcher make regarding the null hypothesis?
    A. Reject the null hypothesis
    B. Retain the null hypothesis
    C. Change the null hypothesis
    D. More information is needed before making a decision regarding the null hypothesis

9

Significant Differences
One-Way Analysis of Variance (ANOVA)

This chapter extends the comparison of two sample means (chapter 8) to the comparison of three or more sample means computed for a single, interval-ratio, dependent variable. The remaining chapters of the book will look at reliable relationships between variables—the other side of the statistical coin.

■ PURPOSE OF ANOVA TESTS

The purpose of this chapter is to present a statistical test, the **one-way analysis of variance (one-way ANOVA)**, that compares means computed from a single dependent variable for three or more groups that are defined by a single categorical (nominal or ordinal) variable. The one-way analysis of variance test is the proper test for making multiple group comparisons of means on a single dependent variable. The fact that there is only one dependent variable makes one-way ANOVA a **univariate** statistical test; all statistical analyses that analyze more than one dependent variable at a time are called **multivariate** tests.

The term "one-way" refers to the fact that the groups are being defined by only one categorical grouping variable (i.e., one independent variable). However, students should be aware that more advanced statistical analyses exist to compare means on a single dependent variable using two or more grouping (independent) variables—one such analysis is called the factorial analysis of variance (factorial ANOVA). Another advanced statistical test, called the multivariate analysis of variance, simultaneously compares multiple sample means on two or more dependent variables. This textbook does not cover factorial ANOVA or multivariate ANOVA (MANOVA) techniques.

Important Concepts Related to Analysis of Variance

The F-Ratio and Logic of ANOVA

In the one-way ANOVA, the specific statistic computed to test for statistically significant differences between the group means is the **F-Ratio**. The F-Ratio works by taking the total variance (variability) observed in the dependent variable and dividing it into two sources: the variance that can be accounted for by reliable differences between the group means on the dependent variable (called **between-group variance**) and the variance that can be attributed to random sampling error, as well as any other sources of error (e.g., measurement error) in the dependent variable (called **within-group variance**). The F-Ratio essentially divides the between-group variance by the within-group variance to determine if the between-group variance exceeds the within-group variance enough to say that the between-group variance is real, reliable, and statistically significant. If the between-group variance does not exceed the within-group variance by very much, the F statistic will not be statistically significant, and it will be concluded that the observed group mean differences are simply the result of random sampling error and measurement error.

FORMULA 9.1: BASIC FORM OF THE F-RATIO

$$\text{F-Ratio} = \frac{\text{Between-Group Variance}}{\text{Within-Group Variance}}$$

Figure 9.1 is a **Venn diagram** (circles used to represent mathematical or logical subsets and relationships) that illustrates how the F-Ratio works. The total circle represents all of the variation observed in the dependent variable. The left side of the circle represents the variation in the dependent variable that can be attributed to the effect of the independent variable (the grouping variable). The right side of the circle represents the variation in the dependent variable that can be attributed to within-group variance, or what I call the *white noise* in the statistical model of the data. This *white noise* is comprised of the individual differences the subjects in the sample bring to the study (sampling error), and any measurement errors involved in collecting the data. As the left side of the circle (comprised of the reliable group differences) becomes substantially larger than the right side of the circle (comprised of sampling and measurement errors), the F-Ratio will become larger until it reaches a magnitude that would result in a decision that statistically significant differences exist between the group means. The greater the ratio of between-group variance to within-group variance, the larger the F statistic, and the more reliable (and statistically significant) the independent variable is in accounting for variation in the dependent variable.

Homogeneity of Variance

As was the case with the independent samples *t*-test, it often is important to determine if our groups have an equal amount of variance around the mean on the dependent variable. In the ANOVA test, this variation of individual scores around the group mean is referred to as within-group variance, since it is comprised of individual differences among subjects comprising the group (sampling error), as well as measurement error. We know that the F-Ratio compares this within-group variance to the reliable between-group variance. But an assumption of the ANOVA is that there is homogeneity of variance, meaning that the within-group variance is the same in each of the groups being compared. If even one sample's within-group variance differs greatly from the other samples, the data suffers from heterogeneity of variance. Figure 9.2 compares homogeneity and heterogeneity of variance.

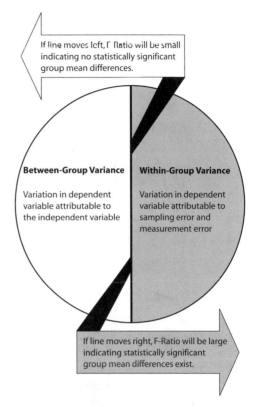

Figure 9.1 Venn Diagram of the F-Ratio

If the number of subjects in each group differs, the one-way ANOVA test is very sensitive to violations of the assumption of homogeneity of variance. Thus, it is best to use equal sample sizes whenever possible when employing the ANOVA test. Most statistical programs test the homogeneity of variance assumption when performing ANOVA so that the robustness of the test can be assessed. Being **robust** means that the test performs accurately even under stressful or less than ideal circumstances. The test will not be very robust when sample sizes are unequal across the groups. But if equal numbers of subjects are in each group, the test is quite robust to violations of the homogeneity of variance assumption.

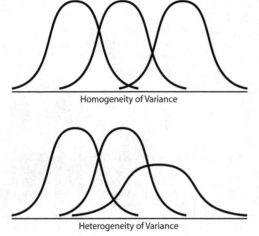

Figure 9.2 Illustration of Homogeneity and Heterogeneity of Variance

Efficiency and the Type I Error Rate

It may have occurred to you that comparisons of multiple group means could be conducted by performing all pair-wise comparisons possible from the groups using independent samples *t*-tests. For example, comparisons between three groups could be conducted by running three *t*-tests comparing: group 1 versus group 2; group 1 versus group 3; and group 2 versus group 3. Mathematically, the results regarding statistical significance will be the same whether these comparisons are made using a one-way ANOVA or using three separate *t*-tests. Remember how a statistical test has a 5% Type I error rate (or the level at which alpha is set), meaning there is a 5% chance that a true null hypothesis will be rejected simply by chance. If three *t*-tests are performed, there is a 15% chance (3 × .05) that one of the null hypotheses will be rejected (statistical significance will be concluded) when it should not have been. Conducting a single one-way ANOVA allows all three comparisons to be made simultaneously while maintaining a 5% Type I error rate. Thus, researchers try to use the most efficient statistical tests possible to make the process more concise and, more importantly, to keep the Type I error rate at a minimum.

■ RESEARCH EXAMPLE

Our research example for the one-way ANOVA asks the following research question: Is there a statistically significant difference in the average number of technical violations (one year postsentencing) across three random samples of offenders assigned to: probation only

($\bar{X}_1$), intensive supervision probation ($\bar{X}_2$), and shock probation ($\bar{X}_3$)? This research question will be answered in two phases. First, the F statistic will be used to test the overall **main effect** of the independent variable, indicating whether significant group differences exist between any of the three group means. Lastly, if the answer is affirmative in that at least two groups have significantly different means, then we will use **post hoc** (meaning "after the fact") tests to determine exactly where the significant differences lie. For example, there may be significant differences between two of the groups, yet neither group is significantly different from the third; or all three groups may be determined to be different from each other. We will discuss post hoc tests in more detail later in the chapter.

Five-Step Model for Hypothesis Testing

Step 1: Make Assumptions

There are three assumptions of the one-way ANOVA test, and they are the same as the assumptions accompanying the independent samples t-test:

1. Use of independent random samples. (This ensures sample representativeness and informs the statistical test to account for between-group differences.)
2. The dependent variable is measured at the interval-ratio level. (This allows for the calculation of a mean.)
3. Homogeneity of variance. (Prevents errors in the statistical test due to differences in dispersion around the point of central tendency across each of the samples.)

Step 2: State Hypotheses

Remember that hypotheses are always stated in terms of population parameters. In the one-way ANOVA test, the null hypothesis indicates that the population means for each group are equal to each other. For our research question the null hypothesis states that the average number of technical violations is equal for the regular probation, the intensive supervision probation, and shock incarceration populations. The alternative hypothesis states that at least one population mean is statistically significantly different from another population mean. Symbolically, the hypotheses would be:

$$H_0: \mu_1 = \mu_2 = \mu_3$$
$$H_1: \text{at least one } \mu \text{ differs from another } \mu$$

Step 3: Select Sampling Distribution and Specify Decision Criteria

In this step we specify the statistical test and other things (degrees of freedom and alpha) we will be using to determine whether to reject the null hypothesis. In our example comparing three forms of probation, we are comparing more than two means on a single dependent variable, thus the one-way ANOVA test will be conducted. This test uses the F-Ratio sampling distribution to make the determination of statistical significance. The general form of the F-Ratio sampling distribution is presented in figure 9.3.

The F sampling distribution is made up of all the possible outcomes of randomly drawing a regular probation sample and computing their average number of technical violations, then randomly drawing an intensive supervision probation sample and computing their average number of technical violations, then randomly drawing a shock probation sample and computing their average number of technical violations, and then subtracting the three means from each other. Slight differences in means will cause the test statistic to fall outside the critical region and close to the central tendency point ($p > \alpha$), will cause the null hypothesis to be retained, and the observed differences will be attributed to random sampling variability. Large differences between any of the group means will cause the test statistic to fall inside the critical region located in the positive tail of the sampling distribution ($p < \alpha$), will cause the null hypothesis to be rejected, and the observed differences will be considered real and reliable (repeatable across other samples from the populations).

Similar to the chi-square distribution, the F-distribution can only be zero or greater (due to squaring of numbers in the computations),

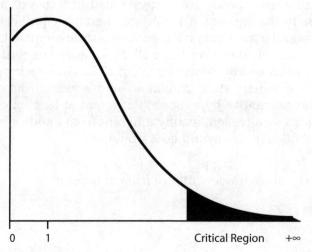

**Figure 9.3
General Form of the F-Distribution**

so there is only one critical region tail. As was the case with the chi-square and *t*-test distributions, there are many F-Ratio sampling distributions corresponding to two primary factors: the number of samples or groups being compared and the sample sizes of those groups. The F-distribution is positively skewed and becomes less skewed as the number of groups and sample sizes increase. The F-distribution maps out all of the possible outcomes for the F-Ratio that compares between- and within-group variances. An obtained F-Ratio of 1.0 would indicate that between- and within-group variances are equal. An obtained F < 1.0 would indicate that there is more within-group (white noise) variance than reliable between-group variance. An obtained F > 1.0 would indicate that there is more between-group variance in the statistical model than within-group variance. The more reliable the independent (grouping) variable is in accounting for variations in the dependent variable, the greater in value will be the F-Ratio, and the more likely it will be determined to be a statistically significant result by falling inside the critical region of the F-distribution.

As was the case with previously learned statistical tests, the decision of which F-distribution to apply to a particular research situation is based on the degrees of freedom, which for the F-Ratio is based primarily on two things: the number of groups being compared and the overall sample size.

In our example comparison of the three probation samples, we will randomly select 3 regular probation offenders, 3 intensive supervision probation offenders, and 3 shock probation offenders. (Note that these sample sizes are unrealistically small so that hand calculations can be demonstrated easily.) Alpha will be set at .05. For the F-Ratio two different degrees of freedom are employed. The first is called the **degrees of freedom for between-group variance (dfb)** and is computed as dfb = $k - 1$ (k denotes the number of groups being compared). The second is called the **degrees of freedom for within-group variance (dfw)** and is computed as dfw = $N - k$ (the overall sample size minus the number of groups). While not used in calculations of the F-Ratio (but appearing on the computer printout), there also is a **degrees of freedom for the total variance (df)** in the dependent variable and is computed as df = $N - 1$. Only the **dfb** and **dfw** are necessary for the analysis. These decision criteria can be summarized for our example as follows:

One-Way ANOVA; α = .05;
dfb = $k - 1 = 3 - 1 = 2$; dfw = $N - k = 9 - 3 = 6$

In research vernacular, we would say that we are running an ANOVA with 2 and 6 degrees of freedom, with an alpha of .05.

Step 4: Compute the Test Statistic

In this step the data from each of the samples are used to compute their respective means on the interval-ratio dependent variable (number of technical violations). The F-Ratio is then computed to compare the three probation samples' means. Use the SPSS Application at the end of the chapter for the example data set and the SPSS steps to do the calculations.

The hand calculations for analysis of variance tests are very laborious, but will be demonstrated for pedagogical purposes. Some necessary definitions include: the **Sum of Squares Total (SST)**—total variance in the dependent variable; **Sum of Squares Between (SSB)**—variance in the dependent variable attributed to between-group differences; **Sum of Squares Within (SSW)**—variance in the dependent variable attributed to within-group differences (sampling and measurement errors); **Mean Square Between (MSB)**—population variance estimate for between-groups, calculated as SSB/dfb; **Mean Square Within (MSW)**—population variance estimate for within-groups, calculated as SSW/dfw; and $\bar{X}_G$ = grand or overall mean on the dependent variable. N_K denotes the sample size for a given group. $\bar{X}_K$ denotes the group mean for a given group.

While the data set is located at the end of the chapter, it also is presented in table 9.1, along with a column labeled X^2, since these values will be used in the hand calculations of the F-Ratio.

Table 9.1 Hypothetical Data Set for Three Probation Samples (X = Number of Technical Violations)

Regular Probation ($N_K = 3$)		Intensive Supervision Probation ($N_K = 3$)		Shock Probation ($N_K = 3$)	
X	X^2	X	X^2	X	X^2
5	25	8	64	6	36
2	4	6	36	4	16
1	1	8	64	7	49
8	30	22	164	17	101
$\bar{X}_K = 2.6667$		$\bar{X}_K = 7.3333$		$\bar{X}_K = 5.6667$	

Formula 9.2 below allows for the computation of the F-Ratio by hand:

FORMULA 9.2: ONE-WAY ANOVA

Step 1: Compute

$$\bar{X}_G = \frac{(5+2+1+8+6+8+6+4+7)}{9} = \frac{47}{9} = 5.2222$$

Chapter Nine ■ Significant Differences: One-Way Analysis of Variance

Step 2: Compute
$$SST = \Sigma X^2 - N(\bar{X}_G)^2$$
$$= (30 + 164 + 101) - 9(5.2222)^2$$
$$= 295 - 9(27.2714)$$
$$= 295 - 245.4426$$
$$= 49.56$$

Step 3: Compute
$$SSB = \Sigma N_K (\bar{X}_K - \bar{X}_G)^2$$
$$= 3(2.6667 - 5.2222)^2 + 3(7.3333 - 5.2222)^2$$
$$+ 3(5.6667 - 5.2222)^2$$
$$= 3(-2.5555)^2 + 3(2.1111)^2 + 3(.4445)^2$$
$$= 3(6.5306) + 3(4.4567) + 3(.1976)$$
$$= 19.5918 + 13.3701 + .5928$$
$$= 33.56$$

Step 4: Compute
$$SSW = SST - SSB = 49.56 - 33.56 = 16.00$$

Step 5: Compute
$$MSB = \frac{SSB}{dfb} = \frac{33.56}{2} = 16.78$$

Step 6: Compute
$$MSW = \frac{SSW}{dfw} = \frac{16.00}{6} = 2.67$$

Step 7: Compute
$$F\text{-Ratio} = \frac{MSB}{MSW} = \frac{16.78}{2.67} = 6.29$$

The computer printout resulting from using the data set and SPSS steps at the end of the chapter is listed below:

Descriptives

Number of Technical Violations

	N	Mean	Std. Deviation	Std. Error	95% Confidence Interval for Mean		Minimum	Maximum
					Lower Bound	Upper Bound		
Regular Probation	3	2.67	2.082	1.202	-2.50	7.84	1	5
Intensive Supervision Probation	3	7.33	1.155	.667	4.46	10.20	6	8
Shock Probation	3	5.67	1.528	.882	1.87	9.46	4	7
Total	9	5.22	2.489	.830	3.31	7.14	1	8

Test of Homogeneity of Variances

Number of Technical Violations

Levene Statistic	df1	df2	Sig.
.778	2	6	.501

ANOVA

Number of Technical Violations

	Sum of Squares	df	Mean Square	F	Sig.
Between Groups	33.556	2	16.778	6.292	.034
Within Groups	16.000	6	2.667		
Total	49.556	8			

The first results box provides descriptive statistics on the three samples indicating sample size (N), mean ($\bar{X}$), standard deviation, standard error of the mean, 95% confidence interval for the mean, and minimum and maximum values on the dependent variable.

The second results box presents Levene's Test for Homogeneity of Variance (Levene statistic, its degrees of freedom, and significance value). Note that the Levene's Test for Homogeneity of Variance yielded $p \geq .05$ so the null hypotheses should be retained and equal variances assumed. Thus, the analysis of variance test should be accurate since this assumption has been upheld.

The third results box reports the analysis of variance test of the main effect of the "sanction" variable in accounting for between-group differences on the dependent variable. This table contains the sum of squares (between, within, and total), the degrees of freedom (between, within, and total), the mean square estimates (between and within), the F-Ratio, and the significance level of the F-Ratio.

Step 5: Make a Decision

Because the probability (*p*-value) associated with the obtained F-Ratio is less than our prespecified alpha level ($p < \alpha$), we should conclude that the test statistic falls inside the critical region of the F-Ratio sampling distribution. We should reject the null hypothesis of equal group means and conclude that the overall main effect is statistically significant, meaning that at least one sample's mean is significantly different from another. We will have to probe this main effect using post hoc tests in order to find out exactly where the significant differences lie.

As was the case in the previous chapters, determination of statistical significance can also be made manually through the use of critical values tables found in the appendices. Remember that while computer output tells us whether the *p*-value is *less than* the alpha level (which would cause us to reject the null hypothesis), critical values tables provide the critical value of the test statistic that needs to be exceeded by the obtained test statistic in order for the test statistic to fall into the critical region causing rejection of the null hypothesis. The critical values table for the F-distribution is presented in appendix D. The table presents critical values of F for two alpha levels, .05 and .01. The degrees of freedom for between-groups (dfb) are displayed across the top of the table, and the degrees of freedom for within-groups (dfw) are displayed down the rows. The researcher should find the critical value of F that corresponds with the dfb and dfw for any particular analysis. In our probation research example we will use the table for alpha = .05. Since we have dfb = 2 and dfw = 6, the $F_{(critical)} = 5.14$. Since our $F_{(obtained)} = 6.29$, it can be concluded that the obtained statistic does fall into the critical region of the F-distribution, warranting a rejection of the null hypothesis and a conclusion that at least two of the samples' means differ significantly from one another.

POST HOC PROBING

Now that we know there is a statistically significant main effect (meaning we obtained a statistically significant F-Ratio), we need to use post hoc testing to probe for answers as to where the significant differences lie. We would not do any post hoc probing if we had retained the null hypothesis when testing the overall main effect. Post hoc tests essentially break the main effect hypothesis that compares all group means simultaneously into pairwise comparisons of group means. We have already discussed the problem with inflated Type I error rates when using multiple pairwise comparisons. All post hoc tests suffer from this problem.

There are many different post hoc tests. The primary distinction is how they handle the Type I error rate problem. For example, some post hoc tests start by comparing the means that are the farthest apart. If they are found to be statistically significantly different from each other, the next two farthest apart means are compared. Once two means are determined not to be significantly different from each other, the comparison tests end because all remaining pairs are lesser apart than the last statistically significant pair. By running the pairwise comparison tests in this manner, the Type I error rate is reduced by the elimination of pairwise comparisons that would have come after the last significant pair. Other tests work in the opposite direction, starting with a comparison of the two means closest together and moving outward until two means are found to be statistically significantly different from each other. At that point, all larger pairs will be significantly different from each other. The ways to approach the problem of inflated Type I error rates differs with each type of post hoc test. Rather than present all of them here, we will look only at the most frequently employed test, the **Tukey HSD post hoc test**. It would be very laborious to perform the hand calculations for post hoc testing, thus it will be presumed that such computations will be facilitated by a statistical software package like SPSS.

The Tukey HSD post hoc test yields two types of output. The first is a table presenting all of the multiple comparisons possible. The difference between the means is reported for each pairwise comparison, along with the standard error of the difference and the significance level (p-value). Statistically significant differences can be identified by comparing the p-value to alpha, or more simply by the asterisks in the mean differences column of the table.

The second type of output yielded by the Tukey HSD post hoc test is a table that groups homogeneous subsets of means. Using the alpha = .05 criterion, the table groups means that are not significantly different from each other into subsets. If the overall main effect is not significant, meaning that post hoc testing was unnecessary, all of the group means will appear in the same subset. But if the null hypothesis for the main effect is rejected, meaning that at least two means are significantly different from each other, then two or more subsets will appear in the table. It is a matter of preference regarding which to use.

Using our probation research example, the output for the post hoc testing is presented below:

Chapter Nine ■ Significant Differences: One-Way Analysis of Variance

Post Hoc Tests

Multiple Comparisons

Dependent Variable: Number of Technical Violations
Tukey HSD

(I) Type of Probation	(J) Type of Probation	Mean Difference (I-J)	Std. Error	Sig.	95% Confidence Interval Lower Bound	95% Confidence Interval Upper Bound
Regular Probation	Intensive Supervision Probation	-4.667*	1.333	.030	-8.76	-.58
	Shock Probation	-3.000	1.333	.140	-7.09	1.09
Intensive Supervision Probation	Regular Probation	4.667*	1.333	.030	.58	8.76
	Shock Probation	1.667	1.333	.470	-2.42	5.76
Shock Probation	Regular Probation	3.000	1.333	.140	-1.09	7.09
	Intensive Supervision Probation	-1.667	1.333	.470	-5.76	2.42

* The mean difference is significant at the .05 level.

Homogeneous Subsets

Number of Technical Violations

Tukey HSD[a]

Type of Probation	N	Subset for alpha = .05 — 1	Subset for alpha = .05 — 2
Regular Probation	3	2.67	
Shock Probation	3	5.67	5.67
Intensive Supervision Probation	3		7.33
Sig.		.140	.470

Means for groups in homogeneous subsets are displayed.
a. Uses Harmonic Mean Sample Size = 3.000.

The first post hoc results box reports the first portion of the Tukey HSD post hoc test used to probe for the location of the statistically significant differences. The column labeled (I) lists the three types of probation, column (J) lists the comparison groups. Thus, each row of the table identifies the two groups being compared on their averages for the dependent variable. The column labeled "Mean Difference (I − J)" reports the difference between the two means being compared. The standard error of that difference is reported as well as the significance levels (p-values) associated with each pairwise comparison. Any p-values that are less than alpha should be concluded to correspond with statistically significant group differences. SPSS also denotes the mean differences that are statistically significant with an asterisk. Lastly, the table presents the 95% confidence intervals for each mean difference.

The second post hoc results box is labeled "Homogeneous Subsets" and lists each group, their sample sizes, and their means. The means are grouped into subsets according to the predetermined alpha level (.05 by default). Groups that are not statistically significantly different are placed in the same subset, while groups that are significantly different are placed in separate subsets. The significance level for the comparisons of means within each subset are reported at the bottom of the table. If the means in a subset are not statistically significantly different from each other, the *p*-value will be greater than .05.

For our probation research example, the multiple comparisons table indicated that only one pairwise comparison is statistically significant: regular probation and intensive supervision probation (ISP). The shock probation sample was not found to differ significantly from either of the other two groups with respect to their average number of technical violations. The homogeneous subsets table tells us the same thing. It indicates that there are two distinct subsets of means: (1) regular probation and shock probation and (2) ISP and shock probation. This tells us that the regular probation sample mean and the ISP sample mean are significantly different from each other (evident because they appear in two different subsets). It also tells us that the shock probation sample mean is not significantly different from the other two probation samples' means since it appears in both subsets. For reporting purposes you will need to know the group means so that you can talk about which ones are higher or lower than the others. The means appear in the homogeneous subsets table, but can be printed with their standard deviations under "options" when running the one-way ANOVA.

The following is an example of how the results of the analysis of our example data would be tabled and reported:

> A study of random samples of offenders sentenced to regular probation (N = 3), intensive supervision probation (N = 3), and shock probation (N = 3) was conducted to determine if differences in their average number of technical violations could be detected one year after sentencing. A one-way analysis of variance (ANOVA) was performed in order to test for significant differences across the three sample means (see table 9.2). The results indicated that the main effect was statistically significant ($F_{2, 6}$ = 6.29, p < .05). A Tukey HSD post hoc test revealed that the intensive supervision probation (ISP) sample had significantly more technical violations (M = 7.33; SD = 1.16) than the regular probation sample (M = 2.67; SD = 2.08). The shock probation sample (M = 5.67; SD = 1.53) was not found to differ significantly from either the regular probation or the ISP samples. However, the results should be inferred with caution due to the low sample sizes employed in this study.

Table 9.2 One-Way ANOVA Test of Differences between Probation Samples' Average Number of Technical Violations

Type of Probation	N	Mean	SD	Location of Significant Differences
Regular Probation	3	2.67	2.08	Regular Probation vs. ISP
ISP	3	7.33	1.16	
Shock Probation	3	5.67	1.53	

$F_{2,6} = 6.29$
$p < .05$

SUMMARY

In this chapter you have learned the purpose and method of conducting tests of differences between multiple sample means. You also learned how to perform post hoc testing and how to report the results. These techniques were demonstrated through an SPSS application that employed a hypothetical research scenario in the field of criminal justice. While this was the last test of group differences presented in this textbook, you learned that more advanced tests exist (e.g., factorial ANOVA and multivariate ANOVA).

KEY TERMS

One-Way Analysis of Variance (One-Way ANOVA)
Univariate
Multivariate
F-Ratio
Between-Group Variance
Within-Group Variance
Venn Diagram
Robust
Main Effect
Post Hoc
Degrees of Freedom for Between-Group Variance (dfb)
Degrees of Freedom for Within-Group Variance (dfw)
Degrees of Freedom for Total Variance (df)
Sum of Squares Total (SST)
Sum of Squares Between (SSB)
Sum of Squares Within (SSW)
Mean Square Between (MSB)
Mean Square Within (MSW)
Tukey HSD Post Hoc Test

SPSS Application: One-Way ANOVA

1. Create the following "probation" data set.

Subject	Type of Probation (Sanction) (1 = Regular Probation; 2 = Intensive Supervision Probation; 3 = Shock Incarceration)	Number of Technical Violations (Violations)
01	1	5
02	1	2
03	1	1
04	2	8
05	2	6
06	2	8
07	3	6
08	3	4
09	3	7

2. Perform the One-Way ANOVA Test:
    i. Analyze
        ii. Compare Means
        iii. One-Way ANOVA
            iv. Move "Violations" variable to the "Dependent List"
            v. Move "Sanction" variable to the "Factor" Box
            vi. Click on "Options" Button
                vii. Check "Descriptive" Box
                viii. Check "Homogeneity of Variance Test" Box
            ix. Click on "Continue"
            x. Click on "Post Hoc" Button
                xi. Check "Tukey" Box
                xii. Click on "Continue"
        xiii. Click on "OK"

SPSS Assignment

1. Create the "alternative school" data set below. This fictitious data set represents a random sample of 16 juvenile delinquents from an alternative school who volunteered to participate in a study of their self-reported delinquent behavior. The juveniles were asked how many times they had taken something that did not belong to

"Alternative School" Data Set:

Juvenile	Race/Ethnicity (1 = White; 2 = Black; 3 = Hispanic;) 4 = Other)	Number of Self-Reported Thefts in Past 12 Months (thefts)
01	1	9
02	2	1
03	3	6
04	4	10
05	1	13
06	2	9
07	3	7
08	4	16
09	1	4
10	2	3
11	3	14
12	4	5
13	1	8
14	2	3
15	3	7
16	4	3

them over the past 12 months. The race/ethnicity (white, black, Hispanic, other) of the juveniles was collected as well.

2. Perform a one-way analysis of variance to determine whether the number of self-reported thefts differs by the race/ethnicity of the juvenile. Perform a Tukey HSD post hoc test to probe for statistically significant differences if the main effect is found to be statistically significant.

3. Write a couple of paragraphs summarizing the results of the analyses performed in step 2. Be sure to table your results.

Multiple-Choice Questions

1. Homogeneity of variance means that _____.
   A. Within-group variance is the same in each of the groups
   B. Between-group and within group variances are the same
   C. Within-group variance is different across the groups
   D. Between-group and within group variances are different

2. Running multiple *t*-tests rather than a one-way ANOVA has the effect of _____.
   A. Reducing the Type I error rate
   B. Reducing homogeneity of variance
   C. Increasing the Type I error rate
   D. Increasing homogeneity of variance

3. The one-way ANOVA tests for differences between how many groups?
   A. One
   B. Two
   C. Three or More
   D. None—ANOVA does not test for group differences

4. Each subset in Tukey's post hoc homogeneous subsets analysis contains _____.
   A. Group means that are not statistically significantly different from each other
   B. Group means that are statistically significantly different from each other
   C. Asterisks that indicate groups that are statistically different from each other
   D. Asterisks that indicate groups that are not statistically different from each other

5. The F-distribution is _____.
   A. Negatively Skewed
   B. Positively Skewed
   C. Normally Distributed
   D. Bimodal

6. If the X variable indicates group membership and an ANOVA indicates that there are statistically significant group differences on the Y variable, then it also can be concluded that X and Y are _____.
   A. Independent of each other
   B. Statistically unrelated to each other
   C. Neutral
   D. Statistically related to each other

Chapter Nine ■ Significant Differences: One-Way Analysis of Variance   191

7. The larger the F-Ratio, the _____.
   A. More likely the between-group differences are statistically significant
   B. More likely the within-group differences are statistically significant
   C. Less likely the between-group differences are statistically significant
   D. Less important the statistical findings

8. The purpose of post hoc probing is to _____.
   A. Increase the likelihood of achieving statistical significance
   B. Identify the largest group mean
   C. Determine where statistically significant group differences exist
   D. Identify the smallest group mean

9. The F-Ratio indicates the amount that _____ exceeds _____.
   A. Between-Group Variance; Total Variance
   B. Between-Group Variance; Within-Group Variance
   C. Within-Group Variance; Between Group Variance
   D. Within-Group Variance; Total Variance

10. One problem with post hoc testing is that it _____.
    A. Often yields inaccurate results
    B. Is difficult to perform
    C. Increases the Type II error rate
    D. Increases the Type I error rate

Section Three

INFERENTIAL STATISTICS
TESTS OF ASSOCIATION

10

Significant Relationships
Bivariate Correlation

This final section of the book examines statistical relationships between interval-ratio variables. In this chapter, we examine the relationship between two interval-ratio variables. The next chapter extends the relationship by using one interval-ratio variable to predict another interval-ratio variable (simple linear regression). The final chapter presents techniques to explore the ability of multiple, interval-ratio, independent variables to predict a single, interval-ratio, dependent variable (multiple linear regression).

Early in this textbook, we used the analogy of a statistical significance coin. One side of the coin represented statistical tests of significant group differences, typically on an interval-ratio dependent variable. The other side of the coin represented statistical tests of significant relationships between variables. You learned that if statistically significant group differences were found for an interval-ratio dependent variable, then flipping the coin over would reveal that the grouping variable was statistically significantly related to the dependent variable. The research question asked (i.e., a question of differences between groups or a question of relationships between variables) determines the side of the coin from which you are operating. Asking the question one way (testing for group differences on the dependent variable) and finding statistical significance means that statistical significance also will be found if the question is asked the other way (testing the relationship between the grouping variable and the dependent variable). Conversely, a finding of no statistically significant group differences on the dependent variable would translate into a finding of a nonsignificant relationship between the grouping and dependent variables. Which side of the statistical significance coin a researcher chooses to use depends on whether the research question would be asked most logically as a between-group-differences question or a relationship-between-variables question. The underlying math (applied linear algebra) used to answer both kinds of questions is the same. The preference of technique often is driven by traditional, as well as trendy, methods found in the professional literature of a discipline.

PURPOSE OF TESTS OF ASSOCIATION

The purpose of this chapter is to present a statistical test, the **bivariate correlation**, that examines relationships between two interval-ratio variables. Sometimes the correlation and similar tests are referred to as **tests of association,** since they determine if the variation observed on one variable is associated with the variation observed on the other variable. More specifically, the correlation tests to determine if changes in value on one variable are related to changes in value on the other variable. If the two variables are found to be statistically associated (correlated) with each other, the test provides additional information as to how strongly the two variables are related to each other (called the **strength of the relationship**), as well as whether the value changes on the two variables are moving in the same or opposite directions (called the **direction of the relationship**). We will discuss both strength and direction of the relationship later in the chapter.

The researcher may have identified one variable as an independent variable and the other as a dependent variable in the context of the overall research objectives, but the correlation statistical test does not require specification of independence and dependence. It simply answers the research question, "Is variable X reliably related to variable Y?" As long as the two variables are interval-ratio variables, the correlation is the appropriate statistical test to answer the question. However, correlation tests may serve as a precursor to tests of prediction (covered in chapters 11 and 12) where the independent (cause) and dependent (effect) variables must be specified. When the researcher has specified independent and dependent variables, the independent variable is always the X variable and is sometimes referred to as the **predictor variable**; the dependent variable is always the Y variable and is sometimes referred to as the **criterion variable**.

IMPORTANT CONCEPTS RELATED TO BIVARIATE CORRELATION

Measures of Association

There actually is a family of techniques that examines the association of variables. The most common measure of association is the **Pearson product-moment correlation coefficient** (typically and simply referred to as correlation, and symbolized by the letter ***r***). The Pearson product-moment correlation coefficient (*r*) is the only measure of association covered in this chapter since it is the most commonly used of all of the techniques found in the association measures family. It is suitable only for use with two interval-ratio variables that are normally distributed.

There are several other measures of association that have been developed to handle special circumstances surrounding data. For example, if one of the variables being tested for association is dichotomous, and coded 0 and 1 (called **dummy coding**, which allows for the requirements of interval-ratio data to be upheld), the **point-biserial correlation coefficient** is the most appropriate measure of association to use. If both of the variables are dichotomous and dummy coded, the **phi correlation coefficient** is the appropriate measure of association to use. Another research situation might involve a test of the relationship between two ordinal variables, or even two interval-ratio variables that deviate greatly from normality, and would be most appropriately tested using the **Spearman rank-order correlation coefficient**. Again, this chapter focuses on the Pearson product-moment correlation (hereafter referred to as correlation) and will not mention the more specialized measures of association again.

Scatterplots

My preference is to teach correlation in a very visual way. We will begin with a discussion of how scatterplots are generated. Next we will discuss other important concepts surrounding the correlation statistic, using the scatterplot as a tool for understanding those concepts.

Scatterplots are graphs of X-Y coordinates, meaning they are graphs of each subject's paired values on the X (predictor) and Y (criterion) variables. For example, if we wanted to know if the number of hours that students study each week (X) is correlated with their GPA (Y), the scatterplot would be generated by plotting dots on a graph corresponding to each student's X and Y values. The X (predictor) variable is arrayed along the horizontal axis; the Y (criterion) variable is arrayed along the vertical axis. Each dot in the graph represents a single subject's X-Y coordinate. A hypothetical example of the X and Y values for 10 students is presented in table 10.1. See if you can find the dot that corresponds with the first student's X-Y coordinate (3 on X; 2.7 on Y) on the scatterplot presented in figure 10.1.

Covariation

The degree to which changes in value on one variable are associated with changes in value on the other variable comprises the **covariation**

Table 10.1 Hypothetical Data for 10 Students (Number of Hours Studied/Week and GPA)

Student	Number of Study Hours/Week (X)	GPA (Y)
01	3	2.7
02	2	1.8
03	8	4.0
04	1	2.9
05	7	4.0
06	6	3.6
07	2	2.1
08	7	3.9
09	5	3.1
10	3	1.9

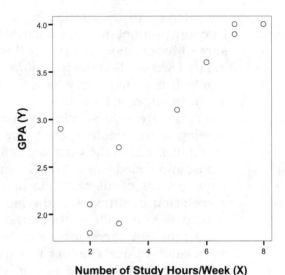

Figure 10.1 Scatterplot of Hypothetical Data in Table 10.1 (Strong Relationship; $r = .87$)

of the X and Y variables. If Y-values change as a function of changes in the X-values, then the X and Y variables covary. If Y-value changes do not correspond with changes in X-values, then the X and Y variables do not covary. The correlation statistic tells us the degree to which this covariation exists. If two variables are correlated with each other, there will be covariation between them.

In the scatterplot presented in figure 10.1, we can see that X and Y do covary since the dots are lining up fairly well in a diagonal line. This means that for each 1-unit (1-value) change on X, there is a consistent change in values on Y. If X and Y did not covary, a diagonal pattern of dots would not be observed, and it would be concluded that the two variables are not correlated with each other. The scatterplot indicates that the number of hours a student studies is associated with his/her GPA.

Strength of Relationship

The correlation statistic (r) ranges in value from 0 to $|1|$, meaning it ranges from zero to the absolute value of 1. The absolute value of a number means that it can be either negative or positive. On a number line, a –1 is the same unit-distance from zero as is a +1; a –3 is three units away from zero, just as is a +3. We will discuss the significance of whether the correlation is negative or positive in a moment. The focus in this section is on the absolute value of the obtained correlation since it tells us the strength of the relationship between the X and Y variables.

Chapter Ten ■ Significant Relationships: Bivariate Correlation

What is important to the discussion of covariation is that a correlation of zero means that there is no covariation between X and Y. At the other extreme, a correlation of either +1 or –1 means that there is perfect monotonic (one-to-one) covariation, which means that for every 1-unit change in values on X, there is a consistent change in values on Y. Typically, a perfect correlation (+1 or –1) is found only when a variable is correlated with itself (which would not make sense to measure). This means that, realistically, the obtained correlation will likely fall somewhere between zero (no relationship) and |1| (perfect relationship). The closer the obtained correlation is to zero, the weaker the relationship between X and Y. The closer the obtained correlation is to |1|, the stronger the relationship.

Because the dots in figure 10.1 are fitting closely to the formation of a diagonal line, we know that there is a fairly strong relationship between our X and Y variables; this means that the obtained correlation will be quite close to |1|. In fact, $r = .87$ indicates that the two variables are strongly associated with each other. If the two variables had been weakly related to each other, it would be harder to detect the formation of a diagonal line through the dots, and the obtained correlation would be closer to zero.

In order to demonstrate a scatterplot for a much weaker relationship, the X variable will be changed from the number of hours studied per week to the number of nights a student goes out to socialize per week. We still would expect some kind of relationship between the X variable (number of nights out per week) and GPA (Y), but it will probably not be as strong as the relationship between study time and GPA. Table 10.2 presents this revised data set, and figure 10.2 presents its scatterplot.

As the scatterplot in figure 10.2 indicates, the dots are not lining up very well along a diagonal line. The harder it becomes to visualize a line through the X-Y coordinates, the weaker the relationship. The correlation between number of nights out and GPA is –.44, indicating a moderate relationship between the two variables. A comparison of the scatterplots in figure 10.1 and figure 10.2 makes it clear that there is a stronger relationship between the number of hours a student studies each week and his/her GPA than the relationship between the number of nights a student goes out each week and his/her GPA. This is confirmed by the obtained correlations for the number of hours studied/week example ($r = .87$) and the number of nights out/week example ($r = -.44$). In terms of their absolute values, we obtained a correlation that is closer to |1| in the number of hours studied example than in the number of nights out example.

If there were no relationship at all between the X and Y variables, the dots would look similar to a shotgun spray, with dots scattered throughout the graph and with no discernable line formation. Table

Table 10.2 Hypothetical Data Set for 10 Students (Number of Nights Out/Week and GPA)

Student	Number of Nights Out per Week (X)	GPA (Y)
01	3	2.7
02	5	1.8
03	7	4.0
04	5	2.9
05	2	4.0
06	3	3.6
07	5	2.1
08	1	3.9
09	3	3.1
10	6	1.9

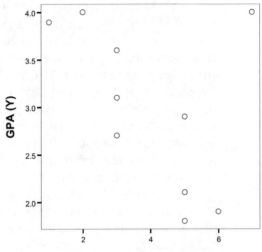

Figure 10.2 Scatterplot of Hypothetical Data in Table 10.2 (Moderate Relationship; $r = -.44$)

10.3 presents a data set where the X variable has been changed to the number of pets that a student owns. We would not expect that the number of pets a student owns would be related to the students' GPA in any way. The scatterplot of this X-Y relationship is presented in figure 10.3. As expected, the dots do not form a diagonal line, and the absolute value of the correlation ($r = .14$) is not far from zero. This correlation would be interpreted as indicating a very weak, almost nonexistent relationship between the X and Y variables.

A final note about the strength of the relationship between two variables has to do with benchmark guidelines for interpreting correlations. Most textbooks do not provide such guidelines because the interpretation of the strength of the relationship should be made in the context of the existing body of research on the topic. For example, the moderate relationship ($r = -.44$) observed for number of nights out per week and GPA might be interpreted as a very strong relationship if all previous research on the topic reported correlations of $|.30|$ or lower. The ultimate interpretation of the strength of the relationship is relative to what has been found previously in other research efforts. But absent a body of literature to provide such a context, the researcher may use the following benchmark guidelines provided by Cohen[1] for the interpretation of correlations: $|.10| - |.29|$ = small correlation (weak relationship); $|.30| - |.49|$ = medium correlation (moderate relationship); $|.50| - |1.00|$ = large correlation (strong relationship).

Table 10.3 Hypothetical Data Set for 10 Students (Number of Pets Owned and GPA)

Student	Number of Pets Owned (X)	GPA (Y)
01	3	2.7
02	4	1.8
03	5	4.0
04	4	2.9
05	2	4.0
06	1	3.6
07	3	2.1
08	5	3.9
09	3	3.1
10	2	1.9

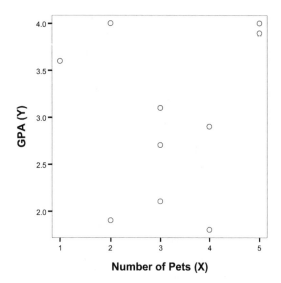

Figure 10.3 Scatterplot of Hypothetical Data in Table 10.3 (Weak Relationship; $r = .14$)

Direction of Relationship

It is now time to address the interpretation of the + and − signs of correlations. We already know that the absolute value of the correlation tells us the strength of the relationship between the X and Y variables. The + and − signs tell us the direction of that relationship. In other words, do the two variables covary directly (in the same direction) or indirectly (in the opposite direction)? If the correlation is positive in value, then the two variables covary directly, meaning that as values increase on the X variable, they also increase on the Y variable. Conversely, if the correlation is negative in value, then the two variables covary indirectly, meaning that as values increase on the X variable, they decrease on the Y variable.

Figure 10.1 presented a strong X-Y relationship where the correlation ($r = .87$) was positive in value. As students studied more hours per week, their GPAs also increased. Take a look at figure 10.1 and observe how the line being formed by the dots starts out near the point of origin (where X and Y axes intersect) and extends to the upper right side of the graph. Positive correlations will always graph in this manner.

Figure 10.2 presented a moderate X-Y relationship where the correlation ($r = −.44$) was negative in value. As students went out more nights per week, their GPAs decreased. For every increase in X, we see a decrease in Y. Take a look at figure 10.2 and observe how the line being formed by the dots starts in the upper left side of the graph and extends to the bottom right side of the graph. Negative correlations will always graph in this manner.

Figure 10.3 presented a weak X-Y relationship where the correlation ($r = .14$) was positive in value. However, since the relationship is weak, the dots do not form a line. But the statistical software is indicating that if there is any relationship there at all, it is leaning toward being a positive one.

Outliers

Earlier in this text you learned about outliers, which are extreme scores. If outliers exist in either the X or Y variables, they may be present in the scatterplot of the X-Y coordinates. Even if the X and Y variables each seem to be normally distributed and absent of outliers, the X-Y coordinates form a new data distribution that may end up having outliers. The best way to detect these outliers is through a visual inspection of the scatterplots. A visual inspection of figure 10.2 reveals an outlier since most of the dots fall on a line that extends from the upper left to the lower right portions of the scatterplot, indicating that as the number of nights out per week increases, GPA tends to decrease. But a single dot on the top, right side of the graph indicates that the student who went out seven nights per week, yet had a 4.0 GPA, is an outlier. His X-Y coordinate did not fit the general pattern of the rest of the students. Removing this outlier from the data set would result in a stronger correlation since the outlier becomes a source of *white noise* for the analysis. However, the data should first be checked for the possibility that the outlier resulted from miscoded data. Visual inspections of scatterplots should be used to "clean" the data, as well as to identify subjects for whom the overall pattern does not apply.

Nonlinearity

Correlations measure the degree to which the X-Y coordinates fit a line. Thus, they describe the strength and direction of the *linear* relationship between X and Y. If the X-Y coordinates are not related in a linear fashion (and there are many possible kinds of nonlinear relationships), the correlation will not accurately describe the X-Y relationship. Table 10.4 presents data for 10 inmates regarding the length of time served (in years) on a 10-year sentence, and the number of disciplinary infractions incurred during their incarceration. Figure 10.4 presents a scatterplot of this data.

The correlation obtained for this data is $r = .06$, meaning that the statistical software was unable to detect a linear relationship between X and Y. This makes sense since the dots in the scatterplot do not form a straight line. But they do form a curved line, indicating that the rela-

Chapter Ten ■ Significant Relationships: Bivariate Correlation

Table 10.4 Hypothetical Data Set for 10 Inmates (Time Served and Number of Disciplinary Infractions)

Inmate	Time Served in Years (X)	Number of Disciplinary Infractions (Y)
01	1	1
02	2	3
03	4	5
04	3	4
05	6	5
06	7	3
07	8	1
08	7	4
09	8	2
10	2	2

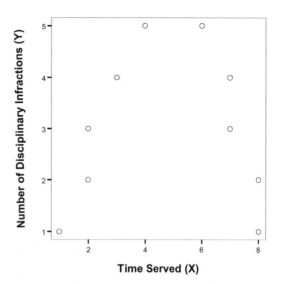

Figure 10.4 Scatterplot of Hypothetical Data in Table 10.4 (Curvilinear Relationship; $r = .06$)

tionship between X and Y is curvilinear. The obtained correlation tells us that no relationship exists between X and Y, but clearly the dots do reveal some kind of an X-Y relationship. We can see that when inmates were in the early portion of their 10-year sentences, they did not commit many disciplinary infractions. When they reached the middle of their sentences, and were the furthest from the two points of freedom (beginning of sentence and end of sentence), they committed the most infractions. But as they approached the end of their sentences, they were less likely to commit an infraction. Thus, an upside down U fits the X-Y coordinates, describing a very real relationship between time served and number of disciplinary infractions. If we analyzed this data using a linear test like correlation, we would have missed the relationship altogether. Statistical techniques that handle nonlinear data are not covered in this textbook; they are more advanced techniques. But it is important to examine scatterplots in order to determine if a low correlation result accurately describes a weak relationship between variables, or if it is an inappropriate test of a curvilinear relationship.

Homoscedasticity

When the X-Y relationship is consistent throughout the scatterplot, the relationship is said to have **homoscedasticity**. When the dots in the scatterplot are close to forming a line for one half of the X-Y coordinates, but are more scattered away from the line for the other half of the X-Y coordinates, the data lack homoscedasticity—we would say that the data display **heteroscedasticity**. With the exception of the outlier, the data displayed in figure 10.2 display homoscedasticity, meaning that the general relationship pattern of increased nights out corresponding with lower GPAs is as consistent a relationship for students who stay in most nights as it is for those who go out most nights. The data displayed in figure 10.1 display heteroscedasticity, meaning that the general relationship pattern of studying more hours corresponding with higher GPAs is not consistent throughout the scatterplot; the pattern is more true for students who study many hours per week than for students who study few hours per week. This pattern is evident because the dots form a tighter line in the upper half of the X-distribution than in the lower half.

Heteroscedasticity is often caused by correlating variables where one or both are skewed. The best way to address the problem is to look at skewness in the individual variables before correlating them. Some statistical techniques normalize data by replacing outliers with the mean for the variable (but this involves changing subjects' scores) or by performing data transformations such as taking the logarithm of the variable (but this requires interpretations of the results that must be reported in log units instead of the raw units of the original data). My preference in handling skewness is to completely remove outliers that are causing the skewness.

Restricted Range

The final concept pertaining to correlations has to do with **restricted ranges** on either the X or the Y variable. Ideally, the scatterplot will extend through the full range of X and of Y. In order to test to see if Y-values change as a function of X-value changes, there has to be change (variation) on both of the variables. If there is full variability on X and no variability on Y, the scatterplot will appear as a horizontal line (see figure 10.5); there is no change in Y-values to allow the graph to move in a vertical way. Conversely, if there is full variability on Y and no variability on X, the scatterplot will appear as a vertical line (see figure 10.6); there is no change in X-values to allow the graph to move in a horizontal manner. Restricted ranges on either the X or Y variables will lead to a lower correlation than would have occurred otherwise.

Research Example

We will demonstrate a correlational analysis with an example about drug courts. A random sample of 15 adult drug offenders from a large county's drug court has been selected to investigate the relationship between time spent in substance-abuse counseling and exit scores on a scale that measures the degree to which drug use is per-

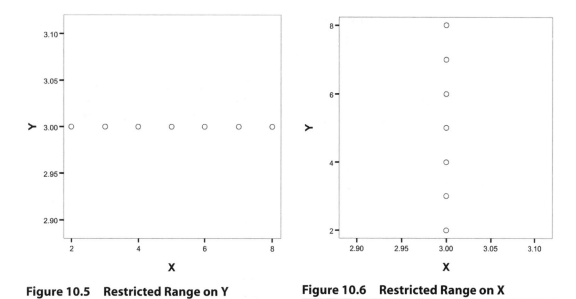

Figure 10.5 Restricted Range on Y

Figure 10.6 Restricted Range on X

ceived in a favorable light. The expectation would be that increased time spent in substance-abuse counseling would result in less favorable attitudes toward drug use (a negative correlation). Our research example asks the following research question: Is there a statistically significant relationship between the number of hours spent in substance-abuse counseling and scores on the Pro-Drug Use Attitude Scale (1 = least favorable; 10 = most favorable)?

Five-Step Model for Hypothesis Testing

Step 1: Make Assumptions
There are four assumptions of the Pearson correlation:

1. Use of a random sample. (This ensures sample representativeness and allows for generalizability of results.)

2. Both variables are measured at the interval-ratio level. (This allows for the assessment of X-Y covariation and all mathematical computations.)

3. The sampling distribution is normally distributed. (This ensures that areas under the curve are accurate and will lead to a proper decision regarding statistical significance.)

4. The X and Y variables are related in a linear fashion, with homoscedasticity, and there is an absence of outliers and restricted range problems. (Allows for proper interpretation of the X-Y relationship.)

Step 2: State Hypotheses

Remember that hypotheses are always stated in terms of population parameters. The population parameter for the correlation statistic (r) is the Greek letter rho (ρ). The null hypothesis states that there is not a reliable relationship between the two variables in the population ($\rho = 0$). The alternative hypothesis states that there is a reliable relationship between the two variables in the population ($\rho \neq 0$). For our example research scenario, the null hypothesis states that increases in time spent in substance-abuse counseling are not associated with either higher or lower scores on the Pro-Drug Use Attitude Scale; any observed covariation is the result of random sampling variability and measurement error. The alternative hypothesis states that increased time spent in substance-abuse counseling is reliably associated with changes in scores on the Pro-Drug Use Attitude Scale. Symbolically, the hypotheses would be:

$$H_0: \rho = 0$$
$$H_1: \rho \neq 0$$

Step 3: Select Sampling Distribution and Specify Decision Criteria

In this step we specify the statistical test and other criteria (one-tailed or two, degrees of freedom, and alpha) we will be using to determine whether to reject the null hypothesis or not. In our example assessing the relationship between hours of counseling and drug use attitudes, we are testing the association between two interval-ratio variables, thus the Pearson correlation test will be conducted. This test uses the correlation (r) sampling distribution to make the determination of statistical significance. The general form of the r sampling distribution is presented in figure 10.7.

The r sampling distribution is made up of all possible outcomes of randomly drawing a sample (for a specified sample size) from the population of offenders who have completed drug court in the study county, computing the correlation between the two variables (number of hours of substance-abuse counseling and scores on the Pro-Drug Use Attitude Scale), and plotting the obtained correlation for that sample. This process is repeated until all possible samples, for the given sample size, have been selected. The obtained correlations that are plotted will form the shape and areas under the curve that make up the sampling distribution for r. The more closely associated the two variables, the farther inside the critical regions (tails of the curve) the obtained correlation will fall, leading to a conclusion of statistical significance ($p < .05$). The less closely associated the two variables, the farther outside the critical regions the obtained correlation will fall, leading to a conclusion of nonsignificance ($p > .05$).

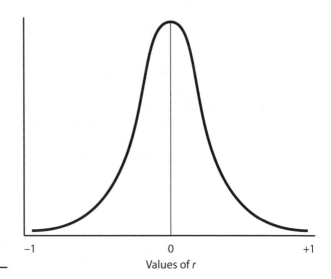

Figure 10.7 The *r* Sampling Distribution

As we have seen several times before, there is a family of *r* sampling distributions, which are determined by the degrees of freedom for the particular data set. For the correlation statistic, the degrees of freedom are calculated as df = N – 2, where N is the number of X-Y pairs or coordinates. As N (and df) increase the *r* sampling distribution becomes more center-peaked, thinner-tailed, and normal in shape.

A determination of whether to use a one-tailed or two-tailed test must be made. My preference is to always perform a two-tailed test so that unexpected findings are not missed. However, if a researcher only wanted to test for a direct relationship (positive correlation) between X and Y, the upper half of the *r* sampling distribution should be used. If the researcher only wanted to test for an indirect relationship (negative correlation), the lower half of the *r* sampling distribution should be used.

For our research application example assessing the relationship between time spent in substance-abuse counseling and drug use attitudes, we will randomly select 15 drug court offenders and record the number of hours of substance-abuse counseling they received (X), as well as their scores on the Pro-Drug Use Attitude Scale (Y). Since both of these variables are interval-ratio, we will use the Pearson correlation to test the linear relationship between the two variables. The test will be two-tailed and alpha will be set at .05. The degrees of freedom will be computed as df = N – 2 = 15 – 2 = 13. These decision criteria can be summarized for our example as follows:

$$\text{Pearson Correlation; two-tailed;}$$
$$\alpha = .05; \text{ df} = N - 2 = 15 - 2 = 13$$

Section Three: Inferential Statistics—Tests of Association

Step 4: Compute the Test Statistic

In this step the data collected on the study sample are used to compute the correlation statistic. The data set is presented below in the columns labeled X and Y as part of the hand calculations. Use the SPSS Application at the end of the chapter for the example data set and the SPSS steps to do the calculations using a computer.

The definitional formula for the Pearson correlation allows the reader to see exactly how the correlation coefficient works. It makes it clear that the statistic takes the cross-product of the standard scores on X and Y (their covariance) and divides it by their combined standard deviations. Formula 10.1 presents the definitional formula for the correlation coefficient.

FORMULA 10.1: DEFINITIONAL FORMULA FOR THE PEARSON CORRELATION

$$r = \frac{\Sigma(X - \mu_X)(Y - \mu_Y)}{\sqrt{\left[\Sigma(X - \mu_X)^2\right]\left[\Sigma(Y - \mu_Y)^2\right]}}$$

The definitional formula for the Pearson correlation coefficient is very cumbersome to use. In response to this problem, various mathematicians have provided algebraic reworkings of the formula to ease hand calculations. Formula 10.2 presents the most commonly used computational formula for the Pearson correlation. It yields the same answer as the definitional formula but requires fewer calculations. It

Table 10.5 Computing Table for Research Application (Correlation between Number of Hours of Substance-Abuse Counseling and Scores on the Pro-Drug Use Attitude Scale)

Offender	Hours of Counseling (X)	Score on Pro-Drug Use Attitude Scale (Y)	X^2	Y^2	XY
01	9	6	81	36	54
02	17	4	289	16	68
03	23	1	529	1	23
04	28	2	784	4	56
05	6	9	36	81	54
06	11	7	121	49	77
07	14	4	196	16	56
08	18	5	324	25	90
09	25	2	625	4	50
10	30	1	900	1	30
11	4	4	16	16	16
12	16	3	256	9	48
13	12	8	144	64	96
14	18	4	324	16	72
15	5	7	25	49	35
Σ	236	67	4650	387	825

Chapter Ten ■ Significant Relationships: Bivariate Correlation

requires that a computing table be set up to organize the computations. The numbers in the summation (Σ) row of the table are the values that should be plugged into the formula. See the computing table and hand calculations for our research application in table 10.5 on the previous page.

FORMULA 10.2: COMPUTATIONAL FORMULA FOR THE PEARSON CORRELATION

$$r = \frac{N\Sigma XY - (\Sigma X)(\Sigma Y)}{\sqrt{\left[N\Sigma X^2 - (\Sigma X)^2\right]\left[N\Sigma Y^2 - (\Sigma Y)^2\right]}}$$

The hand calculations of r for our research application are:

$$r = \frac{15(825) - (236)(67)}{\sqrt{\left[15(4650) - (236)^2\right]\left[15(387) - (67)^2\right]}}$$

$$r = \frac{12375 - 15812}{\sqrt{[69750 - 55696][5805 - 4489]}}$$

$$r = \frac{-3437}{\sqrt{(14054)(1316)}}$$

$$r = \frac{-3437}{\sqrt{18495064}}$$

$$r = \frac{-3437}{4300.589}$$

$$r = -.799$$

The computer printout resulting from using the data set and SPSS steps at the end of the chapter is listed below:

Correlations

		# of Hours of Substance Abuse Counseling (X)	Score on Pro-Drug Use Attitude Scale (Y)
# of Hours of Substance Abuse Counseling (X)	Pearson Correlation	1	-.799**
	Sig. (2-tailed)		.000
	N	15	15
Score on Pro-Drug Use Attitude Scale (Y)	Pearson Correlation	-.799**	1
	Sig. (2-tailed)	.000	
	N	15	15

**. Correlation is significant at the 0.01 level (2-tailed).

The correlations results box lists all variables across the columns and down the rows of the table. This allows for every variable to be correlated with each other (which is helpful when simultaneously performing all possible correlations for many variables). This also means that each correlation will be presented twice, but only needs to be interpreted once. Remember that variables correlated with themselves yield correlations of 1.0. A diagonal can be drawn through the 1s in the table, and correlations can be interpreted in either the top half or the bottom half of the table. The choice of halves will not affect the results, since the two halves are mirror images of each other. Three pieces of information are provided in the cells of the table: the Pearson correlation test statistic value; the two-tailed significance value (p-value); and the sample size (N). Statistically significant correlations at the $\alpha = .05$ level are denoted by a single asterisk; significant correlations at the $\alpha = .01$ level are denoted by two asterisks.

A scatterplot of the X-Y coordinates appears as follows:

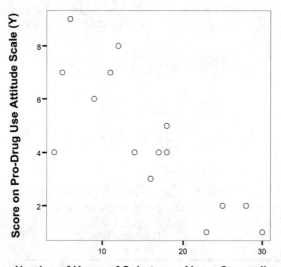

Step 5: Make a Decision

Because the probability (p-value) associated with the obtained correlation is less than our prespecified alpha level ($p < \alpha$), we should conclude that the test statistic falls inside the critical region of the r sampling distribution. We should reject the null hypothesis statement that the observed covariation is due to random sampling variability and measurement error. We have found support for the alternative hypothesis, which states that the observed covariation reflects a statistically significant (reliable and repeatable) relationship between the two variables.

As was the case in the previous chapters, determination of statistical significance also can be made manually through the use of critical values tables found in the appendices in the back of the book. Remember that while computer output tells us whether the *p*-value is *less than* the alpha level, which would cause us to reject the null hypothesis, critical values tables provide the critical value of the test statistic that needs to be *exceeded* by the obtained test statistic in order for the test statistic to fall into the critical region, leading to a rejection of the null hypothesis. The critical values table for the *r* distribution is presented in appendix E. The table presents critical values of *r* for $\alpha = .05$ for each possible degree of freedom. Only positive values of the Pearson correlation are provided since the negative side of the sampling distribution mirrors the positive side. The researcher should find the critical value of *r* that corresponds with the df for the data set. In our drug court research example the df = 13, so $r_{(critical)} = \pm .514$. Since our $r_{(obtained)} = -.799$, it can be concluded that the obtained statistic does fall into the critical region of the *r* distribution, warranting a rejection of the null hypothesis and a conclusion that the two variables are negatively correlated with each other. The number of hours an offender spends in substance-abuse counseling is reliably associated with his/her attitude toward drug use. Specifically, the more hours spent in substance-abuse counseling, the less favorable the attitude toward drug use.

The following is an example of how the results of the analysis of our example data would be reported:

> A study of a random sample of 15 drug court offenders sentenced to substance-abuse counseling was conducted to determine if time spent in counseling had an impact on attitudes toward drug use. For each subject, the number of hours spent in substance-abuse counseling and their exit score on the 10-point Pro-Drug Use Attitude Scale (1 = least favorable; 10 = most favorable) were recorded. A Pearson correlation test revealed that there was a statistically significant relationship between the number of hours of counseling subjects had received and their scores on the Pro-Drug Use Attitude Scale ($r = -.799$, $p < .01$). The two variables were found to be negatively correlated, meaning that as the number of counseling hours received increased, the attitudes toward drug use became less favorable.

STATISTICAL SIGNIFICANCE VERSUS PRACTICAL SIGNIFICANCE

By this point in the textbook you have learned that increased sample size makes sampling distributions become more normal in shape, more center-peaked, and thinner-tailed. This has the effect of making it easier to reject the null hypothesis. The *r* sampling distribution is very sensitive to increases in sample size. This means that if the sample size is large enough, even very small correlations will be determined to be statistically significant. The interpretation of how meaningful a statistically significant correlation is depends on its practical and theoretical importance. It is possible that a very large sample could yield a statistically significant correlation of .07. But how meaningful would that finding be? Yes, statistical significance was obtained, but the value of the correlation indicates that the relationship between X and Y is practically zero. This discussion of assessing the practical significance of a statistically significant finding is relevant not just for the Pearson correlation, but for all of the statistical tests presented in this textbook.

SUMMARY

In this chapter you have learned the purpose and method of conducting the bivariate correlation test of the linear relationship between two interval-ratio variables. You learned how to generate and interpret scatterplots and the Pearson correlation. The many issues surrounding Pearson correlation, namely covariation, outliers, nonlinearity, homoscedasticity, and restricted range, were all discussed. The Pearson correlation was demonstrated through an SPSS application that employed a hypothetical research scenario in the field of criminal justice. Finally, a discussion regarding statistical significance versus practical significance was presented.

Note

[1] Cohen, J. (1988). *Statistical Power Analysis for the Behavioral Sciences* (2nd ed.). Hillsdale, NJ: Lawrence Erlbaum Associates.

KEY TERMS

Bivariate Correlation
Tests of Association
Strength of the Relationship
Direction of the Relationship
Predictor Variable
Criterion Variable
Pearson Product-Moment Correlation Coefficient (*r*)
Dummy Coding
Point-Biserial Correlation Coefficient
Phi Correlation Coefficient
Spearman Rank-Order Correlation Coefficient
Scatterplot
Covariation
Homoscedasticity
Heteroscedasticity
Restricted Range

SPSS Application: Bivariate Correlation

1. Create the following "drug court" data set.

Offender	Hours of Counseling (X)	Score on Pro-Drug Use Attitude Scale (Y)
01	9	6
02	17	4
03	23	1
04	28	2
05	6	9
06	11	7
07	14	4
08	18	5
09	25	2
10	30	1
11	4	4
12	16	3
13	12	8
14	18	4
15	5	7

2. Perform the Pearson correlation test:
   i. Analyze
      ii. Correlate
         iii. Bivariate
            iv. Move the X and Y variables into the "Variables" Box
            v. Click on "OK"

3. Generate a Scatterplot:
   i. Graphs
      ii. Legacy Dialogs
         iii. Scatter/Dot
            iv. Click "Define"
               v. Move the X variable into the X axis box
               vi. Move the Y variable into the Y axis box
               vii. Click on "OK"

SPSS Assignment

1. Create the "school counselor" data set below. This fictitious data set represents a random sample of 15 high school students who have received counseling from their school counselor. They were asked to fill out three inventories measuring their self-esteem, anxiety, and depression levels on 10-point scales (1 = lowest amount of the trait; 10 = highest amount of the trait).

   "School Counselor" Data Set:

Student	Self-Esteem	Anxiety	Depression
01	6	1	2
02	7	1	3
03	5	8	6
04	2	10	8
05	5	5	4
06	10	7	6
07	1	2	3
08	3	3	5
09	7	6	4
10	3	6	7
11	2	8	6
12	8	5	5
13	6	6	4
14	10	9	8
15	4	10	9

2. Generate bivariate correlations between all three inventories (i.e., self-esteem and anxiety; self-esteem and depression; anxiety and depression).

3. Generate scatterplots for all three bivariate relationships.

4. Write a couple of paragraphs summarizing the results of the analyses performed in steps 2 and 3. Discuss any apparent problems with the scatterplots in terms of outliers, heteroscedasticity, restricted range, and nonlinearity.

Chapter Ten ■ Significant Relationships: Bivariate Correlation   **215**

MULTIPLE-CHOICE QUESTIONS

1. Variables used in a bivariate correlation analysis need to be measured at the _____ level of measurement.
   A. Interval/Ratio
   B. Ordinal
   C. Nominal
   D. Any of the Above

2. A negative correlation means that _____.
   A. Increases on X are associated with increases on Y
   B. Decreases on X are associated with increases on Y
   C. Decreases on X are associated with decreases on Y
   D. The relationship between X and Y is small

3. _____ means that the X-Y coordinates are consistently associated across the scatterplot.
   A. Homoscedasticity
   B. Heteroscedasticity
   C. Significance
   D. Correlation

4. The purpose of a bivariate correlation is to _____.
   A. Determine if two group means are significantly related to each other
   B. Determine if two group means are significantly different from one another
   C. Identify statistically significant differences between groups
   D. Identify statistically significant relationships between interval/ratio level variables

5. Restricted ranges on X or Y can cause the correlation to _____.
   A. Decrease
   B. Increase
   C. Stay the Same
   D. None of the Above

6. The criterion variable is also known as the _____.
   A. Categorical Variable
   B. Dummy Variable
   C. Dependent Variable
   D. Independent Variable

7. Which type of graph should be used to visually examine the X-Y coordinates?
   A. Error Box Plot
   B. Criterion and Predictor Graph
   C. Scatterplot
   D. Histogram

8. The bivariate correlation indicates the _____ and _____ of the relationship between two variables.
   A. Significance; Strength
   B. Strength; Direction
   C. Importance; Direction
   D. Direction; Importance

9. The degree to which changes in value on one variable are associated with changes in value on the other variable comprises the _____ of the X and Y variables.
   A. Homoscedasticity
   B. Heteroscedasticity
   C. Variation
   D. Covariation

10. A significant correlation of .77 indicates that the relationship between two variables is _____.
    A. Positive and Weak
    B. Positive and Moderate
    C. Positive and Strong
    D. Nonexistent

11

Significant Relationships
Simple Linear Regression

This chapter extends the concepts of the previous chapter (using bivariate correlation to assess the relationship between two interval-ratio variables) to the concept of using one interval-ratio variable to predict another interval-ratio variable. This technique is called **simple linear regression (SLR)**, but may also be referred to as **bivariate regression** since it examines the predictive relationship between two variables. The next (and final) chapter of this book extends this concept even further by presenting **multiple linear regression** techniques to explore the ability of multiple, interval-ratio, independent variables to predict a single, interval-ratio, dependent variable.

▬ Purpose of Simple Linear Regression

The primary purpose of SLR techniques is to examine the ability of a single independent variable (called the **predictor variable**, or X) to predict values on a single dependent variable (called the **criterion variable**, or Y). Simple linear regression is used to determine not only if the predictor variable predicts values on Y in a linear fashion but also to assess the extent and nature of its predictive ability. This chapter presents the statistical concepts and tests that comprise SLR.

The examples used throughout chapter 10 on bivariate regression can easily be converted to examples for SLR: Does the number of hours students study predict their GPA? Does the number of nights students go out per week predict their GPA? Does the length of time served predict the number of disciplinary infractions inmates receive? Does the number of hours spent in substance-abuse counseling predict drug court offenders' scores on the Pro-Drug Use Attitude Scale? While the previous chapter examined the statistical association between the two variables in each respective example, this chapter goes one step further to examine the ability of the predictor variable to predict the criterion variable. Here is the general form of the research question for SLR: Is the predictor variable (X) a reliable predictor of the criterion variable (Y)? If that question is answered in the affirmative, then additional statistics are used to determine the extent of the predictive value of X in relation to Y.

IMPORTANT CONCEPTS RELATED TO SIMPLE LINEAR REGRESSION

Scatterplots

Scatterplots are graphs of X-Y coordinates, which you learned about when learning bivariate correlation. They are graphs of each subject's paired values on the X (predictor) and Y (criterion) variables. You learned that the more closely the dots in a scatterplot form a straight line, the more closely associated the two variables. Simple linear regression takes the visualized straight line and actually plots the line onto the scatterplot so that it best fits the X-Y coordinates, indicating the ability of X to predict Y. The ability to plot the line comes from the algebraic formula for a line, which will be discussed shortly.

Table 11.1 presents hypothetical data that will be used to demonstrate these concepts and will also serve as the application example so that the many computational exercises throughout the chapter will be consistent. The example uses an unusually small sample size (N = 10) so that mathematical computations are easy. The data are based on the

Table 11.1 Hypothetical Data for 10 Offenders (Number of Prior Arrests Predicting Number of Future Arrests)

Offender	Number of Arrests Prior to Incarceration (X)	Number of Future Arrests (Y)
01	3	2
02	5	5
03	6	7
04	8	9
05	9	9
06	2	6
07	5	4
08	3	4
09	7	5
10	8	6

well-supported theory that the number of arrests that an offender has had prior to incarceration is a good predictor of the number of arrests an offender will have after release; past behavior is a good predictor of future behavior. Figure 11.1 presents the scatterplot of the X-Y relationship for these data.

It is apparent in figure 11.1 that the dots do a fairly good job of forming a line, which indicates a positive correlation, since the dots extend from the intersection of the X and Y axes to the upper right side of the graph. In fact, the obtained correlation for these data is .70, which should be interpreted as a strong, direct relationship between X and Y. The next sections walk you through the simple linear regression technique that will tell us more about the ability of prior arrests (X) to predict future arrests (Y).

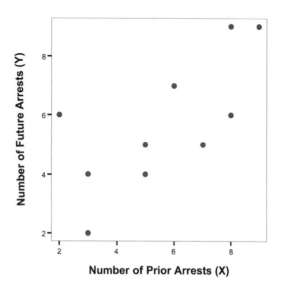

Figure 11.1   Scatterplot of Hypothetical Data in Table 11.1 (Strong Relationship; $r = .70$)

The Regression of Y on X

When we want to know if X predicts Y, we have to perform the **regression of Y on X** to get the answer. Regressing Y on X means that we mathematically determine the manner in which observed Y values are a function of values observed on X. Once the regression formula is specified, we determine how well the equation fits the observed data for Y; in other words, how good of a job does the equation that is based on values of X do in predicting values of Y? You may remember from your early math classes that there is a formula for the generation of a straight line. In statistical regression this straight line is called the **regression line** and is generated by pairing the observed values of X with the predicted values of Y, based on the prediction equation specifying the manner in which Y is a function of X. Formula 11.1 presents the equation for the regression line.

FORMULA 11.1: EQUATION FOR THE REGRESSION LINE OF Y ON X

$Y' = a_y + b_y X$

Where: Y' = the predicted value for Y for a given value of X
b_y = the regression coefficient for the regression of Y on X
a_y = the regression constant of the regression of Y on X

Further definition of this equation in necessary. The symbol Y' is the predicted value of Y that will result from solving the right side of the equation. We want to know what the predicted values of Y would be for each possible value of X so that a comparison can be made between the Y-values that were predicted and the actual Y-values observed in the data set. The more identical the predicted and observed values of Y, the better the job X does in predicting Y.

The symbol b_y represents the **regression coefficient** for the regression of Y on X. It tells us the **slope of the regression line**, which is the amount of change in the predicted values of Y for each 1-unit change on X. The regression coefficient is based on the correlation between X and Y and their respective standard deviations. Formula 11.2 presents the formula for computing the regression coefficient that would be plugged into formula 11.1:

FORMULA 11.2: EQUATION FOR THE REGRESSION COEFFICIENT (b_Y)

$$b_y = r\left(\frac{s_y}{s_x}\right)$$

Where: r = the correlation between X and Y
s_y = the sample standard deviation for Y
s_x = the sample standard deviation for X

Because the correlation between X and Y is imbedded into the regression coefficient, it informs the regression line about the strength and direction of the X-Y relationship. The larger the regression coefficient, the stronger the relationship. If the regression coefficient is positive in value, then a 1-unit increase in X will result in a b_y-unit *increase* in Y. If the regression coefficient is negative in value, then a 1-unit increase in X will result in a b_y-unit *decrease* in Y.

The final element of formula 11.1 that needs further definition is a_y, which is the **regression constant** of the regression of Y on X. It represents the **Y-intercept** of the regression line, which is the point where the regression line crosses the Y-axis. In other words, it is the predicted value of Y when X equals zero. Formula 11.3 presents the equation for the regression constant.

Chapter Eleven ■ Significant Relationships: Simple Linear Regression

FORMULA 11.3: EQUATION FOR THE REGRESSION CONSTANT (a_y)

$$a_y = \bar{Y} - b_y\bar{X}$$

Where: $\bar{Y}$ = sample mean for Y
b_y = regression coefficient
$\bar{X}$ = sample mean for X

In our example data set (table 11.1), we need the means and standard deviations for X and Y, and the correlation between X and Y, before we can use formulas 11.1 through 11.3. These values are:

$\bar{X} = 5.60$
$s_x = 2.413$
$\bar{Y} = 5.70$
$s_y = 2.214$
$r = .703$

Now formulas 11.1 through 11.3 can be computed in the following order:

From formula 11.2:

$$b_y = r\left(\frac{s_y}{s_x}\right) = .703\left(\frac{2.214}{2.413}\right) = .703(.91753) = .645$$

From formula 11.3:
$a_y = \bar{Y} - b_y\bar{X} = 5.70 - (.645)(5.60)$
$= 5.70 - 3.612 = 2.088$

From formula 11.1:
$Y' = a_y + b_yX = 2.088 + (.645)X$

These computations revealed that the equation for our example regression line is: $Y' = 2.088 + .645X$. This equation tells us that the regression line crosses the Y-axis at $Y = 2.088$, and that the slope is .645, meaning that for every 1-unit change in X, there will be a predicted .645 increase in Y.

Figure 11.2, on the following page, presents the scatterplot from figure 11.1, with the addition of the regression line for the data set imposed onto the graph. This line is the best-fitting possible line that could be drawn through the X-Y coordinates to minimize the distance of all dots from the line. Tilting the line in either direction will cause some dots to be disproportionately further from the line than others. It is a similar concept to the mean being the mathematical center point from all values in the variable. The regression line is the mathematical, one-dimensional center point in a two-dimensional space (X-Y axes) for all of the X-Y coordinates in the data set.

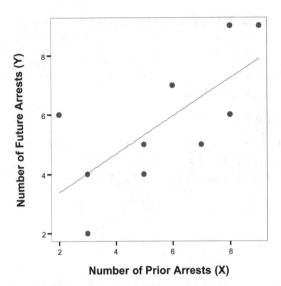

Figure 11.2 Plot of Regression Line on Scatterplot for the Example Data Set

When SLR is performed in SPSS, a results box reports the regression coefficient (b_y) and the regression constant (a_y), as well as the t-tests (and p-values) that determine if the coefficients are statistically significantly different from zero. The coefficients results box for our example can be found at the bottom of the page. The results box provides coefficients in both unstandardized (original metric of the X variable) and standardized (X converted to z-scores) form. The purpose of including **standardized regression coefficients** will be apparent when we move into the next chapter (when we will have multiple predictors instead of just one), since z-scores will allow us to compare the relative predictive strength of each predictor variable in the analysis. In SLR it is best to use the **unstandardized regression coefficients**.

The results box reports the regression constant ($a_y = 2.088$), its standard error, and a t-test to determine if the coefficient is significantly different from zero. We typically don't interpret the t-test for the regression constant. The results box also reports the regression coefficient for X ($b_y = .645$), its standard error, and a t-test (and p-value) to determine if it is significantly different from zero. We hope to get a statistically significant t-statistic ($p < .05$), since the regression coefficient indicates the strength and direction of the relationship between X and Y. Our obtained regression coefficient is significantly different from zero ($t = 2.797, p < .05$). If the t-test had been nonsignificant, we would have to conclude that b_y differed from zero simply due to ran-

Coefficients[a]

Model		Unstandardized Coefficients		Standardized Coefficients	t	Sig.
		B	Std. Error	Beta		
1	(Constant)	2.088	1.395		1.496	.173
	Number of Prior Arrests (X)	.645	.231	.703	2.797	.023

a. Dependent Variable: Number of Future Arrests (Y)

dom sampling variability and measurement error, meaning that there was not a statistical relationship between the predictor and criterion variables (X and Y). One last thing to note regarding this coefficients results box is that unstandardized regression coefficients are labeled B, but refers to the lower-case b_y found in the regression line equation. Once a regression coefficient has been converted to a standardized regression coefficient (z-score), it is labeled Beta. When performing SLR report the B; when performing multiple linear regression (next chapter) report the Beta.

The important thing is for you to be able to see how the regression constant and regression coefficient that appear in the results box correspond to doing the calculations by hand. This should provide you with a better understanding of how the regression equation is derived and interpreted. As we determined through hand calculations, our example regression equation is Y′ = 2.088 + .645X.

Errors of Prediction

The regression equation yields the predicted value of Y (Y′) once an observed value of X is plugged into the equation. The first offender's X-Y coordinate from our example data set (table 11.1) is 3 prior arrests (X) and 2 future arrests (Y). Plugging the X-value into the regression equation (formula 11.1) yields: Y′ = 2.088 + .645X = 2.088 + .645(3) = 2.088 + 1.935 = 4.023. This means that offenders with 3 prior arrests (X) would be predicted to have 4.023 future arrests (Y′). This offender actually had 2 future arrests, so there is some error in the prediction. Table 11.2 presents all of the predicted values of Y for each observed value of X, based on this equation for the regression line.

A glance at the regression line plotted in figure 11.2 makes it clear that some dots are closer to the line than others. Since the regression line represents the predicted values of Y for each observed value of X, the further a dot is from the line, the worse the job the regression equation did in predicting Y for that particular X-Y coordinate. The distance an X-Y coordinate (dot) is from the line, the greater the **error of prediction** for that particular subject. If most of the dots lie

Table 11.2 Predicted Values of Y for Observed Values of X

Offender	Number of Arrests Prior to Incarceration (X)	Predicted Number of Future Arrests (Y′)
01	3	4.023
02	5	5.313
03	6	5.958
04	8	7.248
05	9	7.893
06	2	3.378
07	5	5.313
08	3	4.023
09	7	6.603
10	8	7.248

close to the line, the regression equation is doing a pretty good job of predicting values on Y using observed values of X. If most of the dots are scattered away from the line, the regression equation is doing a poor job of predicting Y. As stated in the last section, the regression line represents the best possible fit of a line to the observed data; it will yield the least amount of errors in prediction than if the line had been positioned any other way.

Errors of prediction (Y – Y′), also called **residuals**, can be computed simply by subtracting the predicted value of Y from the observed value of Y. There will be positive errors (Y – Y′ > 0), meaning the regression equation underpredicted for an X-Y coordinate; and there will be negative errors (Y – Y′ < 0), meaning the regression equation overpredicted for an X-Y coordinate. All of the errors of prediction (residuals) will total to zero, which is something we observed with deviation scores and the mean, indicating that the regression line (like the mean) is the mathematical center point of the observed data. The fact that residuals add up to zero means that the regression equation underpredicts as much as it overpredicts since they cancel each other out when summed. Table 11.3 adds the errors of prediction to our data set.

It is helpful to plot the errors of prediction (residuals) along a vertical axis to make sure that they appear random across all values of X. If the dots are close to the center line (indicating 0 residuals) for one range of values on X but scattered away from the center line for another range of values on X, it would be an indication that there is a pattern to the residuals. Figure 11.3 displays the residual plot for our example data set. The residuals appear to be fairly random, so we

Table 11.3 Errors of Prediction (Number of Prior Arrests Predicting Number of Future Arrests)

Offender	Number of Arrests Prior to Incarceration (X)	Number of Future Arrests (Y)	Predicted Number of Future Arrests (Y′)	Errors of Prediction (Y – Y′)
01	3	2	4.023	–2.023
02	5	5	5.313	–0.313
03	6	7	5.958	1.042
04	8	9	7.248	1.752
05	9	9	7.893	1.107
06	2	6	3.378	2.622
07	5	4	5.313	–1.313
08	3	4	4.023	–0.023
09	7	5	6.603	–1.603
10	8	6	7.248	–1.248
Σ				0.000

Chapter Eleven ■ Significant Relationships: Simple Linear Regression

should not worry that the prediction equation works better for some values of X than others.

Predictive Accuracy

The next concept we need to discuss concerns the overall **predictive accuracy** of the regression equation. The regression line is fit to the data such that the errors of prediction (residuals), if squared and summed, total to a minimum value. We call this the principle of least squared errors, which is symbolized as follows: $\Sigma (Y - Y')^2$ = minimum value.

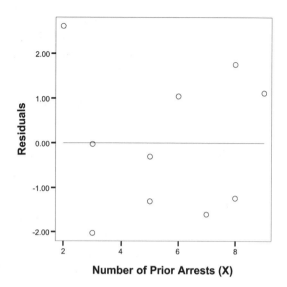

Figure 11.3 Plot of Residuals

Knowing the principle of least squared errors in the abstract provides little help in assessing how accurate our predictions really are. There are two primary ways to assess the accuracy of our predictions. The first is called **cross-validation**, which means that the study is replicated on a new sample of data in order to see if similar results are observed. In the case of our example, we would draw a new sample of offenders, total their numbers of prior and future arrests, and perform simple linear regression to see if the same regression line is obtained. When we do research, we generally only have one data set to work with, so cross-validation would not be possible. Yet it is possible to do a literature search to locate similar studies that may have tested the same predictor and criterion variables as your study.

The F-Ratio

The second method of assessing predictive accuracy involves a comparison of predicted variance to error variance. Recall the one-way analysis of variance in chapter 9. Figure 9.1 presented a Venn diagram of the F-Ratio, which divided the total variance observed in the dependent variable into two sources of variance: between-group and within-group. In regression, the between-group variance becomes predicted variance, and the within-group variance becomes error variance. In the one-way ANOVA, the F-Ratio was a ratio of the two sources of variance; a large F-Ratio meant there was more between-group variance than within-group variance, resulting in a statistically significant finding. The same F-Ratio statistic is computed in linear regression. If there is much more predicted variance than error variance in the statistical model, a large, statistically significant F-Ratio will be obtained, indicating that the predictor variable predicts the criterion variable better than when it is not included in the prediction equation.

This revised interpretation of variance is illustrated in figure 11.4. When the dividing line of the diagram moves to the right, there is more predicted variance than error variance, resulting in a large F-Ratio, indicating that the predictor variable is a good predictor of the criterion variable. When the dividing line of the diagram moves to the left, there is more error variance than predicted variance, resulting in a small F-Ratio, indicating that the predictor variable is a poor predictor of the criterion variable. Another way to think of this is to imagine the entire circle being comprised of error variance, meaning that the variation observed in the dependent variable is attributable to sampling variability and measurement error. Once a predictor of the criterion variable is identified, it partials out a piece of that error variance, and attributes that portion to its ability to reliably predict values on Y. When we move into multiple linear regression in the next chapter, we'll see multiple predictor variables carving out their pieces of the variance pie. And as each one does so, the error variance in the prediction model will get smaller and smaller.

For SLR, the computation of the F-Ratio requires that the regression, residual, and total sums of squares be computed. The total sum of squares is computed as $\Sigma(Y - \bar{Y})^2$, the regression sum of squares is computed as $\Sigma(Y' - \bar{Y}')^2$, and the residual sum of squares are computed by subtracting the regression sum of squares from the total sum of squares. Table 11.4 presents the computation table used to obtain the total and regression sums of squares. We obtained a total sum of

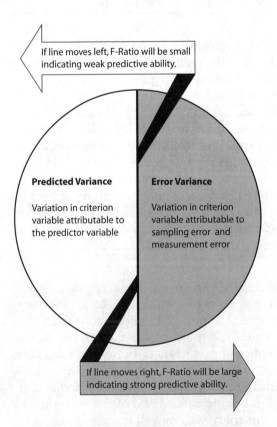

Figure 11.4   Venn Diagram of the F-Ratio

Table 11.4 SLR Sum of Squares Computing Table

Offender	Number of Arrests Prior to Incarceration (X)	Number of Future Arrests (Y)	Predicted Number of Future Arrests (Y')	Total Sum of Squares $(Y - \bar{Y})^2$	Regression Sum of Squares $(Y' - \bar{Y}')^2$
01	3	2	4.023	13.69	2.812
02	5	5	5.313	.49	.150
03	6	7	5.958	1.69	.077
04	8	9	7.248	10.89	2.396
05	9	9	7.893	10.89	4.809
06	2	6	3.378	.09	5.392
07	5	4	5.313	2.89	.150
08	3	4	4.023	2.89	2.812
09	7	5	6.603	.49	.815
10	8	6	7.248	.09	2.396
Σ	56	57	57	44.10	21.809
	5.6	5.7	5.7		

squares of 44.10 and a regression sum of squares of 21.809. Subtracting the two yields a residual sum of squares of 22.291.

The next step in generating the F-Ratio involves computing the degrees of freedom. The total sum of squares has N − 1 degrees of freedom (in our example, df total = 10 − 1 = 9). The regression sum of squares has k − 1 degrees of freedom, where k = the number of variables in the analysis (in our example, df regression = 2 − 1 = 1). The residual sum of squares has N − k degrees of freedom (in our example, df residual = 10 − 2 = 8).

Now the regression and residual mean squares are computed by dividing each type of sum of squares by its respective degrees of freedom. For our example, mean square regression = 21.809/1 = 21.809. Our mean square residual = 22.291/8 = 2.786. The F-Ratio is obtained by dividing the mean square regression by the mean square residual: F = 21.809/2.786 = 7.828. The computer output for the ANOVA table appears below.

ANOVA[b]

Model		Sum of Squares	df	Mean Square	F	Sig.
1	Regression	21.802	1	21.802	7.822	.023[a]
	Residual	22.298	8	2.787		
	Total	44.100	9			

a. Predictors: (Constant), Number of Prior Arrests (X)
b. Dependent Variable: Number of Future Arrests (Y)

The slight differences in the numbers listed in the printout and the results in table 11.4 indicate rounding error, particularly pertaining to the many calculations used to generate the predicted values for future arrests (Y′) and the regression sum of squares. Recall the use of standard deviations and a correlation to generate the regression equation that yields predicted values of Y. Each time a rounded-off number is used in a subsequent formula, the rounding error compounds. Statistical software packages carry out a number to many more digits than would be practical for our hand calculations, thus slight differences in answers may occur. The resultant computer-generated and hand-calculated F-Ratios were almost identical despite the fact that we rounded off in the thousandths place. A table in appendix G displays the numbers carried out to the 9th decimal for those interested in seeing the calculations performed without rounding error problems.

The fact that the computer-generated F-Ratio (7.822) is statistically significant at the $\alpha = .05$ level indicates that the predictor variable (number of prior arrests) reliably predicts the criterion variable (number of future arrests). That brings us back to the question of how accurately X predicts Y.

The Coefficient of Determination

While SLR makes its determination of statistical significance of the overall prediction model based on the F-Ratio, we are more interested in something called the **coefficient of determination**, symbolized as **R^2**. The coefficient of determination is the percent of total variance in Y that is predicted by X (see formula 11.4).

FORMULA 11.4: COEFFICIENT OF DETERMINATION

$$R^2 = \frac{\text{Predicted Variance}}{\text{Total Variance}}$$

Where: Predicted Variance = Sum of Squares Regression
$(\Sigma(Y' - \bar{Y}')^2)$

Total Variance = Sum of Squares Total $(\Sigma(Y - \bar{Y})^2)$

In the ANOVA table, the total variance in Y (called sum of squares total) was divided into two portions: the predicted variance (called sum of squares regression) and the residual variance (called sum of squares residual). Dividing the predicted variance by the total variance yields the proportion of the total variance that has been predicted or explained by the predictor variable (X). For our example data we obtained: predicted variance = 21.809; total variance = 44.100. These values are now plugged into the formula for the coefficient of determination (formula 11.4):

$$R^2 = \frac{\text{Predicted Variance}}{\text{Total Variance}} = \frac{21.809}{44.100} = .495$$

Our obtained coefficient of determination should be interpreted to mean that 49.5% of the variance in the number of future arrests (Y) is predicted by the number of prior arrests that offenders had (X). Again, this figure differs slightly from the computer-generated value of .494 (49.4%) due to rounding error.

In similar fashion, we can divide the residual variance (22.291) by the total variance (44.100) to obtain the **coefficient of nondetermination** (.505), which is the percent of the total variance in Y that is not predicted or explained by X. For our example, 50.5% of the variance in Y remains unaccounted for by our predictor variable. The coefficient of nondetermination can also be derived simply by subtracting the coefficient of determination from one ($1 - R^2$).

SPSS reports the coefficient of determination in a results box labeled "Model Summary." This box is presented below. The R (.703) that is reported is the correlation between the predictor and the criterion variable and has a straightforward interpretation in SLR; when we move into multiple linear regression, the R will take on a different meaning. Squaring that R yields the R^2 we computed and discussed above.

Also provided is the **adjusted R^2**, which makes the unadjusted R^2 more conservative by estimating the amount of **shrinkage** in R^2 that will occur if the regression equation is applied to a new sample. The reason that shrinkage occurs is that regression equations are created based on the maximal correlations between the variables, what you might call a best case scenario. But when that same regression equation is applied to another sample data set, the expectation is that the correlations will not be as strong as they were in the original data set, meaning that the new data set will overestimate the predictive ability of the predictor(s). The adjusted R^2 estimates how much shrinkage in predictability should occur, and adjusts R^2 in a downward fashion accordingly. For our example data set, the adjusted R^2 is .431, a .063

Model Summary

Model	R	R Square	Adjusted R Square	Std. Error of the Estimate
1	.703[a]	.494	.431	1.669

a. Predictors: (Constant), Number of Prior Arrests (X)

decrease from the computer-generated unadjusted R^2, indicating that there would be a 6.3% decrease in predictability if we apply our regression equation to a new sample of data. The final item included in the model summary box is the standard error of the estimate of R, a value that tends not to be reported.

FIVE-STEP MODEL FOR HYPOTHESIS TESTING

Once we get into regression techniques, we tend not to use the five-step model for hypothesis testing. The primary reason for this is that many hypotheses are at work in a regression analysis, and it becomes too laborious to specify them all. For example, there are the correlation tests, an F-test for the ANOVA table, and *t*-tests for each of the regression coefficients. Each one of these tests could have a five-step model specified for them. The primary purpose of using the five-step model whenever possible is that it helps organize the data analysis process. But once the five-step model becomes too tedious, it is no longer helpful. In general, the researcher should make sure that a random sample has been used if the research intent is to generalize the results to the larger population; interval-ratio predictor and criterion variables should be checked for outliers (individual and bivariate); and calculations and interpretations of the regression constant, regression coefficient, F, R, R^2, and adjusted R^2 should follow the SPSS application steps (at end of chapter) and text provided here. All that remains is an example of how all of this information should be succinctly compiled into a research report.

The following is an example of how the results of the SLR analysis of our example data set would be reported:

> A random sample of 10 offenders who had been released from prison one year prior to data collection was selected. Their arrest records for one year prior to incarceration and for one year following release were examined to test the theory that the number of preincarceration arrests would be a good predictor of the number of postrelease arrests. A simple linear regression analysis was performed. The results (see results table) indicated that the number of preincarceration arrests was a statistically significant predictor of the number of postrelease arrests ($F_{1, 8} = 7.82$, $p = .023$). Each preincarceration arrest of an offender predicted a .645 increase in the number of postrelease arrests (B = .645).
>
> Results Table: Simple Linear Regression Results of Regressing the Number of Postrelease Arrests (Y) on the Number of Preincarceration Arrests (X)

	B	S.E.	Beta	Sig.
Number of Preincarceration Arrests	.645	.231	.703	.023
Constant	2.088			
df	1, 8			
F	7.822			
R^2	.494			
Adjusted R^2	.431			

Summary

In this chapter you have learned the purpose and method of conducting simple linear regression analyses to determine if an interval-ratio predictor variable reliably predicts an interval-ratio criterion variable. You learned how to generate and interpret the regression coefficients, the ANOVA table, and measures of predictive accuracy. The key issues surrounding SLR, namely, the regression of Y on X, errors of prediction, predictive accuracy, cross-validation, and the coefficient of determination, were all discussed. Also, an SLR analysis was demonstrated through an SPSS application that employed a hypothetical research scenario in the field of criminal justice.

Key Terms

Simple Linear Regression (SLR)
Bivariate Regression
Multiple Linear Regression
Predictor Variable
Criterion Variable
Scatterplot
Regression of Y on X
Regression Line
Regression Coefficient
Slope of the Regression Line
Regression Constant
Y-Intercept
Standardized Regression Coefficient
Unstandardized Regression Coefficient
Error of Prediction
Residuals
Predictive Accuracy
Cross-Validation
Coefficient of Determination (R^2)
Coefficient of Nondetermination ($1 - R^2$)
Adjusted R^2
Shrinkage

SPSS Application: Simple Linear Regression

1. Create the following "Future Arrests" data set.

Offender	Number of Arrests Prior to Incarceration (X)	Number of Future Arrests (Y)
01	3	2
02	5	5
03	6	7
04	8	9
05	9	9
06	2	6
07	5	4
08	3	4
09	7	5
10	8	6

2. Perform the Simple Linear Regression Analysis:
    i. Analyze
        ii. Regression
            iii. Linear
                iv. Move the Y variable into the "Dependent" Box
                v. Move the X variable into the "Independent" Box
                vi. Click on "OK"

3. Generate a Scatterplot with Regression Line:
    i. Graphs
        ii. Legacy Dialogs
            iii. Scatter/Dot
            iv. Simple Scatter
            v. Click "Define"
                vi. Move the X variable into the X axis box
                vii. Move the Y variable into the Y axis box
                viii. Click on "OK"
                    ix. Double click on the graph on the output screen
                    x. Elements
                    xi. Click "Fit Line at Total"

Chapter Eleven ■ Significant Relationships: Simple Linear Regression

SPSS ASSIGNMENT

1. Create the "training academy" data set below. This fictitious data set represents a random sample of 15 law enforcement officer trainees who took an entrance exam prior to admission to the training academy and a proficiency exam upon completion of the academy. Both exams ranged from 0–100. The director of the academy wants to determine if the scores received on the entrance exam predict the scores received on the proficiency exam.

   "Training Academy" Data Set:

Trainee	Entrance Exam (X)	Proficiency Exam (Y)
01	68	88
02	60	80
03	100	100
04	61	80
05	69	89
06	73	92
07	79	98
08	85	99
09	70	90
10	67	87
11	77	84
12	85	97
13	95	99
14	83	94
15	72	90

2. Conduct a simple linear regression analysis to determine if entrance exam scores predict proficiency exam scores.

3. Generate a scatterplot of the relationship between entrance and proficiency exams. Be sure to include the regression line.

4. Write a couple of paragraphs summarizing the results of the analyses performed in steps 2 and 3. Table your results.

Multiple-Choice Questions

1. The _____ is the point where the regression line crosses the Y-axis.
   A. Regression Coefficient
   B. X-Intercept
   C. Y-Intercept
   D. Regression Maximum

2. Errors of prediction (residuals) should total to _____.
   A. −1
   B. 0
   C. +1
   D. The Standard Deviation Value

3. _____ is used to determine if X reliably predicts Y.
   A. Bivariate Correlation
   B. One-Way ANOVA
   C. Independent Samples *t*-Test
   D. Simple Linear Regression

4. _____ is a process used to determine if similar results can be observed when employing a new sample.
   A. Coefficient of Determination
   B. Regression Coefficient
   C. Cross-validation
   D. Logistic Regression

5. The amount of shrinkage in prediction that will occur if the regression equation is applied to a new sample is indicated by the _____.
   A. Adjusted R^2
   B. R^2
   C. F-Ratio
   D. *p*-value

6. The _____ indicates the proportion of total variance in Y that is predicted by X.
   A. Regression Coefficient
   B. Regression Constant
   C. Coefficient of Determination
   D. F-Ratio

7. Simple linear regression only tests if X predicts Y in a linear fashion.
   A. True
   B. False

8. A regression coefficient of .37 indicates that for every 1-unit _____.
   A. Increase in Y there will be a .37 increase in the predicted value of X
   B. Increase in X there will be a .37 increase in the predicted value of Y
   C. Decrease in X there will be a .37 increase in the predicted value of Y
   D. Decrease in Y there will be a .37 increase in the predicted value of X

9. A researcher is interested in determining if the number of delinquent friends is a significant predictor of the number of juvenile arrests. The researcher should run a simple linear regression that _____.
   A. Regresses delinquent friends on juvenile arrests
   B. Regresses mean differences
   C. Regresses juvenile arrests on delinquent friends
   D. Correlates delinquent friends and juvenile arrests

10. A _____ tells us the amount of change in the predicted values of Y for each 1-unit increase in X.
    A. Coefficient of Determination
    B. Regression Coefficient
    C. Cross-validation
    D. Logistic Regression

12

Significant Relationships
Multiple Linear Regression

This chapter extends the concepts of the previous chapter (simple linear regression) to the concept of using multiple, interval-ratio variables to predict another interval-ratio variable. This technique is called **multiple linear regression (MLR)**, reflecting the use of multiple predictors to predict a single criterion variable. Since MLR is an extension of SLR, many of the concepts and techniques you learned in the previous chapter are applicable in this one.

▄ Purpose of Multiple Linear Regression

The primary purpose of MLR techniques is to examine the ability of two or more independent variables (called the **predictor variables**, or X_1, X_2, . . .) to predict values on a single dependent variable (called the **criterion variable**, or Y). Multiple linear regression is used to determine not only if the predictor variables predict values on Y in a linear fashion but also to assess the extent and nature of the predictors' ability to predict Y. This chapter presents the statistical concepts and tests that comprise MLR.

The examples used throughout the last chapter on SLR can be converted to examples for MLR: Do the number of hours students study and the number of nights students go out per week predict their GPA? Does the length of time served and the type of conviction charge predict the number of disciplinary infractions inmates receive? Do the number of hours spent in substance-abuse counseling and the number of AA meetings attended predict drug court offenders' scores on the Pro-Drug Use Attitude Scale? While the previous chapter examined the ability of a single predictor variable to predict the criterion variable, all of the examples listed above employ two predictor variables in the prediction of the criterion variable. Here is the general form of the research question for MLR: Does a linear combination of the predictor variables (X_1, X_2, X_3, . . .) reliably predict the criterion variable (Y)? If that question is answered in the affirmative, then additional statistics are used to determine how well each of the predictor variables predict the criterion variable.

IMPORTANT CONCEPTS RELATED TO MULTIPLE LINEAR REGRESSION

Scatterplots

Scatterplots are the graphs of X-Y coordinates that you learned about in the last two chapters. In MLR, an additional axis is added for each additional predictor variable. A regression model with two predictors and one criterion variable requires a three-dimensional graph. Regression models with three predictors and one criterion variable require a four-dimensional graph, and so on. It is difficult for us to visually examine graphs beyond three dimensions, but it is interesting to note that mathematics continues to work in nth-dimensional space. We will be using two predictor variables in our example throughout this chapter, requiring a three-dimensional graph. The third axis appearing in a three-dimensional graph is called the X_2-axis (sometimes called the Z-axis).

In SLR, the scatterplots graphed each subject's paired values on the X (predictor) and Y (criterion) variables. In MLR with two predictor variables, the scatterplot graphs each subject's corresponding values on the X_1 (first predictor), X_2 (second predictor), and Y (criterion) variables. You learned in SLR that the more closely the dots in a scatterplot form a one-dimensional straight line, the more closely the two variables are associated. In MLR with two predictor variables, the more closely the dots fit a two-dimensional plane, the more closely the two variables are associated. If we were to employ three predictor variables, association would be assessed by how closely the dots fit a three-dimensional ellipse, and so on. Multiple linear regression with two predictors takes the visualized regression plane and actually plots it onto the scatterplot so that it best fits the X_1-X_2-Y coordinates, indicating the ability of X_1 and X_2 to predict Y. The ability to plot the plane comes from the algebraic formula for a plane, which will be discussed shortly.

Table 12.1 presents hypothetical data that will be used to demonstrate these concepts and will also serve as the application example so that the many computational exercises throughout the chapter will be consistent. The example uses an unusually small sample size (N = 10) so that mathematical computations are easy. The data are an exten-

Chapter Twelve ■ Significant Relationships: Multiple Linear Regression 239

Table 12.1 Hypothetical Data for 10 Offenders

Offender	Number of Arrests Prior to Incarceration (X_1)	Age (X_2)	Number of Future Arrests (Y)
01	3	37	2
02	5	30	5
03	6	27	7
04	8	29	9
05	9	22	9
06	2	28	6
07	5	33	4
08	3	34	4
09	7	30	5
10	8	40	6

sion of the example used throughout the SLR chapter and are based on the well-supported theories that the number of arrests that an offender has had prior to incarceration is a good predictor of the number of arrests an offender will have after release and that younger inmates will have more postrelease arrests than older inmates. Figure 12.1 presents the scatterplot of the X_1-X_2-Y relationship for these data.

Each dot in figure 12.1 represents a single subject's values on the three variables: number of prior arrests (X_1), age (X_2), and number of postrelease arrests (Y). Soon we will discuss the plotting of a regression plane onto the scatterplot, as well as how it was determined that there is a strong relationship (R = .86) between these three variables.

Multiple Correlation

In SLR, you learned that bivariate regression is based on the bivariate correlation between the predictor and criterion variables. Multiple linear regression is based on the **multiple corre-**

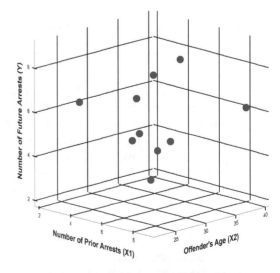

Figure 12.1 Scatterplot of Hypothetical Data in Table 12.1 (Strong Relationship; R = .86)

lation (R) between a linear combination of the predictor variables and the criterion variable. The regression equation resulting from an analysis specifies the manner in which the predictor variables are linearly combined. But before discussing the mathematics behind multiple correlation, it may be more useful to obtain a conceptual understanding through the use of Venn diagrams.

Figure 12.2 depicts a Venn diagram of a multiple correlation between three variables (X_1, X_2, and Y). Each circle represents the total variance in a variable. Where the circles overlap, there is shared variance between the variables; this shared variance is computed as the squared correlation (r^2) between the two variables. We are interested in how much shared variance there is between Y and the predictor variables. The more variance in Y that is shared with the predictor variables, the better the job the predictor variables do in predicting Y and the larger the multiple correlation (R). The less that the circles of the predictor variables overlap with the Y-circle, the worse the job the predictor variables do in predicting Y and the smaller the multiple correlation.

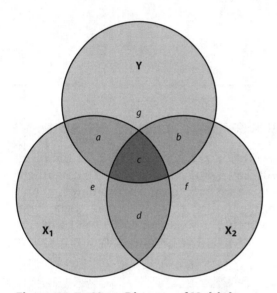

Figure 12.2 Venn Diagram of Multiple Correlation (R)

In figure 12.2, specific areas (some overlapping and some unique) of the circles are labeled *a, b, c, d, e, f, g*. The letter *a* represents the amount of variance in Y that is uniquely explained by X_1 (also called the squared **semi-partial correlation** between X_1 and Y). The letter *b* represents the amount of variance in Y that is uniquely explained by X_2 (the squared semi-partial correlation between X_2 and Y). The letter *c* represents the amount of variance in Y that is simultaneously explained by X_1 and X_2 (redundant predictive ability). The letter *d* represents the amount of shared variance between X_1 and X_2 that does not predict Y. The letters *e* and *f* represent the unique portions of variance in X_1 and X_2 that are not shared with any other variable. The letter *g* represents the portion of Y that is unexplained (unpredicted) by X_1 and X_2; it remains as error variance in the regression model until other significant predictors are identified.

In MLR, the areas *a, b,* and *c* are summed to indicate the amount of variance in Y that is explained (predicted) by the combined use of

X_1 and X_2. This area, representing the predicted variance, is quantified as the squared multiple correlation (R^2); taking the square root of this number gives us the multiple correlation (R) between X_1, X_2, and Y. Areas *d, e, f,* and *g* become part of the error variance. The primary goal in MLR is to identify additional predictors that will predict (overlap with) the variance in Y, thus increasing predicted variance, while not adding too much error variance (nonoverlapping area) to the overall regression model.

Generating the multiple correlation between X_1, X_2, and Y by hand is rather tedious (and may be considered optional material). The steps are provided using the data from our example:

Step 1: Compute the means, standard deviations, and correlations for all three variables. These are listed in table 12.2:

Table 12.2 Descriptive Statistics for Example Data Set

Offender	Number of Arrests Prior to Incarceration (X_1)	Age (X_2)	Number of Future Arrests (Y)
01	3	37	2
02	5	30	5
03	6	27	7
04	8	29	9
05	9	22	9
06	2	28	6
07	5	33	4
08	3	34	4
09	7	30	5
10	8	40	6
	M = 5.60; SD = 2.413	M = 31.0; SD = 5.185	M = 5.70; SD = 2.214
		$r_{X1Y} = .703$ $r_{X2Y} = -.668$ $r_{X1X2} = -.266$	

Step 2: Find the proportion of variance in Y that is predicted by X_1 (area *a* + *c* in figure 12.2). It is the squared bivariate correlation between X_1 and Y:

$r^2_{X1Y} = (.703)^2 = .494$

Step 3: Find the unique proportion of variance in Y that is predicted by X_2 (area *b* in figure 12.2). This requires that the regression equation of regressing X_2 on X_1 be computed. This regression equation is: $X'_2 = a_{x2} + b_{x2}X_1$

Where:

$$b_{X2} = r_{X1X2}\left(\frac{s_{X2}}{s_{X1}}\right)$$

$$= -.266\left(\frac{5.185}{2.413}\right)$$

$$= -.266(2.1488)$$

$$= -.5716$$

$$a_{X2} = \bar{X}_2 - b_{X2}\bar{X}_1$$

$$= 31.0 - (-.5716)(5.60)$$

$$= 31.0 + 3.20$$

$$= 34.20$$

Using these values, we get the following regression equation for the regression of X_2 on X_1:

$$X'_2 = 34.20 + (-.572)X_1$$

By plugging all of the observed values of X_1 into the regression equation, we obtain the predicted values of X_2. We also need to compute the residuals of regressing X_2 on X_1 by subtracting each predicted value of X_2 from each observed value of X_2 ($X_2 - X'_2$). Table 12.3 presents the predicted values and residuals of regressing X_2 on X_1:

Table 12.3 Predicted Values and Residuals from Regressing X_2 on X_1

Offender	Age (X_2)	Predicted Age (X'_2)	Residuals ($X_2 - X'_2$)
01	37	32.48	4.52
02	30	31.34	-1.34
03	27	30.77	-3.77
04	29	29.62	-.62
05	22	29.05	-7.05
06	28	33.06	-5.06
07	33	31.34	1.66
08	34	32.48	1.52
09	30	30.20	-.20
10	40	29.62	10.38

Now we can find the unique proportion of variance in Y that is predicted by X_2 (area b in figure 12.2). It is the squared semi-partial correlation between X_2 and Y. It is computed by regressing X_2 on X_1 and correlating the residuals with Y (hand calculations for this correlation are not presented):

$$r^2_{Y(X1.X2)} = (-.499)^2 = .249$$

Step 4: Find the proportion of variance in Y that is predicted by X_1 and X_2. This is the area represented by $a + b + c$ in figure 12.2, and is the squared multiple correlation between X_1, X_2, and Y. It is computed by summing the proportions of variance (squared correlations) that resulted from steps 2 and 3:

$$R^2_{Y.X1.X2} = .494 + .249 = .743$$

This value is the coefficient of determination, meaning that 74.3% of the total variance in Y (number of future arrests) is explained by X_1 (number of prior arrests) and X_2 (age). We will say more about this coefficient of determination later on in this chapter. The multiple correlation (R) between X_1, X_2, and Y is obtained by taking the square root of the coefficient of determination:

$$R = \sqrt{.743} = .862$$

The multiple correlation (R) should be interpreted as a bivariate correlation in terms ranging from 0 to 1 and providing information about the strength of the relationship between the variables, but R never takes on a negative value, so it never informs us as to the direction of the relationships between the variables. That information comes from the regression coefficients themselves.

Performing the SPSS steps at the end of the chapter for the MLR application example yields the "Model Summary" results box on the bottom of the page. It confirms the multiple correlation (R) and coefficient of determination (R^2) for our example data set computed above. It also reports the adjusted R^2, which makes the R^2 more conservative by accounting for expected shrinkage from using the resultant regression equation on a new sample. The standard error for the multiple correlation is provided as well, but typically is not reported in research reports.

In particular, researchers want to know the R, R^2, and adjusted R^2 for their MLR analysis since they provide information about the performance of all of the predictors in their ability to predict values on Y. Given the high value of R (.862), we know there is a strong relationship between Y and the linear combination of X variables. Given the high value of R^2 (74.3%), we know that our predictors are doing a very

Model Summary

Model	R	R Square	Adjusted R Square	Std. Error of the Estimate
1	.862[a]	.743	.670	1.272

a. Predictors: (Constant), Offender's Age (X2), Number of Prior Arrests (X1) good job of predicting values on Y. The amount of shrinkage does seem to be considerable (going from 74.3% to 67.0%), but it is not unexpected given the small sample size of our study (statistics become more stable with larger sample sizes). But knowledge regarding the relative importance of one predictor over another must be obtained through the results of regressing Y on X_1 and X_2.

The Regression of Y on X_1 and X_2

When we want to know if X_1 and X_2 reliably (statistically significantly) predict Y, we have to perform a **regression of Y on X_1 and X_2** to get the answer. Regressing Y on X_1 and X_2 means that we mathematically determine the manner in which observed values on Y are a function of values jointly observed on X_1 and X_2. Once the regression formula is specified, we determine how well the equation fits the observed data for Y; in other words, how good of a job does the equation that is based on values of X_1 and X_2 do in predicting values of Y? You may remember from your previous math classes that there is a formula for the generation of a plane. In statistical regression this plane is called the **regression plane** and is generated by associating the observed values of X_1 and X_2 with the predicted values of Y, based on the prediction equation specifying the manner in which Y is a function of X_1 and X_2. Formula 12.1 presents the equation for the regression plane.

FORMULA 12.1: EQUATION FOR THE REGRESSION PLANE OF Y ON X_1 AND X_2

$$Y' = a_y + b_1 X_1 + b_2 X_2$$

Where: Y' = the predicted value for Y for given values of X_1 and X_2

a_y = the regression constant of the regression of Y on X_1 and X_2

b_1 = the regression coefficient for the regression of Y on X_1

b_2 = the regression coefficient for the regression of Y on X_2

Further definition of this equation in necessary. The symbol Y' is the predicted value of Y that will result from solving the right side of the equation. We want to know what the predicted values of Y would be for each possible value of X_1 and X_2 so that a comparison can be made between the Y-values that were predicted and the actual Y-values observed in the data set. The more identical the predicted and observed values of Y, the better the job X_1 and X_2 do in predicting Y.

The symbol b_1 represents the **regression coefficient** for the regression of Y on X_1, and reflects the correlation between Y and X_1 as well as the correlation between X_1 and X_2; it tells us the amount of change in the predicted values of Y for each 1-unit change on X_1. The symbol b_2

represents the regression coefficient for the regression of Y on X_2 and reflects the correlation between Y and X_2, as well as the correlation between X_1 and X_2. It tells us the amount of change in the predicted values of Y for each 1-unit change on X_2. These regression coefficients indicate the amount of weight each variable has in predicting Y.

The symbol a_y represents the **regression constant** of regressing Y on X_1 and X_2. It is the predicted value of Y when both of the predictors take on the value of zero. The regression constant, along with the regression coefficients, also allow for the plotting of the regression plane.

No matter how many predictor variables are included in the regression model, formula 12.1 is the formula that is used; additional $b_k X_k$ components would be added for each additional predictor variable (the subscript k refers to each additional predictor) and would take the following general form:

$$Y' = a_y + b_1 X_1 + b_2 X_2 + \ldots + b_k X_k$$

We will not compute the regression equation for our MLR application example by hand since the calculations become very cumbersome at this advanced level of statistics. The chapter on SLR provided enough detailed information on the specifics of the math behind regression to give you a conceptual grounding in the technique. With the ease of accessing statistical software, it is unlikely that anyone would ever perform the hand calculations anymore. Readers who are interested in the mathematical details of MLR should consult Tabachnick and Fidell.[1]

Using the SPSS steps at the end of the chapter for our application example, the regression computations (using formula 12.1) revealed that the equation for the regression plane is:

$$Y' = 9.642 + .519 X_1 - .221 X_2$$

This equation tells us that the regression plane crosses the Y-axis at Y = 9.642, when both predictors take on the value of zero. It tells us that for each 1-unit increase in the number of prior arrests (X_1) an offender has, there will be a .519 increase in the predicted number of future arrests (Y'). It also tells us that for each 1-unit increase in age (X_2), there will be a .221 decrease in the predicted number of future arrests (Y').

These values are reported in the "Coefficients" results box of the SPSS output located below.

Model		Unstandardized Coefficients		Standardized Coefficients	t	Sig.
		B	Std. Error	Beta		
1	(Constant)	9.642	3.091		3.119	.017
	Number of Prior Arrests (X1)	.519	.182	.565	2.844	.025
	Offender's Age (X2)	-.221	.085	-.517	-2.602	.035

a. Dependent Variable: Number of Future Arrests (Y)

The coefficients results box reports the unstandardized regression coefficients (b_1 and b_2) and the regression constant (a_y), as well as their standard errors. Also reported are the **standardized regression coefficients (Beta coefficients)**, which are the **unstandardized regression coefficients** that have been converted to z-scores. The conversion to z-scores takes the predictors out of their original metrics (which are not readily comparable) and gives them a standardized metric that allows us to compare the predictors in terms of their ability to predict Y. We can see from the results box that the number of prior arrests an offender has is a better predictor (Beta = .565) of future arrests than is age (Beta = –.517), since the prior arrests predictor has a Beta with a larger absolute value (disregarding + and –) than the age predictor. We usually report the Beta rather than the unstandardized coefficient (labeled B) when writing up MLR analyses (or else we report both unstandardized and standardized regression coefficients).

The t-tests (and p-values) that determine if the coefficients are statistically significantly different from zero are reported as well. The significance values are all less than .05, so we would conclude that all of the coefficients are significantly different from zero, meaning each predictor variable has weight in the regression equation. This finding indicates that both of our predictors reliably predict values of Y.

Figure 12.3 presents the scatterplot from figure 12.1 with the addition of the regression plane for the data set imposed on the graph. This plane is the best-fitting possible surface that could be drawn through the X_1-X_2-Y coordinates to minimize the distance of all dots from the plane. The floor and ceiling of the plane are determined by the regression constant and the regression coefficients. Tilting the plane in any direction will cause some dots to be disproportionately farther from the plane than others. The regression plane is the mathematical, two-dimensional center point in a three-dimensional space (X_1-X_2-Y axes) for all of the X_1-X_2-Y coordinates in the data set.

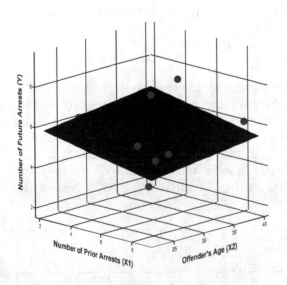

Figure 12.3   Plot of Regression Plane on Scatterplot for the Example Data Set

Errors of Prediction

The regression equation yields the predicted value of Y (Y') once observed values of X_1 and X_2 are plugged into the equation. The first offender's X_1-X_2-Y coordinate from our example data set (table 12.1) is 3 prior arrests (X_1), 37 years of age (X_2), and 2 future arrests (Y). This particular offender's X_1-X_2-Y coordinate (dot) can be found in the bottom, back corner of the graph in figure 12.3. Plugging the X_1 and X_2 values into the regression equation (formula 12.1) yields:

$$Y' = 9.642 + .519X_1 - .221X_2$$
$$= 9.642 + .519(3) - .221(37)$$
$$= 9.642 + 1.557 - 8.177$$
$$= 3.022$$

This means that offenders with 3 prior arrests (X_1), and who are 37 years old (X_2), would be predicted to have 3.022 future arrests (Y'). Table 12.4 presents all of our subjects' Y-scores, as well as their predicted values of Y (Y') given their observed values of X_1 and X_2.

The first offender in our data set, who was predicted to have 3.022 future arrests, actually had 2 future arrests, so there is a small amount of **error of prediction**. In chapter 11, this subject was predicted to have 4.023 future arrests when prior arrests was the only predictor in the regression equation, so the error of prediction is smaller now that we have added a second reliable predictor (X_2) to the regression model.

Errors of prediction (Y – Y'), also called **residuals**, can be computed simply by subtracting the predicted value of Y from the observed value of Y. There will be positive errors (Y – Y' > 0), meaning

Table 12.4 Errors of Prediction (Number of Prior Arrests and Age Predicting Number of Future Arrests)

Offender	Number of Arrests Prior to Incarceration (X_1)	Age (X_2)	Number of Future Arrests (Y)	Predicted Number of Future Arrests (Y')	Errors of Prediction (Y – Y')
01	3	37	2	3.022	–1.022
02	5	30	5	5.607	–.607
03	6	27	7	6.789	.211
04	8	29	9	7.385	1.615
05	9	22	9	9.451	–.451
06	2	28	6	4.492	1.508
07	5	33	4	4.944	–.944
08	3	34	4	3.685	.315
09	7	30	5	6.645	–1.645
10	8	40	6	4.954	1.046
Σ					.026

the regression equation underpredicted for those X_1-X_2-Y coordinates; and there will be negative errors (Y − Y' < 0), meaning the regression equation overpredicted for those X_1-X_2-Y coordinates. All of the errors of prediction (residuals) will total to approximately zero (allowing for rounding error), which is something we observed with deviation scores around a mean and with SLR residuals, indicating that the regression plane (like the mean and regression line) is the mathematical center point of the observed data. While not practical for hand calculations, the residuals would have added up to exactly zero if we had not rounded off any decimals in any of the numbers resulting from calculations used to generate the predicted values of Y (including means, standard deviations, correlations, and regression coefficients). The fact that residuals add up to approximately zero means that the regression equation underpredicts as much as it overpredicts since they cancel each other out when summed. Table 12.4 presents the errors of prediction for our MLR analysis.

It is helpful to visualize errors of prediction as well. A glance at the regression plane plotted in figure 12.3 makes it clear that some dots are closer to the plane than others. Since the regression plane represents the predicted values of Y for jointly observed values of X_1 and X_2, the further an X_1-X_2-Y coordinate (dot) is from the plane, the worse the job the regression equation did in predicting Y (and the greater the error of prediction) for that particular X_1-X_2-Y coordinate. If most of the dots lie close to the regression plane, the regression equation did a good job of predicting values on Y using observed values of X_1 and X_2. If most of the dots are scattered away from the regression plane, the regression equation did a poor job of predicting Y. The regression plane represents the best possible fit of a two-dimensional plane to the three-dimensional plot of the observed data; it will yield the least amount of errors in prediction than if the plane had been positioned in any other way.

Predictive Accuracy

The next concept we need to discuss concerns the overall **predictive accuracy** of the regression equation. The regression plane is fit to the data such that the errors of prediction (residuals), if squared and summed, total to a minimum value. We call this the principle of least squared errors, which is symbolized as follows: $\Sigma(Y - Y')^2$ = minimum value.

As with SLR, knowing the principle of least squared errors in the abstract provides little help in assessing how accurate our predictions really are. There are two primary ways to assess the accuracy of our predictions. The first is called **cross-validation**, which means that the study is replicated on a new sample of data in order to see if similar results are observed. In the case of our example, we would draw a new sample of offenders, total their numbers of prior and future arrests, record their ages, and perform multiple linear regression to see if the same regression plane was obtained. When we do research, we generally only have one data set to work with, so cross-validation would not be possible. Yet it is possible to do a literature search to locate similar studies that may have tested the same predictor and criterion variables as your study.

The F-Ratio

The second method of assessing predictive accuracy involves a comparison of predicted variance to error variance by computing the F-Ratio. This discussion of predicted and error variances was covered in detail in chapter 11 and will not be repeated to that extent here. The reader should review figure 11.4 and the discussion of partitioning variance in the criterion variable, as well as the F-Ratio test.

In SLR, there was only one predictor variable partitioning predicted variance out of the criterion variable. In MLR, there are two or more variables partitioning predicted variance from the total variance in Y. If the linear combination of the predictors is able to explain more of the variance in Y than the amount that is left to error variance, then the F-Ratio will be large and statistically significant. If the predictors are not able to explain enough of the variance in Y, meaning that too much of that variance is left to error variance, then the F-Ratio will be small and nonsignificant. Any variance that the predictor variables bring to the regression model that is not shared variance with Y gets added into the pool of error variance as well. This means that it is important to have **predictive efficiency**, meaning the regression model should include the predictors that have the most shared variance with Y, as well as the least amount of unshared (error) variance.

As with SLR, the computation of the F-Ratio requires that the regression, residual, and total sums of squares be computed; however, the calculations are a bit different. The residual sum of squares is computed as $\Sigma(Y - Y')^2$ and reflects the remaining variance in Y not explained by the predictor variables (error variance). The regression sum of squares is computed as $\Sigma(Y' - \bar{Y}')^2$, which is the way it was computed for SLR. The total sum of squares in MLR is computed by adding together the residual and regression sums of squares. Table 12.5 on the next page presents the computation table used to obtain the residual and regression sums of squares. For our example data set, we obtained a residual sum of squares of 11.3039 and a regression sum of squares of 32.7899. Adding the two yields a total sum of squares of 44.0938. These numbers differ slightly from the computer output below due to rounding error.

Table 12.5 MLR Sum of Squares Computing Table

Offender	Number of Arrests Prior to Incarceration (X_1)	Age (X_2)	Number of Future Arrests (Y)	Predicted Number of Future Arrests (Y')	Residual Sum of Squares $(Y - Y')^2$	Regression Sum of Squares $(Y' - \bar{Y}')^2$
01	3	37	2	3.02	1.0404	7.1824
02	5	30	5	5.61	.3721	.0081
03	6	27	7	6.79	.0441	1.1881
04	8	29	9	7.39	2.5921	2.8561
05	9	22	9	9.45	.2025	14.0625
06	2	28	6	4.50	2.2500	1.4400
07	5	33	4	4.95	.9025	.5625
08	3	34	4	3.69	.0961	4.0401
09	7	30	5	6.65	2.7225	.9025
10	8	40	6	4.96	1.0816	.5476
Σ				57.01	11.3039	32.7899

The next step in generating the F-Ratio involves computing the degrees of freedom. The total sum of squares has N – 1 degrees of freedom (in our example, df = 10 – 1 = 9). The regression sum of squares has k – 1 degrees of freedom, where k equals the number of variables in the analysis (in our example, df regression = 3 – 1 = 2). The residual sum of squares has N – k degrees of freedom (in our example, df residual = 10 – 3 = 7).

Now the regression and residual mean squares are computed by dividing each type of sum of squares by its respective degrees of freedom. For our example, mean square regression = 32.7899/2 = 16.39495. Our mean square residual = 11.3039/7 = 1.61484. The F-Ratio is obtained by dividing the mean square regression by the mean square residual: F = 16.39495/1.61484 = 10.15268. Again, these numbers differ slightly from the computer output below due to rounding error. The computer output for the ANOVA table appears below.

ANOVA[b]

Model		Sum of Squares	df	Mean Square	F	Sig.
1	Regression	32.766	2	16.383	10.119	.009[a]
	Residual	11.334	7	1.619		
	Total	44.100	9			

a. Predictors: (Constant), Offender's Age (X2), Number of Prior Arrests (X1)
b. Dependent Variable: Number of Future Arrests (Y)

The fact that the obtained F-Ratio is statistically significant at the α = .05 level indicates that the overall regression model, comprised of two predictor variables (number of prior arrests and age), reliably predicts the criterion variable (number of future arrests). And since the *t*-tests for the regression coefficients (presented earlier) were all statistically significant, we know that both predictor variables meaningfully predict variance in Y. That brings us back to the question of how accurately X_1 and X_2 predict Y.

The Coefficient of Determination

While MLR makes its determination of statistical significance of the overall prediction model based on the F-Ratio, we are more interested in the **coefficient of determination (R^2)**. The coefficient of determination is the percent of total variance in Y that is predicted by X_1 and X_2 (see formula 12.2). This is the same coefficient of determination we computed when determining the multiple correlation (R) for our variables earlier in this chapter (see section on multiple correlation).

FORMULA 12.2: COEFFICIENT OF DETERMINATION

$$R^2 = \frac{\text{Predicted Variance}}{\text{Total Variance}}$$

We computed the predicted variance (regression sum of squares) and the total variance (total sum of squares) above. Dividing the predicted variance by the total variance yields the proportion of the total variance that has been predicted or explained by the predictor variables (X_1 and X_2). For our example data using our hand calculations we obtained: predicted variance = 32.7899; total variance = 44.0938. These values are now plugged into the formula for the coefficient of determination (formula 11.4):

$$R^2 = \frac{\text{Predicted Variance}}{\text{Total Variance}} = \frac{32.7899}{44.0938} = .7436$$

Our obtained coefficient of determination should be interpreted to mean that 74.4% of the variance in the number of future arrests (Y) is predicted by the number of prior arrests that offenders had (X_1) and their age (X_2).

In similar fashion, we can divide the residual variance (11.3039) by the total variance (44.0938) to obtain the **coefficient of nondetermination** (.2564), which is the percent of the total variance in Y that is not predicted or explained by X_1 and X_2. For our example, 25.6% of the variance in Y remains unaccounted for by our predictor variables. The coefficient of nondetermination can also be derived simply by subtracting the coefficient of determination from one (**1 – R^2**). The

SPSS results box reporting the R, R^2, and adjusted R^2 was presented in the multiple correlation section earlier in this chapter.

TYPES OF MULTIPLE LINEAR REGRESSION

There are several types of MLR, and the distinctions are based on the order and manner in which the predictor variables are entered into the regression equation. The reason order matters is that once a predictor is allowed to partial out the amount of variance in Y that it predicts, there is less available or unexplained variance left for other predictors to claim. In fact, given the tendency for predictors to be highly intercorrelated, there usually is not very much unexplained variance in Y left for predictors to claim once the first few predictors for a model have been selected.

It is important to remember that we should strive for predictive efficiency because if we just toss a bunch of predictors into a regression model, each one will bring so much error variance with them that the overall model likely will be nonsignificant (there will be too much residual variance relative to regression variance). Researchers often wish to conduct regression analyses that allow them to assess the ability of a number of predictors to predict a single criterion variable. Thus, there are several options in MLR that provide the researcher some control over variable entry order.

Direct Enter Method

When using the **direct enter method** in MLR, all of the predictors submitted to the analysis are included in the order in which they were listed in the SPSS command. This method should be used when theoretical (or other) reasons provide a clear rationale for which variables should be included in the analysis. For example, a researcher may want to test a theory that specifies that offenders who have a lot of prior arrests and are young will have more future arrests than their counterparts (the theoretical underpinning of our example analysis). The primary problem with this method is that we will lose predictive efficiency if too many of the predictor variables are highly correlated with each other; this results in **predictive redundancy** at the expense of predictive efficiency. In fact, if two variables are correlated at .98 or higher, they have so much predictive redundancy (called **multicollinearity**) that one of the variables should be excluded from the model. We have used direct regression throughout this chapter.

Stepwise Regression Methods

The alternative to using direct regression is stepwise regression, where the computer sequentially adds predictor variables to the regression model based on their contributions to the overall predicted variance (R^2) of the regression model. In the absence of a compelling theoretical reason to use direct regression when employing multiple predictor variables, stepwise regression is the best method to use. This is true primarily because it enhances predictive efficiency. There are three types of stepwise regression.

Forward stepwise regression selects predictor variables in the order of greatest-to-least amount of increase in R^2. It stops selecting predictors for the model once the increase in R^2 is no longer statistically significant. This method is useful for identifying the order of importance of predictors, but since the method stops *stepping* (selecting predictors) once increases in R^2 are no longer statistically significant, it doesn't have a chance to reassess predictive redundancy once several predictors have been entered into the model.

Backward stepwise regression starts out by selecting all of the predictor variables simultaneously, similar to the direct enter method. Then it removes predictors one at a time in the order of least-to-greatest amount of decrease in R^2. It stops removing predictors from the model once removing a predictor would cause a statistically significant decrease in R^2. Some researchers conducting exploratory research prefer to use backward stepwise regression since it identifies the maximum number of predictors that yield a statistically significant overall regression model. However, these models have the greatest risk of suffering from predictive redundancy, which is often referred to as **overspecification of the regression model**.

Stepwise regression combines forward and backward stepwise regression. It starts out in a forward stepwise manner, selecting variables that yield the greatest increase in R^2. However, at any point that a variable that was previously selected becomes redundant to other selected predictors, it takes backward stepwise action by removing the predictor. Stepwise regression results in regression models that have the most predictive efficiency and thus is the recommended method when predictive efficiency is a goal. My personal experience has been that unless theory compels a particular entry order, stepwise regression is the best method to use.

Handling Nominal Level Variables

Because of the mathematics involved in an MLR analysis, all variables submitted to the analysis need to be measured at the interval-ratio level. There is a way to transform nominal variables (and ordinal variables treated as nominal) so that they can be submitted to MLR as well. It is called **dummy coding** and is based on the argument that two categories coded 0 and 1 actually meet the requirements of interval-ratio data (equal distances between values of the variable). Typically the 0 indicates an absence of the trait being measured and 1 indicates the presence of the trait being measured, unless the variable cannot have an absence of trait (e.g., gender), wherein the assignment of 0 and 1 to the two categories would be arbitrary. This means that dichotomous (two-category) nominal variables can be dummy coded 0 and 1 and submitted to the MLR analysis.

Polytomous (multicategory) nominal variables must be split out into separate variables (called **vectors**) for each category of the variable and then each vector is dummy coded 0 and 1 to indicate the presence or absence of the trait represented by that vector. The number of vectors required for a categorical variable is $k - 1$, where k is the number of categories in the variable. The reason that one less vector is needed than the number of categories of the variable is that once values for a subject are known on all of the $k - 1$ vectors, the score on the missing vector is known. For example, if race were a variable with four categories (black, white, Hispanic, other), only three vectors would be required to code this variable. If we created dummy coded vectors for the first three categories, and if a subject received a score of zero on all three of those vectors, we would know that person fell into the "other" race category. If the subject received a score of 1 on any of the $k - 1$ dummy coded vectors, we would know that person received a zero on the missing vector. If we used four vectors for all four categories of the race variable, the computer would detect that as being redundant mathematical information, and you would get an error in your computer output.

There is no loss of information with dummy coding, but remember our discussion of predictive efficiency, which described how it is common for the first few variables entered into an MLR analysis to claim the explainable variance in Y. A polytomous nominal variable requiring a number of dummy coded vectors can greatly compromise predictive efficiency.

There are many more complexities and nuances of multiple linear regression than are covered in this chapter. You could take entire courses devoted to the study of MLR. The point of this chapter was to provide you with enough capability and conceptual understanding in the technique to perform some basic analyses and to be able to interpret most of the MLR analyses reported in research studies.

The following is an example of how the computer-generated results of the MLR analysis of our example data set would be reported:

> A random sample of 10 offenders, who were released from prison one year prior to data collection, was selected. The number of arrests during the one year prior to incarceration and the one year following release were recorded. Their ages at the time of release

from prison were recorded as well. In an attempt to test the theory that the number of preincarceration arrests and the offender's age would be good predictors of the number of postrelease arrests, a multiple linear regression analysis was performed. The direct regression results (see results table) indicated that both predictors significantly predicted future arrests ($F_{2,7} = 10.119, p < .05$). The number of preincarceration arrests was the strongest predictor (Beta = .565, $p < .05$), confirming that increases in prior arrests are associated with increases in future arrests. Age also was determined to be a statistically significant predictor (Beta = –.517, $p < .05$) of the number of postrelease arrests, confirming that increases in age are associated with decreases in criminal activity. The overall regression model explained 74.3% of the total variance in the number of future arrests variable.

Results Table: Direct Regression Results of Regressing the Number of Postrelease Arrests (Y) on the Number of Preincarceration Arrests (X_1) and Age (X_2)

	B	S.E.	Beta	Sig.
Number of Preincarceration Arrests	.519	.182	.565	.025
Age	–.221	.085	–.517	.035
Constant	9.642			
df	2, 7			
F	10.119			
R^2	.743			
Adjusted R^2	.670			

■ SUMMARY

In this chapter you have learned the purpose and methods of conducting multiple linear regression analyses to determine if multiple interval-ratio predictor variables reliably predict an interval-ratio criterion variable. You learned how to generate and interpret the regression coefficients, the ANOVA table, and measures of predictive accuracy. The key issues surrounding MLR—multiple correlation, the regression of Y on multiple predictor variables, errors of prediction, predictive accuracy, cross-validation, the coefficient of determination, direct and stepwise regression methods, and dummy coding—were all discussed. Also, an MLR analysis was demonstrated through an SPSS application that employed a hypothetical research scenario in the field of criminal justice.

Note

[1] Tabachnick, B. & Fidell, L. (1996). *Using Multivariate Statistics* (3rd ed.). New York: Harper Collins.

KEY TERMS

Multiple Linear Regression (MLR)
Predictor Variable
Criterion Variable
Scatterplot
Multiple Correlation (R)
Semi-Partial Correlation
Regression of Y on X_1 and X_2
Regression Plane
Regression Coefficient
Regression Constant
Standardized Regression Coefficient (Beta Coefficient)
Unstandardized Regression Coefficient
Error of Prediction
Residuals
Predictive Accuracy
Cross-Validation
Predictive Efficiency
Coefficient of Determination (R^2)
Coefficient of Nondetermination ($1 - R^2$)
Direct Enter Method
Predictive Redundancy
Multicollinearity
Forward Stepwise Regression
Backward Stepwise Regression
Overspecification of the Regression Model
Stepwise Regression
Dummy Coding
Vectors

SPSS APPLICATION: MULTIPLE LINEAR REGRESSION

1. Open the "future arrests" data set you created in chapter 11 and add the predictor variable "age."

Offender	Number of Arrests Prior to Incarceration (X_1)	Age (X_2)	Number of Future Arrests (Y)
01	3	37	2
02	5	30	5
03	6	27	7
04	8	29	9
05	9	22	9
06	2	28	6
07	5	33	4
08	3	34	4
09	7	30	5
10	8	40	6

Chapter Twelve ■ Significant Relationships: Multiple Linear Regression

2. Perform the Multiple Linear Regression Analysis:
   i. Analyze
      ii. Regression
         iii. Linear
            iv. Move the Y variable into the "Dependent" Box
            v. Move the X_1 and X_2 variables into the "Independent" Box
            vi. Click on "OK"
3. Generate a scatterplot. (You do not have to include the regression plane. The current version of SPSS does not provide a point and click option to add the plane to the scatterplot. Syntax must be used to generate the plane.)
   i. Graphs
      ii Legacy Dialogs
         iii. Scatter/Dot
         iv. Click on 3-D Scatter
         v. Click "Define
            vi. Move the Y variable into the Y axis box
            vii. Move the X_1 variable into the X axis box
            viii. Move the X_2 variable into the Z axis box
            ix. Click on "OK"

SPSS Assignment

1. Open the "training academy" data set you created for chapter 11 and add the gender variable (see below). This fictitious data set represents a random sample of 15 law enforcement officer trainees who took an entrance exam prior to admission to the training academy and a proficiency exam upon completion of the academy. Both exams ranged from 0–100. The officer's gender was recorded as well (dummy coded 0 = female; 1 = male) and should be added to the data set. The director of the academy wants to determine if the scores received on the entrance exam and the gender of the officer predict the scores received on the proficiency exam.

2. Conduct a multiple linear regression analysis to determine if entrance exam (X_1) scores and gender (X_2) predict proficiency exam scores (Y).

3. Generate a scatterplot of the relationship between the entrance exam scores (X_1), gender (X_2), and the proficiency exams (Y).

4. Write a couple of paragraphs summarizing the results of the analyses performed in steps 2 and 3. Table your results.

"Training Academy" Data Set:

Trainee	Entrance Exam (X_1)	Gender (0 = female; 1 = male) (X_2)	Proficiency Exam (Y)
01	68	1	88
02	60	1	80
03	100	1	100
04	61	0	80
05	69	1	89
06	73	0	92
07	79	0	98
08	85	1	99
09	70	0	90
10	67	1	87
11	77	1	84
12	85	0	97
13	95	0	99
14	83	1	94
15	72	1	90

MULTIPLE-CHOICE QUESTIONS

1. When predictor variables are entered into a multiple linear regression model in the order they were submitted to the analysis, the analysis is using the _____ method.
   A. Forward Stepwise
   B. Backward Stepwise
   C. Central Enter
   D. Direct Enter

2. _____ allow for a comparison of predictors in terms of their ability to predict Y.
   A. Standardized Regression Coefficients
   B. Unstandardized Regression Coefficients
   C. Coefficients of Determination
   D. Unstandardized Residuals

3. Scatterplots created for a multiple linear regression analysis with two predictor variables have _____ axes.
   A. Three
   B. Two
   C. One
   D. None

4. A squared semi-partial correlation between Y and X_2 indicates the amount of variation in _____.
   A. Y that is not explained by X_2
   B. Y that is uniquely explained by X_2
   C. X_2 that is not explained by Y
   D. X_2 that is uniquely explained by Y

5. The purpose of multiple linear regression is to examine the ability of _____.
   A. A single dependent variable to predict values on the independent variables
   B. Two or more dependent variable to predict values on the independent variable
   C. Two or more independent variables to predict values on the dependent variable
   D. A single dependent variable to predict values on one independent variable

6. In a multiple linear regression analysis with two predictors and Y, the regression plane is comprised of _____.
   A. Observed Y-X_1-X_2 coordinates
   B. Residuals associated with predicting Y based on Y, X_1, and X_2
   C. Predicted Y-X_1-X_2 coordinates
   D. Observed Y-X_1-X_2 residuals

7. The *t*-test in a multiple regression analysis is used to test whether the regression coefficients are significantly different from _____.
   A. Each other
   B. The mean of Y
   C. One
   D. Zero

8. _____ are also known as Beta coefficients.
   A. Unstandardized Regression Coefficients
   B. Standardized Regression Coefficients
   C. Coefficients of Determination
   D. Residuals

9. The regression surface on a scatterplot in multiple linear regression with two predictor variables is a _____.
   A. Plane
   B. Line
   C. Curve
   D. Cone

10. Standardized regression coefficients convert unstandardized regression coefficients to _____.
    A. Means
    B. Probabilities
    C. z-scores
    D. Correlations

Appendices
Statistical Tables

Appendix A Areas under Normal Distribution   262
Appendix B Critical Values of t 263
Appendix C Critical Values of Chi-Square Distribution   264
Appendix D Critical Values of F-Distribution   265
Appendix E Critical Values of r Distribution   266
Appendix F Random Digits Table   267
Appendix G Computations for Simple Linear Regression Analysis Example   268

Appendix A Areas under Normal Distribution

z	0.00	0.01	0.02	0.03	0.04	0.05	0.06	0.07	0.08	0.09
0.0	0.0000	0.0040	0.0080	0.0120	0.0160	0.0199	0.0239	0.0279	0.0319	0.0359
0.1	0.0398	0.0438	0.0478	0.0517	0.0557	0.0596	0.0636	0.0675	0.0714	0.0754
0.2	0.0793	0.0832	0.0871	0.0910	0.0948	0.0987	0.1026	0.1064	0.1103	0.1141
0.3	0.1179	0.1217	0.1255	0.1293	0.1331	0.1368	0.1406	0.1443	0.1480	0.1517
0.4	0.1554	0.1591	0.1628	0.1664	0.1700	0.1736	0.1772	0.1808	0.1844	0.1879
0.5	0.1915	0.1950	0.1985	0.2019	0.2054	0.2088	0.2123	0.2157	0.2190	0.2224
0.6	0.2258	0.2291	0.2324	0.2357	0.2389	0.2422	0.2454	0.2486	0.2518	0.2549
0.7	0.2580	0.2612	0.2642	0.2673	0.2704	0.2734	0.2764	0.2794	0.2823	0.2852
0.8	0.2881	0.2910	0.2939	0.2967	0.2996	0.3023	0.3051	0.3078	0.3106	0.3133
0.9	0.3159	0.3186	0.3212	0.3238	0.3264	0.3289	0.3315	0.3340	0.3365	0.3389
1.0	0.3413	0.3438	0.3461	0.3485	0.3508	0.3531	0.3554	0.3577	0.3599	0.3621
1.1	0.3643	0.3665	0.3686	0.3708	0.3729	0.3749	0.3770	0.3790	0.3810	0.3830
1.2	0.3849	0.3869	0.3888	0.3907	0.3925	0.3944	0.3962	0.3980	0.3997	0.4015
1.3	0.4032	0.4049	0.4066	0.4082	0.4099	0.4115	0.4131	0.4147	0.4162	0.4177
1.4	0.4192	0.4207	0.4222	0.4236	0.4251	0.4265	0.4279	0.4292	0.4306	0.4319
1.5	0.4332	0.4345	0.4357	0.4370	0.4382	0.4394	0.4406	0.4418	0.4429	0.4441
1.6	0.4452	0.4463	0.4474	0.4484	0.4495	0.4505	0.4515	0.4525	0.4535	0.4545
1.7	0.4554	0.4564	0.4573	0.4582	0.4591	0.4599	0.4608	0.4616	0.4625	0.4633
1.8	0.4641	0.4649	0.4656	0.4664	0.4671	0.4678	0.4686	0.4693	0.4699	0.4706
1.9	0.4713	0.4719	0.4726	0.4732	0.4738	0.4744	0.4750	0.4756	0.4761	0.4767
2.0	0.4772	0.4778	0.4783	0.4788	0.4793	0.4798	0.4803	0.4808	0.4812	0.4817
2.1	0.4821	0.4826	0.4830	0.4834	0.4838	0.4842	0.4846	0.4850	0.4854	0.4857
2.2	0.4861	0.4864	0.4868	0.4871	0.4875	0.4878	0.4881	0.4884	0.4887	0.4890
2.3	0.4893	0.4896	0.4898	0.4901	0.4904	0.4906	0.4909	0.4911	0.4913	0.4916
2.4	0.4918	0.4920	0.4922	0.4925	0.4927	0.4929	0.4931	0.4932	0.4934	0.4936
2.5	0.4938	0.4940	0.4941	0.4943	0.4945	0.4946	0.4948	0.4949	0.4951	0.4952
2.6	0.4953	0.4955	0.4956	0.4957	0.4959	0.4960	0.4961	0.4962	0.4963	0.4964
2.7	0.4965	0.4966	0.4967	0.4968	0.4969	0.4970	0.4971	0.4972	0.4973	0.4974
2.8	0.4974	0.4975	0.4976	0.4977	0.4977	0.4978	0.4979	0.4979	0.4980	0.4981
2.9	0.4981	0.4982	0.4982	0.4983	0.4984	0.4984	0.4985	0.4985	0.4986	0.4986
3.0	0.4987	0.4987	0.4987	0.4988	0.4988	0.4989	0.4989	0.4989	0.4990	0.4990
3.1	0.4990	0.4991	0.4991	0.4991	0.4992	0.4992	0.4992	0.4992	0.4993	0.4993
3.2	0.4993	0.4993	0.4994	0.4994	0.4994	0.4994	0.4994	0.4995	0.4995	0.4995
3.3	0.4995	0.4995	0.4995	0.4996	0.4996	0.4996	0.4996	0.4996	0.4996	0.4997
3.4	0.4997	0.4997	0.4997	0.4997	0.4997	0.4997	0.4997	0.4997	0.4997	0.4998
3.5	0.4998	0.4998	0.4998	0.4998	0.4998	0.4998	0.4998	0.4998	0.4998	0.4998
3.6	0.4998	0.4998	0.4999	0.4999	0.4999	0.4999	0.4999	0.4999	0.4999	0.4999
3.7	0.4999	0.4999	0.4999	0.4999	0.4999	0.4999	0.4999	0.4999	0.4999	0.4999
3.8	0.4999	0.4999	0.4999	0.4999	0.4999	0.4999	0.4999	0.4999	0.4999	0.4999
3.9	0.49995	0.49995	0.49996	0.49996	0.49996	0.49996	0.49996	0.49996	0.49997	0.49997

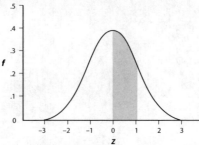

Appendix B Critical Values of t

df	α (Two-Tailed)						
	0.2	0.1	0.05	0.02	0.01	0.001	0.0001
1	3.078	6.314	12.706	31.821	63.657	636.619	6366.198
2	1.886	2.920	4.303	6.695	9.925	31.598	99.992
3	1.638	2.353	3.182	4.541	5.841	12.924	28.000
4	1.533	2.132	2.776	3.747	4.604	8.610	15.544
5	1.476	2.015	2.571	3.365	4.032	6.869	11.178
6	1.44	1.943	2.447	3.143	3.707	5.959	9.082
7	1.415	1.895	2.365	2.998	3.499	5.408	7.885
8	1.397	1.860	2.306	2.896	3.355	5.041	7.120
9	1.383	1.833	2.262	2.821	3.250	4.781	6.594
10	1.372	1.812	2.228	2.764	3.169	4.587	6.211
11	1.363	1.796	2.201	2.718	3.106	4.437	5.921
12	1.356	1.782	2.179	2.681	3.055	4.318	5.694
13	1.35	1.771	2.160	2.650	3.012	4.221	5.513
14	1.345	1.761	2.145	2.624	2.977	4.140	5.363
15	1.341	1.753	2.131	2.602	2.947	4.073	5.239
16	1.337	1.746	2.120	2.583	2.921	4.015	5.134
17	1.333	1.740	2.110	2.567	2.898	3.965	5.044
18	1.33	1.734	2.101	2.552	2.878	3.922	4.966
19	1.328	1.729	2.093	2.539	2.861	3.883	4.897
20	1.325	1.725	2.086	2.528	2.845	3.850	4.837
21	1.323	1.721	2.080	2.518	2.831	3.819	4.784
22	1.321	1.717	2.074	2.508	2.819	3.792	4.736
23	1.319	1.714	2.069	2.500	2.807	3.767	4.693
24	1.318	1.711	2.064	2.492	2.797	3.745	4.654
25	1.316	1.708	2.060	2.485	2.787	3.725	4.619
26	1.315	1.706	2.056	2.479	2.779	3.707	4.587
27	1.314	1.703	2.052	2.473	2.771	3.690	4.558
28	1.313	1.701	2.048	2.467	2.763	3.674	4.530
29	1.311	1.699	2.045	2.462	2.756	3.659	4.506
30	1.31	1.697	2.042	2.457	2.750	3.646	4.482
40	1.303	1.684	2.021	2.423	2.704	3.551	4.321
60	1.296	1.671	2.000	2.390	2.660	3.460	4.169
100	1.292	1.660	1.984	2.364	2.626	3.390	4.053
∞	1.282	1.645	1.960	2.326	2.576	3.291	3.750

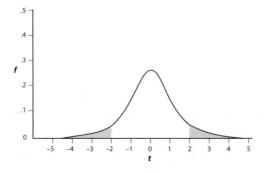

Appendix C Critical Values of Chi-Square Distribution

df	α				
	0.05	0.02	0.01	0.001	0.0001
1	3.84	5.41	6.63	10.83	15.14
2	5.99	7.82	9.21	13.82	18.42
3	7.81	9.84	11.34	16.27	21.11
4	9.49	11.67	13.28	18.47	23.51
5	11.07	13.39	15.09	20.51	25.74
6	12.59	15.03	16.81	22.46	27.86
7	14.07	16.62	18.48	24.32	29.88
8	15.51	18.17	20.09	26.12	31.83
9	16.92	19.68	21.67	27.88	33.72
10	18.31	21.16	23.21	29.59	35.56
11	19.68	22.62	24.72	31.26	37.37
12	21.03	24.05	26.22	32.91	39.13
13	22.36	25.47	27.69	34.53	40.87
14	23.68	26.87	29.14	36.12	42.58
15	25.00	28.26	30.58	37.70	44.26
16	26.30	29.63	32.00	39.25	45.92
17	27.59	31.00	33.41	40.79	47.57
18	28.87	32.35	34.81	42.31	49.19
19	30.14	33.69	36.19	43.82	50.80
20	31.41	35.02	37.57	45.31	52.39
21	32.67	36.34	38.93	46.80	53.96
22	33.92	37.66	40.29	48.27	55.52
23	35.17	38.97	41.64	49.73	57.08
24	36.42	40.27	42.98	51.18	58.61
25	37.65	41.57	44.31	52.62	60.14
26	38.89	42.86	45.64	54.05	61.66
27	40.11	44.14	46.96	55.48	63.16
28	41.34	45.42	48.28	56.89	64.66
29	42.56	46.69	49.59	58.30	66.15
30	43.77	47.96	50.89	59.70	67.63

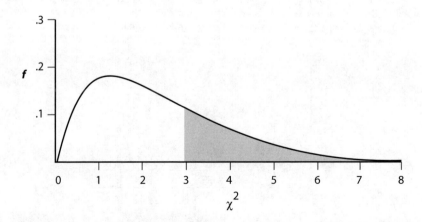

Appendix D Critical Values of F-Distribution (dfb = between-groups degrees of freedom, dfw = within-groups degrees of freedom)

Part A: $\alpha = 0.05$

dfw	\ dfb → 1	2	3	4	5	6	7	8	9	10	11	12
2	18.5	19.0	19.2	19.3	19.4	19.4	19.4	19.4	19.4	19.4	19.4	19.4
3	10.1	9.55	9.28	9.12	9.01	8.94	8.89	8.85	8.81	8.79	8.76	8.74
4	7.71	6.94	6.59	6.39	6.26	6.16	6.09	6.04	6.00	5.96	5.93	5.91
5	6.61	5.79	5.41	5.19	5.05	4.95	4.88	4.82	4.77	4.74	4.71	4.68
6	5.99	5.14	4.76	4.53	4.39	4.28	4.21	4.15	4.10	4.06	4.03	4.00
7	5.59	4.74	4.35	4.12	3.97	3.87	3.77	3.73	3.68	3.64	3.60	3.57
8	5.32	4.46	4.07	3.84	3.69	3.58	3.50	3.44	3.39	3.35	3.31	3.28
9	5.12	4.26	3.86	3.63	3.48	3.37	3.29	3.23	3.18	3.14	3.10	3.07
10	4.96	4.10	3.71	3.48	3.33	3.22	3.14	3.07	3.02	2.98	2.94	2.91
11	4.84	3.98	3.59	3.36	3.20	3.09	3.01	2.95	2.90	2.85	2.82	2.79
12	4.75	3.89	3.49	3.26	3.11	3.00	2.91	2.85	2.80	2.75	2.72	2.69
15	4.54	3.68	3.29	3.06	2.90	2.79	2.71	2.64	2.59	2.54	2.51	2.48
20	4.35	3.49	3.10	2.87	2.71	2.60	2.51	2.45	2.39	2.35	2.31	2.28
25	4.24	3.39	2.99	2.76	2.60	2.49	2.40	2.34	2.28	2.24	2.21	2.16
30	4.17	3.32	2.92	2.69	2.53	2.42	2.33	2.27	2.21	2.16	2.13	2.09
40	4.08	3.23	2.84	2.61	2.45	2.34	2.25	2.18	2.12	2.08	2.04	2.04
60	4.00	3.15	2.76	2.53	2.37	2.25	2.17	2.10	2.04	1.99	1.95	1.92
120	3.92	3.07	2.68	2.45	2.29	2.17	2.09	2.02	1.96	1.91	1.87	1.83

Part B: $\alpha = 0.01$

dfw	\ dfb → 1	2	3	4	5	6	7	8	9	10	11	12
2	98.5	99.0	99.2	99.2	99.3	99.3	99.4	99.4	99.4	99.4	99.4	99.4
3	34.1	30.8	29.5	28.7	28.2	27.9	27.7	27.5	27.3	27.2	27.1	27.1
4	21.2	18.0	16.7	16.0	15.5	15.2	15.0	14.8	14.7	14.5	14.4	14.4
5	16.3	13.3	12.1	11.4	11.0	10.7	10.5	10.3	10.2	10.1	9.99	9.89
6	13.7	10.9	9.78	9.15	8.75	8.47	8.26	8.10	7.98	7.87	7.79	7.72
7	12.2	9.55	8.45	7.85	7.46	7.19	6.99	6.84	6.72	6.62	6.54	6.47
8	11.3	8.65	7.59	7.01	6.63	6.37	6.18	6.03	5.91	5.81	5.73	5.67
9	10.6	8.02	6.99	6.42	6.06	5.80	5.61	5.47	5.35	5.26	5.18	5.11
10	10.0	7.56	6.55	5.99	5.64	5.39	5.20	5.06	4.94	4.85	4.77	4.71
11	9.65	7.21	6.22	5.67	5.32	5.07	4.89	4.74	4.63	4.54	4.46	4.40
12	9.33	6.93	5.95	5.41	5.06	4.82	4.64	4.50	4.39	4.30	4.22	4.16
15	8.68	6.36	5.42	4.89	4.56	4.32	4.14	4.00	3.89	3.80	3.73	3.67
20	8.10	5.85	4.94	4.43	4.10	3.87	3.70	3.56	3.46	3.37	3.29	3.23
25	7.77	5.57	4.68	4.18	3.86	3.63	3.46	3.32	3.22	3.13	3.06	2.99
30	7.56	5.39	4.51	4.02	3.70	3.47	3.30	3.17	3.07	2.98	2.90	2.84
40	7.31	5.18	4.31	3.83	3.51	3.29	3.12	2.99	2.89	2.80	2.73	2.66
60	7.08	4.98	4.13	3.65	3.34	3.12	2.95	2.82	2.72	2.63	2.56	2.50
120	6.85	4.79	3.95	3.48	3.17	2.96	2.79	2.66	2.56	2.47	2.40	2.34

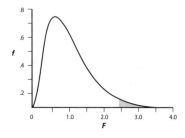

Appendix E Critical Values of *r* Distribution ($\alpha = 0.05$)*

df	r
1	0.997
2	0.950
3	0.878
4	0.811
5	0.754
6	0.707
7	0.666
8	0.632
9	0.602
10	0.576
11	0.553
12	0.532
13	0.514
14	0.497
15	0.482
16	0.468
17	0.456
18	0.444
19	0.433
20	0.423
21	0.413
22	0.404
23	0.396
24	0.388
25	0.381
26	0.374
27	0.367
28	0.361
29	0.355
30	0.349
35	0.325
40	0.304
45	0.288
50	0.273
60	0.250
70	0.232
80	0.217
90	0.205
100	0.195
120	0.174

*For sample sizes not tabulated, either extrapolate or test for significance using the *t*-test.

Appendix F   Random Digits Table

874335	218040	632420	240295	301131	152740	433058	274170
142131	051859	719342	714391	174251	147150	108520	771712
577728	460401	847722	767239	201744	006565	204589	960553
080052	246887	107893	627841	196599	792021	038162	390011
501153	355165	168311	790826	174928	955178	754258	125025
146207	369709	775557	516449	855970	838321	826020	246163
273515	015616	254341	330587	162088	174360	554720	349616
594504	658609	007492	524747	718771	586831	569750	047201
773722	805035	015969	656055	354632	089893	328631	466358
928848	601866	338853	047266	601409	588331	617007	750155
130680	336701	613351	286758	193966	377556	048648	557283
903145	937763	554796	728537	570290	643603	565449	562057
723294	473898	456644	992231	371495	963132	937428	954420
521302	654580	690478	463092	941820	803428	262731	939938
180471	329905	206005	792002	828627	022402	467626	239803
037226	990598	031055	395463	282404	368588	806509	590830
381118	268005	771588	955604	756766	981147	361899	245461
954822	434100	111684	920179	408451	889864	544440	471762
454139	901479	313550	002567	597321	515148	592903	053426
027996	723365	717520	681773	386364	168036	074181	789768
778443	093607	242049	702424	041696	550187	383294	995730
260656	846676	883719	574775	532552	253887	243386	001878
982935	957671	217239	074705	031298	262045	205728	654403
906706	042314	895439	743718	413420	448197	149714	815122
946521	856953	149277	388942	757533	076503	782862	861477
470054	798560	287835	583131	845375	301748	140819	186534
798107	404733	198320	164665	661808	669342	087352	698984
704605	853694	846064	737547	894822	615321	814358	323143
916600	464292	774523	171407	435529	966344	341855	498953
614267	196000	605281	101497	878168	439697	017987	681981
930906	148913	538043	428698	020102	143290	019025	843417
452944	063756	850643	819512	361819	075658	849363	970079
719931	821876	399037	206069	606933	625961	841521	564408
724544	945246	117307	286123	162181	073984	656142	144469
412582	096463	517660	023052	637428	090138	781997	743955
182972	578750	190428	145861	345662	235457	035980	412182
387765	835955	304068	649179	802995	461602	063111	714091
832135	952549	105163	293258	228666	610859	836534	230248
274385	153632	418418	103979	045038	916136	157518	056846
925940	304925	146667	872845	377600	500970	155459	305700

Appendix G Computations for Simple Linear Regression Analysis Example

Prior Arrests	Future Arrests	Predicted Future Arrests	Total SS	Reg. SS	Pred Errors
3	2	4.022938583	13.69	2.812534996	−2.022938583
5	5	5.312985827	0.49	0.149779970	−0.312985827
6	7	5.958009449	1.69	0.066568876	1.041990551
8	9	7.248056693	10.89	2.396479525	1.751943307
9	9	7.893080315	10.89	4.809601268	1.106919685
2	6	3.377914961	0.09	5.392078928	2.622085039
5	4	5.312985827	2.89	0.149779970	−1.312985827
3	4	4.022938583	2.89	2.812534996	−0.022938583
7	5	6.603033071	0.49	0.815468727	−1.603033071
8	6	7.248056693	0.09	2.396479525	−1.248056693
Total		57.000000002	44.1	21.801306782	−0.000000002
Mean = 5.6	Mean = 5.7				

Residual SS   22.298693218

MS Reg   21.801306782
MS Residual   2.787336652
F Ratio   7.821554947

R^2 0.494360698
$1 - R^2$ 0.505639302

Index

Adjusted coefficient of determination, 229
Alpha (type I) errors, 107, 109–110
Alpha, setting, 102–103
Alternative hypothesis, 99
Analysis of variance
 efficiency and type I error rate of, 176
 F-ratio and logic of, 174
 important concepts related to, 174–176
 post hoc testing and, 183–186
 purpose of, 173
 research example of, 176
Assumption
 interval-ratio data, 99
 of nominal data, 99
 of normality, 60, 98
 of randomization, 98

Backward stepwise regression, 253
Beta (type II) errors, 108
Beta coefficients, 246
Beta errors, 108–110
Between-group variance, 174–175, 179
Biased estimators, 50

Bivariate correlation
 Cohen's guidelines for interpreting, 200
 definition of, 196
 important concepts related to, 196–205
 multiple, 239–241, 244
 research example of, 204
 statistic, 198, 200
Bivariate regression, 217. See also Simple linear regression

Cases/subjects, definition of, 6
Central limit theorem, 82, 84
Central tendency, measures of, 28, 38, 40–41, 44–45
Charts
 displaying discrete data with, 25
 interpretation of, 28–29
 variability displayed in, 29
Chi-square distribution, critical values of, 264
Chi-square goodness-of-fit test, 115–124

Chi-square test for independence, 116–117, 125–132
Chi-square tests
 purpose and types of, 115, 117
 research examples of, 117–118
Coefficient
 of determination, 228, 230, 251
 of nondetermination, 229, 251
Cohen's guidelines for interpretation of correlations, 200
Computer statistical packages, 49. See also SPSS
Confidence intervals, 85–89
Continuous vs. discrete variables, 8
Correlation
 bivariate. See Bivariate correlation
 Cohen's guidelines for interpreting, 200
 multiple, 239–241, 244
 statistic, 198, 200
Covariation, 197

269

Criterion (outcome) variables, 96, 196, 217, 237
Critical region, 101–103, 105–106
Critical values of t, 263
Cross-validation, 225, 248
Cumulative frequency/percentage distributions, 20, 22

Data
  definition of, 3
  graphic display of, 27
  interval-ratio, collapsing into score categories, 23–24
  reduction, defined, 37
Decision criteria, specifying
  for chi-square goodness-of-fit test, 119–121
  for chi-square test for independence, 127–129
  for dependent samples t-test, 161–163
  for five-step model for hypothesis testing, 101
  for independent samples t-test, 152–158
  for one-sample t-test, 141–144
  for one-way ANOVA test, 178–179
  for Pearson correlation test, 206–207
Degrees of freedom
  for between-group variance, 179
  for the total variance, 179
  for within-group variance, 179
Dependent samples t-test, 139–140, 158–165

Dependent variables, 8–9
Descriptive statistics
  definition of, 9
  measures of central tendency and dispersion, 37
  normal curve and standard scores, 59–66
  quantitative, 37–38
Deviation scores, 41
Direct enter method of MLR, 252
Direction of the relationship, 196
Discrete vs. continuous variables, 8
Dispersion, measures of, 45, 47–48, 50–52
Distribution sampling, concept of, 79–84
Distributions
  based on score intervals, 23–24
  displaying and graphing, 19–30
  graphing and charting, 25–30
  normal. See Normal curve
  standard normal, 64, 66. See also Standard normal curve
  See also Frequency distributions, Sampling distributions
Dummy coding, 197, 254

Empirical knowledge, definition of, 6
Errors
  Alpha (type I), 107, 109–110
  Beta (type II), 108
  of prediction, 223–224, 247–248
Expected frequency counts, 115

F-distribution, critical values of, 265
Five-step model for hypothesis testing, 97–98, 100–101, 104
  ANOVA, 177–183
  Pearson correlation, 205–211
  simple linear regression, 230
Forward stepwise regression, 253
F-Ratio, 174, 225–226, 249
Frequency counts, observed/expected, 115
Frequency distributions
  cumulative, 20
  cumulative percentage, 22
  definition of, 19
  generation of, 20
  percentage, 21–22
  working with grouped data, 23–24
  See also Distributions

Graphs
  central tendency of, 28–29
  displaying continuous data with, 27
  interpretation of, 28–29
  variability displayed in, 29
Greek letters and mathematical symbols, 41

Heterogeneous vs. homogenous score distribution, 49–50
Heteroscedasticity, 204
Homogeneity of variance, 175–176
Homogeneous subsets, 185
Homoscedasticity, 203

Index

Hypotheses, definition of, 5, 95
Hypothesis testing
  for chi-square goodness-of-fit test, 118–124
  for chi-square test for independence, 126–132
  for dependent samples t-test, 159–165
  five-step model for, 97–98, 100–101, 104
  for independent samples t-test, 151–158
  methods of, 97, 99–101, 104, 106–107
  role in criminal justice research, 95–96

Independent random samples, 148
Independent samples t-test, 139–140, 150–158
Independent variables, 8–9
Index of Qualitative Variation (IQV), 45–46
Inferential statistics
  definition of, 9
  introduction to, 75–89
  logic of, 80
Internal level of measurement, 13
Interquartile range (Q), 46, 48
Interval estimates. *See* Confidence intervals
Interval-ratio
  data, assumption of, 99
  variables, 47. *See also* Bivariate correlation

Joint-frequencies, 125

Kurtosis statistic, 51–52

Leptokurtic distributions, 51–52
Levene's Test for Equality of Variances, 151
Levene's Test for Homogeneity of Variance, 157, 182

Main effect, 177
Matched samples design, 149
Mean
  concept of, 40–41
  standard error of, 81
Mean difference tests, 139–164
Mean of the differences between the paired scores, 161
  standard error of, 161–162
Mean square between (MSB), 180
Mean square regression/residual, 227
Mean square within (MSW), 180
Measurement
  definition of, 9
  levels of, 10–15
Median (Md), 40
Mesokurtic distributions, 51–52
Mode (Mo), 38, 40
Multiple correlation, 239–241, 244
Multiple linear regression
  definition of, 237
  handling nominal level variables in, 253–255
  important concepts related to, 238–252
  purpose of, 237
  types of, 252–253
Multistage cluster sampling, 78
Multivariate tests, 173

Negative skew, 43
Nominal level of measurement, 10–11
Nonlinearity, 202
Nonparametric tests, 115–133
Nonskewed distribution, 43
Normal curve, 59–60, 62
  standard, 64–65
Normal data, assumption of, 99
Normal distribution, 43, 262
Normality theorem, 81
Normality, assumption of, 60, 98
Null hypothesis, 99, 102, 107–108

Observed frequency counts, 115
One-sample t-test, 139–140, 144–147
One-tailed vs. two-tailed tests, 104–106, 143–144, 145, 207
One-way ANOVA, defined, 171. *See also* Analysis of variance (ANOVA)
Ordinal level of measurement, 12–13
Ordinal variables, 47
Outliers, 20, 43, 45, 202
Overspecification of the regression model, 253

Pearson correlation, 205–211
Pearson product-moment correlation coefficient, 196
Percentage distributions, 21–22
Percyrs variable, 68
Phi correlation coefficient, 197

Platykurtic distributions, 52
Point estimates, 85
Point-biserial correlation coefficient, 197
Pooled variance, 155
Population parameters, 100
Positive skew, 43
Post hoc testing, 177, 183, 185–186
Practical significance, 110
Prediction, errors of, 223–224, 247–248
Predictive accuracy, 225, 248, 250–251
Predictive efficiency, 249
Predictor variables, 196, 217, 237
Probability
　normal curve and, 61–62
　sampling techniques, 75–76
p-value, definition of, 107

Qualitative data, defined, 7
Quantitative descriptive statistics, 37–38
Quantitative data, defined, 7

r distribution, critical values of, 266
Random digits table, 267
Random sampling variability, 81, 97
Random selection, 61
Randomization, 61–62, 98
Range, 46, 48
Ratio level of measurement, 14
Regression
　coefficient, 220, 244
　constant, 220, 245
　line, Y-intercept and slope of, 220
　model, overspecification of, 253
　plane, 244
　of Y on X, 219
　of Y on X_1 and X_2, 244
Reliable differences, 96
Repeated-measures t-test, 149
Replication, 100
Research hypothesis, 99
Research questions, 97
Residuals, 247
Restricted ranges, 204
Robustness of testing, 175

Sample mean, 85, 95
Sample representativeness, 76
Sampling
　dependent samples, 149
　independent random samples, 148
　independent vs. dependent, 148–150
　matched samples design, 149
　multistage cluster, 78
　random variability in, 81
　stratified, 78
　systematic random, 77
　techniques, 75–79
Sampling distributions
　concept of, 79–84
　F-ratio, 178
　for five-step model for hypothesis testing, 100
　for one-way ANOVA test, 178–179
　for Pearson correlation test, 206–207
Scatterplots, 197, 201
　multilinear regression and, 238
　simple linear regression and, 218–219
Scientific inquiry process, 5
Score distributions
　heterogeneous vs. homogeneous, 49–50
　measures to describe the shape of, 37
Score intervals, 23–24
Selection bias, 148
Semi-partial correlation, 240
Setting alpha, 102–103
Shrinkage, 229
Significant differences
　in chi-square goodness-of-fit test, 117
　in chi-square test for independence, 116, 118
　in dependent samples t-test, 140, 158
　in independent samples t-test, 139, 152, 154
　in one-sample t-test, 139
　in one-way analysis of variance (ANOVA), 173–186
Significant relationships
　bivariate correlation, 195–212
　multiple linear regression, 237–255
　simple linear regression, 217–230
Simple linear regression
　computations for sample of, 268
　important concepts related to, 218–230
　purpose of, 217
Simple random sampling, 76
Skew, negative and positive, 43

Index

Skewness
  heteroscedasticity and, 204
  negative vs. positive, 43
Slope of the regression line, 220
Spearman rank-order correlation coefficient, 197
SPSS, 40, 44–45
  bivariate correlation using, 213–214
  converting raw scores to z-scores to percentiles with, 67, 69
  generating the skewness statistic with, 56
  multiple linear regression using, 243, 245, 252, 256
  one-way ANOVA calculations using, 181, 188
  random sample generation with, 90, 92
  simple linear regression using, 222, 229–230, 232–233
Squared deviation scores, 42
Standard deviation, 49
Standard error
  of the difference, 155
  of the mean, 81
  of the mean of the differences, 161–162
Standard normal curve, 64–66
Standard scores, 62–63
Standardized regression coefficients, 222, 246
Statistical significance vs. practical significance, 211
Statistical tables, 261–267
Statistically significant differences, 96

Statistics
  basic elements of, 6–10
  definition of, 3
  descriptive vs. inferential, 9
  quantitative descriptive, 37–38
  reasons for studying, 4–5
  role in scientific inquiry, 5
Stepwise regression methods of MLR, 252–253
Stratified sampling, 77–78
Strength of relationship, 196, 200
Subjects/cases, definition of, 6
Sum of squares between (SSB), 180
Sum of squares total (SST), 180
Sum of squares within (SSW), 180
Symbols, mathematical, and Greek letters, 41
Systematic random sampling, 77

Test statistic, 101
Testing. *See* Hypothesis testing
Tests of association, 196
t-tests, 139–165
  dependent samples, 139–140, 158–165
  independent and dependent sampling in, 147–151
  independent samples, 139–140, 151–158
  one-sample, 139–147
Tukey HSD post hoc test, 184
Two-tailed tests, 104–106

Type I and Type II errors, 107–110, 176

Uniform distribution, 43
Unit of analysis, 7
Univariate statistical tests, 173
Unstandardized regression coefficients, 222, 246

Variability
  in charts and graphs, 29
  random sampling, 81
Variables
  continuous vs. discrete, 8
  criterion (outcome), 96
  independent vs. dependent, 8
Variance
  between-group vs. in-group, 174
  definition of, 50
  homogeneity of, 150–151, 157, 175–176
  pooled (standard error of the difference), 155
Vectors, 254
Venn Diagram
  of multiple correlation, 240
  of the F-ratio, 174, 226

White noise, 174
Within-group variance, 174–175, 179
Within-subjects t-test, 149

Y-intercept of the regression line, 220

z-scores, 62–63, 86, 89